WHY O LORD?

Praying our sorrows

DAVID J. COHEN

T0385323

Paternoster:
thinking faith

19 18 17 16 15 14 13   7 6 5 4 3 2 1

First published 2013 by Paternoster
Paternoster is an imprint of Authentic Media Limited
52 Presley Way, Crownhill, Milton Keynes, MK8 0ES.
www.authenticmedia.co.uk

British Library Cataloguing in Publication Data

A catalogue record for this book is available from the British Library

ISBN 978-1-84227-754-6
978-1-78078-303-1 (e-book)

Cover Design by Paul Airy (www.designleft.co.uk)
Printed and bound by CPI Group (UK) Ltd., Croydon, CR0 4YY

Contents

Contents

Contents

In memory of my beloved father, Abraham Cohen
1924-2008

Preface

As I write, some of my friends and colleagues are experiencing deep distress in their lives every day. Others are struggling with the difficult experiences which most people face every day and the questions these experiences raise. As I listen to the latest news, to keep abreast of what's happening in my own country and abroad, I am repeatedly reminded that there are various causes of distress to both individuals and communities and I am prompted to join with many in asking, 'Why, O Lord?'

The Psalter responds to that question and, in so doing, has something important to say to us. I have always had an interest in praying the psalms and have experienced their use in various settings over the years. However, it has become increasingly apparent to me that psalms of distress, those psalms which question, prod, protest and argue, held a critical place in Judeo-Christian history and need to regain a place in our world today. If we, as people of faith, are to engage with our own experiences of distress, and find the grace to stand in solidarity with others in distress, then I believe these psalms are indispensable for that quest.

The intention of this book is twofold. The first goal was to develop a coherent way of looking at psalms of distress in response to the question 'Why, O Lord?' This resulted in the Matrix of Lament. With this model in hand, it then became critical to see what happens when psalms of distress are viewed through this lens. Could people begin to pray with the voice of the psalmist and, in so doing, find a voice for their own sorrows? To this end, I have included the stories of some of those fearless enough to have already embarked on this journey with me, telling their stories when they returned so others might benefit.

Beyond this, it is my hope that what you read here will be a catalyst for you to explore praying all the psalms, and psalms of distress in particular. If you are not familiar with these particular psalms, which make up over a third of the Psalter, or even if you are, please embark on this journey with me. I trust that your journey will reflect the hope expressed in the words of Ann Weems:

> In the godforsaken, obscene quicksand of life,
> there is a defining alleluia
> rising from the souls
> of those who weep,
> and of those who weep with those who weep.
> If you watch, you will see
> the hand of God
> putting the stars back in their skies
> one by one.[1]

In light of your journey, may you experience this kind of rising hope as you reflect on your life, and the life of those around you. Through this book, may you experience a new opportunity to pray your sorrows as you discover the inherent power of these astounding psalms.

David J Cohen
Perth, June 2012

Acknowledgements

This project has evolved over many years, and so a significant number of people have contributed to the content of this book along the way. My interest in praying our sorrows began as a doctoral dissertation in 2002 under the capable supervision of Dr Nancy Ault and Dr Alex Main from Murdoch University, Perth, Western Australia. Recalling our first conversations about my proposal reminds me of the enthusiasm they both showed for my ideas and the encouragement with which they urged me to pursue the research.

The support of my own institution, Vose Seminary, and my colleagues here, over a long period of research has also been a constant encouragement. The time allowed for writing and research, as part of my work, has been of great value in enabling me the freedom to produce this book. It is a privilege to be part of a group that values thinking theologically and reflecting practically on the biblical text and the practice of ministry.

Finally, I would like to thank my wife Christine and my children Ashleigh and Jayden, who have endured the many hours it has taken over the years to get the material into this form. Christine and I have often engaged in conversations about my writing and she has not infrequently offered her expertise to help me clarify my thinking. She has also given her time to proofread the manuscript, for which I am most appreciative.

Abbreviations

AJL	*Australian Journal of Liturgy*
CBQ	*Catholic Biblical Quarterly*
CC	*Christian Century*
CE	Common Era
CUP	Cambridge University Press
Heb.	Hebrew
IJPR	*The International Journal for the Psychology of Religion*
JAAR	*Journal of the American Academy of Religion*
JBL	*Journal of Biblical Literature*
JBS	*Journal of Biblical Studies*
JPCC	*Journal of Pastoral Care and Counseling*
JPsychTheol	*Journal of Psychology and Theology*
JR	*Journal of Religion*
JReligHealth	*Journal of Religion and Health*
JSOT	*Journal for the Study of the Old Testament*
JSSR	*Journal for the Scientific Study of Religion*
JST	*Journal of Supervision and Training*
NET	The NET Bible
NIV	New International Version
OUP	Oxford University Press
Ps.	Psalm
Pss.	Psalms
RevExp	*Review and Expositor*
SBL	Studies in Biblical Literature
SJT	*Scottish Journal of Theology*
Trans.	Translation/translated by
UCP	University of Chicago Press
WBC	Word Biblical Commentary

Bible References

All references are taken from the New Revised Standard Version, unless otherwise stated.

Foreword

How do we pray in times of distress? In recent decades biblical scholars have been looking afresh at the Book of Psalms asking questions about the more than a third that have been called psalms of lament or complaint, psalms in times of distress. What are their components? How do they function in worship and personal devotion, both Jewish and Christian? Are all appropriate for Christians? Some churches use lectionaries prescribing regular reading of all the psalms, but sadly while psalms of praise and thanksgiving are often quoted and sung in some form, little attention has been given to pastoral and personal use of lament psalms. David Cohen's book is refreshing and innovative in its thoughtful, well-founded practicality.

David began theological studies at Vose Seminary when I was Principal and Lecturer in Old Testament. He brought experience as a professional musician and teacher, with a strong Christian commitment enriched by his family's Jewish heritage. Through the years I have been stimulated and blessed through David, as student, friend and now colleague. Conversations are always a delight. After ministry as a pastor, with wider responsibilities in lay training and professional development, he joined the seminary faculty. His sensitive creativity and pastoral heart, blended with academic depth and integrity, are evident in his teaching of Old Testament and Hebrew and leadership in worship.

Building on a long interest in psalms, the solid research undergirding this book brings together a rare combination of biblical scholarship and pastoral understanding of people. Here you will find clarity of writing, lightness in communicating research, and insightful warmth in using the psalms today. He invites you on a journey – and he is a guide always aware of those travelling with him. There are two ground-breaking components. First, his 'Matrix of Lament' moves beyond simply literary structure to embrace psychodynamic features. Second, he is not a scholar whose research leads to, as an addendum, 'my ideas about practical implications'. Rather he tells the stories of what happened when a variety of people tested the matrix over several weeks of guided personal interaction with specific psalms. You hear their voices. On that basis the book has practical guidelines as to how 'you' can journey along the road that some have already tested.

Read and you will be drawn closer to God to whom we pray the psalms in times of calm or distress. Thank you, David.

John Olley

1.

The Journey Begins

In the Psalter we find a collection of prayers which offers us a window through which to view human nature and experience, and a mirror in which we can see ourselves vividly reflected.[1] These qualities, and the Psalter's common use, prompted John Calvin to conclude:

> I have been accustomed to call this, I think not inappropriately, 'An Anatomy of All Parts of the Soul'; for there is not an emotion of which anyone can be conscious that is not here represented as in a mirror. Or rather, the Holy Spirit has here drawn to the life all the griefs, sorrows, fears, doubt, hopes, cares, perplexities, in short all the distracting emotions with which human minds are wont to be agitated.[2]

Doubtless the aesthetic nature of the Psalter, and the wide gamut of experience expressed within it, have provided a significant resource for voicing the deepest feelings and thoughts about God, humankind and the relationship between the two. There is a sense of timelessness about the psalms, yet those who wrote, prayed and sang them share in the familiar experiences of life so markedly expressed throughout the Psalter. It is probably for this reason that psalms have continually featured prominently in Judeo-Christian history. Our focus here is on lament psalms, in particular, and the way in which they can offer a pathway of prayerful expression to God amid distress.

Over the past hundred years or so, many have examined and analyzed psalms in various ways. In part, this has been an attempt to understand why individuals and communities have prayed them throughout the ages. The diversity of this exploration could be summarized as three distinct, and yet complementary perspectives. Some have focused on the original historical setting of the psalms.[3] Others have analyzed the language, style and genre of psalms.[4] Still others have explored the practical application of psalms in worship and pastoral care.[5] From this rich seedbed a significant conversation has sprouted, exploring the relevance of lament psalms as a redeeming pathway for people to embrace, and engage with, their distress.

Perhaps it is these psalms which resonate most deeply with our humanity. They voice a sense of brokenness and vulnerability, common in human experience, as they complain to, and protest before, God. The intentional and systematic use of these psalms by faith communities, throughout Judeo-Christian history, underlines their significance and, in doing this, alerts us to their redeeming qualities for people embracing distress.[6]

This book emerges from, and hopefully enriches, the broader conversation about the nature and purpose of these psalms. Revisiting the past and present conversations about historical context, literary style and the practical use of lament psalms raises a pressing question for me: 'How would it affect a person if they prayed lament psalms when faced with distress?' Asking that question is important for three equally significant reasons. First, these psalms have been used consistently throughout Judeo-Christian history highlighting their value as prayer. Second, the reality is that within some faith communities, use of *any* psalms in an intentional or systematic way has ceased to be common practice. From the latter part of the twentieth century psalms have become increasingly absent from some contexts of personal devotion, pastoral care and corporate worship. This is especially the case in evangelical churches.[7]

Where psalms are occasionally used in these contexts the selection is most often limited to psalms of praise or thanksgiving. Lament psalms, in particular, have largely been ignored. The third reason for asking the question emerges from my experience of parish ministry during which I became increasingly aware, and disturbed, when faith communities struggled to recognize and embrace people who were distressed.

Everyone faces distressing situations, often daily, and they are confronted by varying intensities of crises throughout life but what is the response to this by the wider faith community and particularly from those charged with pastoral care? Perhaps lament psalms could provide a key to this dilemma. It seems today that the typical response to distressing life events is for faith communities, often, to avoid, ignore or even try to suppress the voices of those who are suffering. If there is a response it is often in the form of platitudes such as 'trust in God' or 'pray more', when acknowledgement and validation of the person's experience is of far greater importance. It is critical that people in distress are encouraged to tell their stories and express their thoughts and feelings in a safe and secure environment. Lament psalms are one resource which offers a pathway towards this healthy engagement with distress.

To discover how these psalms can offer the pathway described above, it will be helpful to begin by exploring exactly what these psalms are. We will then consider some of the implications for those with personal distress and what effect using lament psalms as a form of prayer might have. These ideas will be drawn together in what I have called the 'Matrix of Lament'. It is a model that provides a lens through which to view lament psalms and to understand their potential function for people in distress.

Based on the Matrix of Lament we will then explore how a process of lament can be viewed and the psychodynamic movements which are possible for those who pray lament psalms. Beyond this we will listen to stories of some who have been on a journey. Their journey took them from viewing lament psalms through the Matrix of Lament to using them for prayer as a way of engaging with their own distress and reflecting on the experience. It is my hope that, as you join with us on this journey, you too will begin to pray your sorrows and, in doing so, discover the transformative journey through lament to praise.

Our exploration begins by considering some helpful signposts which will enable us to understand more clearly what lament psalms are and how they might function. By doing this we will gain our bearings for the journey ahead. I've listed the signposts below:

Signpost 1   What is lament?
Signpost 2   Lament and ritual
Signpost 3   The language of lament
Signpost 4   Shape and function

In the following few chapters we will consider each signpost in turn and progressively uncover the richness and profound qualities of lament psalms. From this emerging picture we will then see that, while the signposts direct us to some important past and current perspectives on psalms, they also point beyond themselves. Where they point to may be unexplored territory for many people but as the journey begins new vistas will open up offering rich opportunities for personal growth. So, let us begin the journey together.

2.

Signpost 1 – What is Lament?

Lament is not a word used commonly today. Many years ago, on first encountering its use to describe a particular type of psalm, I began to question what the term meant. This led me to consider whether there might be a more helpful way of describing the nature and content of this type of psalm.[1] To understand these psalms it is important first to notice that within the lament genre, which makes up over a third of the biblical psalms, both individual and communal types exist.[2] In other words some were written by, and perhaps only used by, individuals while others were written by, or for, a group of people and used by various communities. Whatever each psalm's origins, history suggests that all lament psalms eventually came to be used by communities in corporate worship and they then became prayers within the liturgies of both synagogue and church.

These psalms contain the thoughts and feelings of individuals and communities in response to distressing experiences. They portray openness and authenticity before God that, on first encounter, may be confronting for some. Whatever a person feels about the language in these psalms they are clearly prayerful in nature.[3] Lest the psalms' words be viewed as an end in themselves, Brueggemann reminds us that they are not the end result of distress but rather an 'invitation to prayers beyond these words'.[4] His observation draws attention to the potential of these psalms when they are voiced as prayer. The words of lament psalms provide a locus of reference; a beginning point for an evolving response to personal distress.

It is interesting that the identity of the lamenter, the cause of the distress and the historical context remain largely unclear from the psalms themselves. However, rather than this being viewed as a weakness, the absence of such information enables these psalms to be used in a wide range of situations by a diversity of people beyond their original context. As a result, the psalms can be used by a particular person, in a particular situation of distress, or by any person, in any situation of distress. An interesting quirk of history saw the later inclusion of the names David, Moses, Solomon and others attached to, and suggesting authorship of, various psalms. While the attributions are all but impossible to authent- icate, they do, at least, reinforce a connection between lamenting and real-life experience. Perhaps these attributions also suggest that prominent figures of the faith experienced distress just as we do and engaged with it through writing and/or praying psalms.

Even though the term 'lament' has been largely unchallenged, as a way of describing the genre, some alternatives have been offered. While, in my view, none of the alternatives we will now briefly explore provide a definitive understanding of these psalms, they each add to our appreciation of their nature and potential func- tion. Let's begin with the word 'lament'. Although a useful term, it can obscure the diversity of expression found in these psalms. For example, the term could suggest that these psalms are solilo- quies or monologues, which they are not. Even a cursory reading suggests that they are more in the form of dialectic between the psalmist, God and others. The others are often characterized as the enemy. Lament also leaves ambiguous whether it encompasses a person's thoughts, feelings, actions or all three.

In one attempt to define lament, Westermann compares and contrasts it with praise, suggesting that together they are two themes underlining a movement in the Psalter. He points out that 'lamentation is the language of suffering [and] . . . praise of God is the language of joy', noting a general shift from more lament at the beginning of the Psalter to more praise towards the end of the collection.[5] So, for Westermann, while lament is present, it must be viewed in contrast to praise to be understood. While he describes this movement from lament to praise over the course of the Psalter, he is also aware of the same dynamic *within* most lament psalms.

I would also hasten to add that, despite Westermann's helpful observations, it should not be assumed the lament to praise movement is uniform within discrete psalms or throughout the Psalter as a whole. The psalms continue to oscillate between the poles of lament and praise from beginning to end, although with a clear movement towards praise.[6] In the same way, individual lament psalms, in themselves, also reflect the same oscillation between lament and praise, perhaps mirroring the lack of uniformity in individual responses to distress. So, understanding the term 'lament' as the language of suffering in contrast to praise which is the language of joy is helpful, but is it enough?

Complaint

Gerstenberger, among others, prefers to characterize lament psalms as complaints. While there is no question that complaint is a significant feature of these psalms the term is, in my view, too narrow a label. Having said, that Gerstenberger's perspective does offer some interesting insights into a *practice* involving these psalms suggesting that, 'individual complaints belonged to the realm of special offices for suffering people whom assisted by their kinsfolk, participated in a service of supplication and curing under the guidance of a ritual expert'.[7]

His observation is helpful in highlighting the practice of praying these psalms, alerting us to the capacity for them to aid those who are suffering distress. From this perspective Gerstenberger draws four notable conclusions about the way these psalms were prayed in ancient Israel. First, he argues that expressing complaint was a legitimate form of prayer for anyone within the faith community. Second, he proposes that the prayerful expression was not *improvised* but, rather, a formal prayer. Third, Gerstenberger emphasizes that the expression had the potential to promote transition through critical, distressing, 'threshold' life experiences.[8] Finally, he remarks that complaint, though it may be expressed by an individual, is not disconnected from the community. Psalms prayed by involving others, as Gerstenberger suggests, display the interconnectedness between the individual and the community.

Broyles also underlines the complaint nature of lament psalms but chooses to focus on the prominence of the plea. Interestingly, he points out that the person in distress 'pleads a case, so it is an argument'.[9] The plea stresses that the psalmist wants a resolution of the complaint through the agency of the divine–human relationship. The psalmist is understandably not content to remain in distress and recognizes or, at least hopes for, efficacy in expressing their suffering to God through prayer. Broyles' emphasis on the plea also reveals the fluid nature of empowerment in the relationship between the person praying, God and others. The plea draws attention to the human need for expressing oneself to a significant other and the internal struggle for a sense of control in a situation which is felt to be out of control. It is also indicative of an intrinsic human desire for resolution to distress.

Disorientation

Brueggemann takes a broader perspective on lament psalms by employing Ricoeur's image of 'disorientation' and characterizes lament psalms as 'songs of disorientation'.[10] Identifying these psalms as 'songs of disorientation' is helpful in highlighting the relational nature of these psalms. While Brueggemann views discrete psalms as being either psalms of orientation, disorientation or reorientation, these three descriptions are also helpful in labelling features *within* individual lament psalms. So, using each of Brueggemann's terms, and applying them to lament psalms, we see that they voice a transition from disorientation through reorientation to orientation within themselves. The engagement depicted in lament psalms does not simply show the struggle with distress but also the deeply relational nature of such an experience. With this in mind, Brueggemann's term 'reorientation', to describe lament psalms, is helpful but it does not reflect the range of experience that these psalms articulate. The examples below, all taken from lament psalms, demonstrate that expressions of disorientation, reorientation and orientation are all evident within them:

1. *Disorientation* – Psalm 88:4–5 – 'I am counted among those who go down to the Pit; I am like those who have no help, like those forsaken among the dead, like the slain that lie in the

grave, like those whom you remember no more, for they are
cut off from your hand.'

2. *Reorientation* – Psalm 35:28 – 'my tongue shall tell of your
righteousness and of your praise all day long.'
3. *Orientation* – Psalm 10:16 – 'The LORD is king for ever and
ever.

Most lament psalms have each of these characteristics, indicating a
progressive intrapsychic shift for the psalmist.[12] It is also another way
of expressing Westermann's view of the movement from lament to
praise. The relational shift is from a position of isolation where God
is at best distant, or at worst absent, to a position where the reality of
God's presence can be acknowledged.

There is no question that lament psalms can be characterized
in all the ways described above. However, while each approach
highlights particular features of these psalms none on its own
encapsulates their content in total. If we were to characterize the
psalms using only *one* of the approaches above we could easily
overlook several other important features that they contain.

Psalms of Distress

With the diversity of approaches outlined above, and having explored
various attempts to understand these psalms, we arrive back at our
first concern. Is lament the best term to capture the nature and content
of these psalms? The common factor in all the approaches is the
recognition that these writings emerged from real-life experiences of
distress. In these prayers the psalmists express experiences ranging
from specific to general distress, using language through which their
experiences can be voiced *and* potentially become an opportunity for
reflection. The language used brings into sharp focus the possibility
of restored relationship between the person and God, despite their
distress. Even if restoration of relationship is not sensed immediately,
the psalms at least voice a wish for divine response and a firm hope
for the future. There is no doubt that the writers of these psalms found
a deep need to voice their distress in some way. It suggests that the
presence of distress, almost involuntarily, results in questions, accu-
sations, complaints, descriptions of the predicament and pleas for

help.[13] In a paradoxical way the distressed person expresses a desire for God's action even when God is perceived to be powerless.

Because of the prevalence of distress in these psalms, it may be that 'psalms of distress' is a more apt way of labelling this genre. However, the other explanations of the genre, discussed above, still need to be included in our perspective to maintain a well-rounded view of the psalms' content. Using 'psalms of distress', to highlight their content, allows us then to describe an action involving these psalms as a lament process.[14] While 'psalms of distress' recognizes the focus of the language contained in these prayers, including complaint and feelings of disorientation, 'lament' underlines the importance of a process involving an articulation of thoughts and feelings around the experience. Finally, distress is a more familiar term for describing stressful experiences of life for people today that, in turn, call for a process of lament.

Of course, even with this label there is a risk of viewing these psalms simplistically. It is important to recognize their complexity just as distressing experiences are complex. This complexity can perhaps be more fully understood and appreciated by those who use these psalms rather than by those who seek to describe them or analyze them. We will explore the idea of using psalms of distress in later chapters but a few observations may be helpful here. Westermann proposes that a psalm of distress 'is the language of suffering'.[15] This reminds us to view these psalms *not* simply as text on a page or literary forms frozen in ancient times but, rather, as words and forms waiting for a new voice to bring them to life. This new voice then plumbs the depths of every person's distress amid the vicissitudes of daily life. Understanding the nature of psalms of distress, and how they might contribute to a process of lament, provides us with a significant signpost at the beginning of our journey in discovering their value.

3.

Signpost 2 – Lament and Ritual

The Liturgical Function

Having alluded to the prominence of psalms of distress in the worship of ancient Israel, we see the next signpost along on our journey to understanding their transformative power. Many have pursued the rather elusive goal of identifying the original setting, or settings, in which psalms were written and used.[1] Although largely inconclusive and at times rather unconvincing, these pursuits have at least highlighted the fact that all psalms emerged from the experiences of real people and were gradually incorporated into the liturgy. It is also probable that the words found in various psalms were used to express worship towards God long before they were recorded as written text.

Although it is all but impossible to identify the authors of psalms of distress, or the details of their distressing experiences, the authenticity of their expression could hardly be questioned.[2] This authenticity, together with the continuing use of these psalms as part of liturgical practice, reinforces the relevance and efficacy of both the form and the content.[3] Including these psalms in the liturgy, and eventually in the Psalter itself, suggests that they offered validation of people's distressing experiences.

This articulation of distress through psalms needs to be viewed in the broader context of covenant. Because the people of Israel were God's covenant people they had permission, as individuals and as a community, to pray to God about their distress. Praying about distress was viewed as an appropriate and normal activity within the context of the divine–human relationship.

So, three important practices permeated the worship life of ancient Israel in relation to distress. First, experiences of distress were intentionally given a language of their own in the form of a psalm genre. Second, these psalms were given a prominent place in the liturgy of ancient Israel and, third, psalms of distress were incorporated in the Psalter making up over a third of the collection, as we now possess it. Beyond the life and times of ancient Israel the Christian tradition has recognized these realities for the best part of two millennia.

Psalms of distress, particularly within the Psalter, have unique literary qualities within the wider corpus of biblical literature.[4] However, beyond their literary uniqueness, when the struggle they record is incorporated in liturgy, their content is forced front and centre for the worshipping community. By definition, including psalms of distress within the liturgy reinforces the need to voice distress in the context of relationship. This type of historical use in both Jewish and Christian liturgy has set an important precedent for using psalms of distress today as a continuing, integrated expression in both personal devotion and corporate worship. It opens another pathway for nurturing the spiritual formation of both individuals and communities of faith.

A focus on the place of psalms of distress within the liturgical context raises a further issue which is integral to the practice of liturgy. All liturgical practice is encased in some form of ritual and so acknowledgement of the use of psalms of distress in liturgy, by default, recognizes the presence of some kind of ritual to accompany them.[5]

Ritual

So, what might be the effect of using psalms of distress with ritual? Before answering this question it is helpful to consider some perspectives on the nature and function of ritual in a general sense. Then we will apply these perspectives specifically to the use of ritual with psalms of distress.

We know that ancient people groups, including those found in the Hebrew Bible, used rituals in many forms. From what has been discovered and surmised about ritual practices clearly many were intentional, while some were more intuitive responses to situations, acted out without much thought.[6] Although ritual is clearly a common part of human behaviour it is not that simple to define. Tom Driver's work is helpful in highlighting a rationale for using rituals which explains both their nature and function. In his extensive work on the subject he argues that we need to understand ritual in three related ways

- [as] often and ideally powerful;
- this power is properly used not to instil conformity to what is old and entrenched but to facilitate various kinds of transformation; and
- the truly ethical kind of transformation is that which results in the increase of freedom.[7]

In light of this rationale, Driver then stresses that practising ritual is not a choice, saying that it 'is not *whether* to ritualize but when, how, where and why'.[8] Perhaps ancient peoples inherently understood this need for ritual response to all kinds of life experience. So, when human distress is viewed in this light it suggests that it is not '*Whether* experiences of distress are ritualized' but, rather, '*How* experiences of distress are ritualized'. The type of rituals used, and the way in which people participate, needs to take into account the power of the actions, the potential for transformation and the ultimate goal of freedom.

This understanding of ritual is also helpful in our contemporary context. Some react against the word 'ritual' but their reaction emerges from the more popular notion of it being a completely static practice which is rigid, repetitive and meaningless. Driver challenges this understanding. While he argues that ritual implies a revisiting of the same action over and again, he goes on to acknowledge that the ritual can change in the process of engagement. The physical activity itself may, or may not, change but understanding it and experiencing it can evolve. He captures this tension by suggesting that, 'As a particular act of ritualizing becomes more and more familiar . . . it comes to seem less like a pathway and more like a shelter'.[9] An appreciation of the need of ritual, and the power of ritual to transform the individual and the community, will influence our thinking about how we engage with distress and how we enter a process of praying our sorrows.

Applying these ideas to the use of ritual, by praying psalms of distress, sees important possibilities emerge. These psalms, prayed in a ritual form, could provide a pathway towards something new. Such a practice could also increasingly provide a place of safety and security or, as Driver puts it, a shelter. It is to this place that a person can return or retreat when faced with various kinds of distress in navigating everyday life.

If, as Driver suggests, ritual is both a pathway and a shelter which can also be transformative, how might this transformation occur? One way of viewing the potential transformation of ritual is to consider that it can transcend a person's cognitive processes and promote expression of emotions. Theodore Jennings is one who suggests that ritual 'is primarily corporeal rather than cerebral, primarily active rather than contemplative, primarily transformative rather than speculative'.[10] His observations stress the holistic nature of ritual for those who engage in such an activity. So, for Jennings, ritual transformation encompasses, but is not limited to, the transformation of thinking and emotions. He proposes that, 'Ritual action does not primarily teach us to *see* differently but to *act* differently. It does not supply a point of view so much as a *pattern of doing*'[11] (italics mine). Ritual, viewed as a 'pattern of doing', implicitly suggests that it may be a way of encouraging a person to act differently, in response to a particular situation, in both a planned and repeated way. In repeating the ritual, a person's thoughts, feelings and behaviours can progressively be transformed as they intentionally respond in a new way to a familiar situation. These observations are of critical importance as we explore new ways of responding to distress through praying psalms of distress within a ritual.

It has also been argued that the efficacy of a ritual is only fully realized when a person is actively engaged in it.[12] This participation involves the use of words *and* action and, while not underplaying the importance of the spoken word, Rappaport suggests that physical action accompanying words is 'performatively stronger' or 'performatively more complete' than simply speaking.[13] While it may be overstated to argue that spoken word is *always* stronger when attached to action, it is important to consider that words bonded to actions *can* form a stronger, and possibly a more complete, 'pattern of doing'.[14] When words and actions form the rit-ual, then this can provide a catalyst for reflection and a deeper level of understanding, becoming potentially transformative.

Victor Turner, in his formative work on the nature of ritual, argues that it is 'prescribed formal behaviour . . . having reference to beliefs in mystical beings and powers'.[15] In this sense ritual can also express an experience of, and beliefs about, God. Ritual connects with the transcendent but it need not be complex or esoteric in nature. In fact, many rituals are simply 'elaborations upon . . . behaviours already known'.[16] Despite any simplicity, elaborations, made possible through ritual, can express something far deeper and more complex. It may be that some thoughts and feelings can only be expressed in actions and so, a non-verbal action in ritual can not only reinforce the verbal but may also transcend it.[17]

A connection between the verbal and the non-verbal in ritual also strengthens the potential of the person to pay attention to what is happening for them in the process. This, in turn, leads to a greater mindfulness about a person's thoughts and feelings when ritual becomes 'a process for marking interest'.[18] Mindfulness and 'marking interest' require intentional self-involvement in a ritual for it to be effective. It invites the participant to observe, to reflect and to make meaning of what takes place.

Levine explains specifically how the use of psalms in ritual can externalize emotions affecting the way a person lives, saying, 'ritual forms in us "a complex permanent attitude," an emotional pattern that governs our individual lives. As metaphor functions within language, so ritual can be a tool for the abstract, symbolic thought. Ritual actions can be regarded as figures of speech, in which a gesture stands symbolically for a complex of ideas and emotions.'[19]

Ritual then acts as a sign which, even if simple, externalizes a collection of thoughts and emotions within the person. When a person's experiences of distress are considered in this light it is interesting to contemplate what the effect might be when their thoughts and feelings around these experiences are externalized through a ritual involving prayer.

Another way of understanding ritual is as a story which can be told and retold because, 'Ritual and story are common ways

15

within a particular social context by which we order and interpret our world'.[20] The emphasis here is twofold. First, ritual can be a vehicle for telling a story, whatever that story might be, and second, the purpose of telling a story through ritual expresses a desire to make sense of what has happened. Telling a story in this way promotes mindfulness about what has taken place and also contributes to the opportunity for transformation within the individual and community.

In expanding on the connection between story and ritual Anderson and Foley go on to identify two distinct types of story using the terms 'mythic' and 'parabolic'.[21] A mythic story is characterized as one in which all struggles and difficulties are successfully resolved and all ends well. In contrast to this, the parabolic story narrates paradox and contradiction, allowing them to be voiced and the tension to remain unresolved. However, rather than concluding that the two types of story are irreconcilable opposites, it is more helpful to view them as an important foil to each other. The mythic stories offer a sense of hope while, 'Parabolic stories invite transformation by opening us to the possibility of something new'.[22] Anderson and Foley contrast the two different functions, saying that, 'Myth may give stability to our story, but parables are agents of change and sometimes disruption'.[23] Understood in this sense, the absence of mythic stories from a person's narrative may leave them bereft of hope, while the absence of parabolic stories may well limit opportunities for transformation and growth. Ritual provides a vehicle for both the mythic and parabolic to be brought together in a coherent and all-encompassing life narrative.

Most psalms of distress contain both these elements as they tell the story of a person's experience.[24] By holding both the mythic and the parabolic together they do not deny the reality of distress, nor the possibility of resolution, but offer an invitation to something new. These psalms present a world which is not being experienced as the person desires or expects. Nevertheless they tell a story of possibility where, at least, a sense of a hopeful future can begin to emerge.

A ritual can provide a safe holding space for the tension between the mythic and the parabolic, allowing for meaning-making to begin. The primary function of combining myth and parable then becomes an opportunity to 'construct meaning and build community'.[25] We can achieve this by, 'tell[ing] stories of life in order to establish meaning and to integrate our remembered past with what we perceive to be happening in the present and what we anticipate for the future'.[26]

It is reasonable then to imagine that the ritualizing of stories of distress can be beneficial for a distressed person. Psalms of distress contain mythic elements which offer hope for the future and perhaps even the present. However, the mythic alone is inadequate and unrealistic if it is not balanced with the parabolic. These psalms also offer parabolic elements which give voice to the paradoxes and the questions which must be asked, even if they cannot be answered. Together, these mythic and parabolic elements facilitate a well-rounded articulation of a person's distressing experience.

What meanings might then emerge when one engages with personal distress in this way? Anderson and Foley's combining of mythic and parabolic is one example of understanding meaning. Of course, meaning is not homogeneous in nature. It is better described as being 'multivalent'.[27] A ritual involving psalms of distress encourages a multiplicity of meanings to emerge from the person's initial engagement with both the mythic and the parabolic stories.

From the meanings that do emerge, one thing is clear: ritualizing psalms of distress offers an opportunity where both the parabolic and the mythic can be brought together and securely contained so that a multiplicity of meanings can safely emerge. In ritual, many stories and meanings are allowed and encouraged to co-exist, opening the possibility of engagement with, reflection on, and perhaps even resolution of personal distress. The connection of a person's own narrative with ritual is the critical factor in this process.

It could also be that, 'Rituals not only construct reality and make meaning; they help us fashion the world as a habitable and hospitable place'.[28] So, ritual also has an efficacy beyond itself in affecting the everyday world of a person. It is important however to reiterate that, while ritual can be observed, this effectiveness is only discovered through participation. Ritual invites the participant to change their world through action.

Given these connections between actions and words, it is important to consider how this might function for a person responding to a situation of distress. Psalms of distress can provide the words for prayer, while a ritual provides a space for these prayers and an opportunity for the words to be acted out. This offers a person an invitation to reflect on their distress by responding to their circumstances in a different way. Undoubtedly greater mindfulness can result in what may be called a 'knowing'. This 'knowing' is not limited to apprehending an idea cognitively, independent of a person's experience, but rather an awareness of what is happening to oneself as a significant by-product of the experience.[29] An emerging mindfulness, through ritualizing, is the key for a transformative process to take place.

Is self-awareness and mindfulness all that results from the combination of words and action in ritual? The bringing together of words and ritual can result in 'action and experience interpenetrat[ing]'.[30] Canda explains the idea further suggesting that, 'Transformation is a process involving a period of de-structuring of a stable condition, a period of extreme fluidity and openness to new possibilities, and a period of restructuring a new stable condition'.[31]

A ritual practice of praying psalms of distress can provide the type of transformation process that Canda identifies where 'de-structuring' can take place. Even when a person is not experiencing distress, a ritual focusing on personal distress may offer an opportunity for the formative process of 'de-structuring' and 'restructuring' to take place.

Whether performed amid distress or not, this is a destabilizing activity. However, despite the destabilization, it is important to reiterate that the ritual also acts as a shelter, offering both safety *and* the opportunity for change. So the 'ritualizing activity [has] the intention of leading somewhere, of going from one condition to another, even though the end may not be clearly in view'.[32] The process could be likened to washing clothes in a washing machine (transformation) rather than simply reading a manual about a washing machine (information). A helpful term which captures this type of process is 'transformance': transformation through performance which, to be effective, by definition, requires participation.[33]

An important aspect to ritual's 'transformance' function is that it is 'confessional'. The person taking part in the ritual accepts personal responsibility for their situation and responds, through ritual, in an attempt to alter their situation. Driver summarizes the significance of this, saying, 'The confessional mode transcends the ritual mode inasmuch as the performers recognize and speak out (confess) their moral responsibility for the rituals they perform'.[34]

Important to the confessional nature of ritual is honesty in expression of the heart. So in ritual we '*act* what we feel, not what we ought to do'.[35] Expressing emotion, questions and imaginings, helps to locate both oneself and God in relation to each other. The ritualizing of this confession is an affirmation of a sense of relationship with oneself, God and others. It 'is to place oneself in the presence of others, whether human or divine, making of oneself a very word of address inviting response'.[36]

In contrast to this, others suggest that ritual can in fact result in a multi-dimensional alienation from oneself and others, which may extend to a sense of distance or alienation from God.[37] It could be that, paradoxically, there is an element of truth in both these views. A sense of relationship *with* oneself, God and others, and alienation *from* oneself, God and others in a ritual illustrates the multivalent potential of the action. However, rather than rejecting one or the other, it suggests a tension point from which integration and transformance can begin to emerge.

Interestingly, all these observations resonate with qualities often found in psalms of distress.[38] Immediately, as a person begins to pray these psalms verbally, he or she is engaged in a confessional process. The psalm's anonymity easily allows its words to become the performer's own confession. The psalm then is no longer simply about expressing the *idea* of personal distress but, rather, it becomes an expression and confession of the person's *own* experience of personal distress.

As alluded to earlier, ritual use of these psalms does not need to be accompanied by a congruent experience of distress. Quesnell explains that it can be '[a] re-presentation so a past reality may be experienced more profoundly; in fact, that it may no longer be past, but the most present reality of all'.[39]

So, as we consider using psalms of distress, it is helpful to view them as either reflecting a person's current lived reality or as a 're-presentation' of past reality. Beyond this there can be great value in seeking to make past reality 'the most present reality of all'. In other words, revisiting past distress, through ritual, opens the opportunity for it to become profoundly available for meaning-making in the present.

All this assumes self-involvement of the person and an assumption that they pray the psalms, in a ritual, to discover something new about themselves and the distress they have experienced. Robert Sweetman describes such a stance as one of 'permeability', explaining the concept as 'the reader's openness to allow what she reads to get under her skin, to change her essential posture towards the text at hand, or perhaps even in life'.[40] Again this underlines the transformative potential of ritual for one who engages in the process.

Ritual, of course, can also be used within a non-religious environment, by people who do, or do not, recognize the existence of a divine other. However, intrinsic to psalms of distress is the belief that a person can pray to God about such experiences. The reality of God's involvement in the ritual process carries special significance for those praying psalms of distress. As highlighted earlier, Victor Turner concluded that ritual assumed 'reference to beliefs in mystical beings and powers'.[41] This acknowledgement of divine presence and involvement has implications for our understanding of how psalms of distress function as prayer in ritual.

Anderson and Foley are again insightful suggesting that ritual:

> is significantly magnified when the divine and human intersect in our storytelling and ritualizing. We are transformed in part because we begin to understand our particular story as part of a larger, transcendent narrative. God has chosen to co-author a redemptive story for us and with us in human history, and in so doing has invited us to reshape radically the horizon of all other storytelling and ritual making.[42]

It is a reasonable assumption that people of faith will inevitably engage in thinking about how God is, or is not, involved in distressing experiences of life. In fact, it seems that distress, perhaps even more than other life experiences, heightens a person's levels of thinking and expression about God's involvement in their situation. This intersection can be both comforting *and* problematic for the distressed person. However, ritual offers a place where the intersection can be acknowledged and the tensions voiced. Ritual becomes a place of significant value where human and divine narratives can interweave.

As a person takes part in ritualizing the intersection of personal narratives it becomes possible for a sacramental word from God to be received by them *in* their distress.[43] It offers a sacred space for both the person and God to speak. Brock suggests that, 'If in ritual we encounter the Ultimate, if in liturgy we meet God on the brink of chaos, then the sacramental response becomes a way of talking about what one took into the Presence of the Holy, what one anticipated happening and what really and finally happened'.[44]

In this sense, then, what began as a story of distress, being told, can potentially be re-authored as a story of transformation. This takes place as the person of faith engages with themselves and God in the context of a ritual.

4.

Signpost 3 – The Language of Lament

Several things can be said about the *function* of the text of psalms of distress *because* of its style and use of language.[1] Having observed this third signpost we will discover that it points to the way in which psalms of distress draw together both narrative and poetic elements. They achieve this in a seamless way to tell the story of distress and, in so doing, gain access to the deepest emotions evoked by such experiences.

Narrative

Doubtless psalms of distress have a distinctive narrative quality. They do not simply record an isolated complaint or even just a specific request of God. Rather, they are richly textured, and at times complex, stories of personal distress incorporating personal responses to these experiences. They tell the story of distress by identifying the characters,[2] sometimes describing a precipitating event, or a plot, providing a climax[3] and often a sense of resolution. Ensconced in poetry, this narrative gives shape to experiences of distress with language that promotes expansive freedom in emotional expression.[4]

With this freedom comes an accompanying sense of movement through re-presenting the story.[5] The movement often gains its impetus from a voiced reflection on the past[6] and the capacity of the psalmist to re-author the story. This, in turn, culminates in the imagining of a hopeful future. Another way of describing the movement is a transition from desolation to consolation.

Of particular interest in the narrative is the interplay between the characters present in psalms of distress; namely, the psalmist, God and others (often characterized as the enemy). Westermann characterizes the interaction between them as a dialectic style of communication.[7] The dialectic reinforces the significance of the relationships between the psalmist, God and enemies in the experience of distress, admitting the struggle and tension in relationships between all these characters.[8]

Evidence in psalms of distress themselves suggests that dialectic, as an integral part of the narrative, provides the impetus for a movement from desolation to consolation.[9] Use of the term 'dialectic' is important as it highlights the often confrontational nature of the encounter between the psalmist, God and the enemy. To this end the language of dialectic is noticeably graphic in many psalms of distress reflecting the nature of the tension present in each of the relationships.[10]

A second way to understand the narrative nature of psalms of distress is to view them as moving stories of disorientation – reorientation – new orientation, a concept discussed earlier.[11] More specifically then, use of these terms enables a person's current experience of distress to be better defined, as well as guiding their movement through distress. The terms are also helpful in naming the movement from confusion to clarity, while at the same time creating an awareness of the possible relational shifts that can take place as distress is successfully negotiated through the dialectic.

The presence of the dialectic, and the shifts in relationship, underline that the narrative of distress is often bound up in multiple relationships. It also underlines the potential to move the distressed person toward a greater understanding of their experience and/or potential resolution. Engaging in the dialectic enables the exploration of relationship as the narrative of distress unfolds. We will look at the finer details of the dialectic in psalms of distress later. However, now we turn to the significance of these psalms as a narrative expressed through poetry.

Poetry

Despite their narrative qualities, poetry is clearly the chosen language for psalms. Brown notes that, 'The power of the psalms lies first and foremost in its evocative use of language. The psalms at once caress and assault the soul.'[12] Poetic language has a subversive capacity to achieve what Brown observes. Poetry acts on the reader or speaker as it 'forms our feeling in the process of expressing it'.[13] In this way, 'Everyday reality is metamorphosed by . . . imaginative variations that work on the real'.[14]

Psalms of distress, then, do not represent fanciful wondering about what life experience might be like but, rather, use metamorphic language to describe a person's actual view of reality. In this sense poetry is complementary to narrative. It contributes to telling the story of distress through forming a metaphorical picture based on a perception, or set of perceptions, arising from real-life experiences. Beyond this, poetry also offers the language for imagining a different reality. These observations hint at the psychodynamic function of psalms of distress, which is largely tied to the use of poetic language. We will examine this in a later chapter. For now it is important to consider some of the unique qualities of Hebrew poetry and how they facilitate the languaging of distress. To do this, it is worthwhile examining a small selection of biblical scholars' perspectives on Hebrew poetry.

Robert Alter describes Hebrew poetry as, 'working through a system of complex linkages of sound, image, word, rhythm, syntax, theme, idea . . . an instrument for conveying densely patterned meaning, and sometimes contradictory meaning'.[15] Of particular significance for us is his last statement about incorporating 'contradictory meaning' which is often present in psalms of distress. This echoes the ideas of parabolic stories which we explored in the last chapter.

Kugel underlines the prominence of patterns and regularity within Hebrew poetry which suggests that it is language which lends itself to use in ritual of various kinds.[16] When applied to psalms of distress, clearly these linguistic parameters create a functionally rich literary tapestry. The consistent use of patterns and regularity, through devices such as parallelism,[17] creates a unique genre of poetic, or dramatic, literature which was not simply to be read, or even heard, but also performed.[18] The most significant device used in Hebrew poetry to achieve a sense of patterning and regularity is parallelism, which enables the contrasting, re-emphasizing or rephrasing of ideas being expressed by the psalmist.

So, in performing psalms of distress as prayer in ritual, the person can voice confronting words and imagery which can evoke powerful responses. These responses can be in the form of thoughts, emotions and actions. The poetry of these psalms provides an incomparable medium for recounting distress by languaging it in a way which is refining but not constrictive to either a person's emotions or their imagination. Poetic language provides for freedom of expression and yet safety in using a method familiar to one who prays regularly with the psalms.[19]

Brown adds that there is power in the psalms' poetic language performing a didactic function, calling it 'poetry with a purpose'.[20] He concludes that in poetry 'metaphors *do* something to enable the reader to perceive something differently'.[21] This being the case, the continuing ritual use of psalms of distress for prayer can offer the person praying instruction in how to perceive their distress differently and respond appropriately to such experiences. A person using these psalms can discover 'powerful ways to stimulate reflection and emotion' through 'iconic metaphor' as the language articulates their experiences.[22] The idea of iconic metaphor is explained by MacCormac who observes that, 'Metaphors not only communicate suggestive and expressive meaning but they also become iconic objects through their fusion of sense with sound'.[23] So psalms of distress potentially offer an iconic representation of a person's experience providing containment and shaping which can then lead to reflection.[24]

To capture both the narrative and poetic qualities of psalms of distress it is helpful to view them as poetic narrative. Seeing the text this way enables us to say more about its efficacy for a person who prays it. Although there are limits to what the written word can express, as it is 'only a partial reflection of the inner word',[25] words are important as a primary mode of human expression. The poetic narrative 'word' found in psalms of distress is best viewed as dialectic consisting of questions and answers.[26] Viewing the language of these psalms in this way is helpful in underlining what they do, and do not, provide. While psalms of distress are a fixed text and a fairly fixed form, that does not 'fix' the accompanying affect and cognition. Rather, as suggested above, they offer a containment which, perhaps paradoxically, frees up the person praying, through a dialectical process of questioning and answering, to move eventually beyond the psalm itself.

When a person engages with the poetic narrative, through the dialectic, they are not left just to ponder the words of the question but to look beyond these words, for an answer. In doing this, their experience is embraced through voicing these word-signs. It is therefore, '[an] entry into the world of ideas'[27] which is discovered as emotions and thoughts are acknowledged. Quinn suggests that the primary function of poetry is expressing emotions.[28] However, the poetry of the psalms achieves this without losing its narrative quality. Taking his thinking a step further Quinn makes the connection between poetry and ritual, suggesting that such a connection 'sets up a counterpoint between sound and sense that refuses to be ignored. The pattern of sound provides the structure and a pattern of thought.' This reinforces the emphases explored in the previous chapter and also suggests that perhaps human beings do not invent rituals as much as rituals invent human beings.[29]

Identifying the poetic narrative language in the psalms of distress also enlivens us to the relationships between the characters. The distressed person is not alone in their distress. The significance of relationship, as a foundation for understanding the function of the poetic narrative we see in these psalms, cannot be overstated. The relationship between entities is as important as the discrete entities involved in any discourse.[30] One result of this, as Bakhtin argues, is that the dialogical[31] relationship between the entities creates a continuing process of defining the characters in terms of their relationship with one another.[32] In speaking about this in regard to psalms of distress Levine states,

> I can experience myself on my own terms – feel pain, feel happiness, and so forth – but I cannot perceive or understand myself except from some point of view outside myself (though any one external point of view will necessarily be limited).[33]

So in the poetic narrative of these psalms, the psalmist is clearly a character in relationship with others. Awareness of these relationships for the psalmist creates a deeper self-awareness *through* an engagement with others in the process.[34] The dialectical mode provides the opportunity for the 'in between' to be experienced, recognized and reflected upon. In other words the true nature of the characters in relationship with each other is only discovered in the communication between them. To this end Bakhtin argues that, 'Dialogic interaction is indeed the authentic sphere where language *lives*. The entire life of language, in any area of its use . . . is permeated with dialogic relationships.'[35]

Interestingly, in psalms of distress, the other characters are God and an enemy. God can be viewed as a kind of 'super-addressee who transcends the present, seeing us from the vantage point of eternity'.[36] Arguably the presence of the divine character in psalms of distress recognizes that a deeper sense of self-understanding can come, eventually, *only* from including the divine other in the process. It seems that recognizing someone or something greater than oneself may be one outcome of an authentic engagement with personal distress. Of course for the person of faith this acknowledgement is foundational; compelled by their belief in a god, and the relational connection they have with that god. For those engaging with distress without a sense of the divine other it begs the question, 'Who is a significant other for me?'

While a superficial reading of psalms of distress might suggest that they are formed purely by the words of the distressed person, this is not always the case. The poetic narrative often includes words spoken by God and the enemy. The technique of 'double-voiced-ness', to use a Bakhtinian term, where God's words or the enemy's words are quoted by the psalmist in distress, performs two significant functions.[37] First, they provide an opportunity for the psalmists to stand somewhat detached from their experience and view it from another perspective (that is, God's and/or the enemy's). Second, double-voicing provides the opportunity for reflecting on the 'in between' as it expresses the nature of the relationship between the person in distress with God and/or the enemy. It is also possible that this provides the added force of the text having a 'rhetorical use . . . intended to persuade [God to respond]'.[38]

The upshot of this dialectical process, and the use of double-voicing, is the creation of a polyphonic discourse which ultimately promotes the emergence of a more richly textured self-expression and deeper self-awareness.[39] It is 'a movement inward through a movement outward, into the open, to a position of vulnerability'.[40] In psalms of distress the author presents an authentic person as they perceive themselves, God and their enemy. By including God as a character in the process these psalms voice a 'relationship and, in that relationship . . . being heard and answered by a Thou'.[41] So, the discourse is not simply about telling; it is also about hearing and responding.

Dialogue or Dialectic?

Thus far we have primarily used the word 'dialectic' to describe the kind of communication present in psalms of distress. This is because it is not sufficient to characterize psalms of distress as dialogue. Rather than the three characters conversing with each other – an implication of using the word 'dialogue' – there is a decidedly argumentative tone, better described as dialectic. Westermann was the first to highlight the dialectic in psalms of distress and the relational dynamic it underlined. He concluded that this dialectic relationship is three-way. That is, the psalmist relates to themselves, to God and to an anonymous enemy. Only the dialectic between the person and God is literally articulated in psalms of distress. However, as mentioned above, the use of double-voicedness means that the words of God[42] or the words of the enemy[43] are not infrequently quoted by the distressed person. It is also reasonable to infer that the psalmist was also engaged in an internal dialectic with themselves.

It seems that the presence of the dialectic is indicative, and perhaps even symptomatic, of a person in distress. It not only voices the person's distress but also says something about the perceived nature of the relationship, or lack of the relationship, with God and with others. The reason for the dialectic, in part, is the struggle for the psalmist with feelings of personal disempowerment amid distress. To explore the nature of this struggle further we will now consider each of the characters involved in this three-way dialectic in turn to discover their significance in these psalms and their importance to a lament process.

The first relationship obvious within the three-way dialectic is that which exists between the person and themselves. Even a cursory reading of psalms of distress reveals distressed people who often describe themselves as those who are in need.[44] Interestingly, they also sometimes characterize themselves as faithful, innocent and upright.[45] Another self-description is found in a subcategory of psalms of distress, usually referred to as 'penitential psalms', where the psalmists describe themselves as having sinned, recognizing the need to confess and repent. These are all attempts by the person to come to terms with themselves amid personal distress.

However, these thoughts and emotions are not experienced alone. A psalm that is used as a form of prayer is, in a sense, speaking to oneself *and* to God about oneself and about God. In psalms of distress psalmists voice thoughts and feelings about themselves and their situation. They are deeply personal, in that they are expressed by the psalmists themselves rather than by someone else on their behalf, and promote vulnerability as the psalmists take ownership of their thoughts and feelings directed toward God in prayer. The way the relationship with the self is articulated in prayer says something about the view the psalmists had of themselves, God and the relationship between the two.

This expression of relationship in the psalms of distress is not often one of harmony but, rather, an articulation of tension and struggle. A significant aspect of this struggle is the elusive nature of self-empowerment, or control, which can affect a person's response to distress. The psalmist desires control over their life, and the situation, but is confronted with a reality where there is a sensed lack of personal empowerment. Ambivalence and ambiguity are obvious in the poetic narrative but there is no attempt to deny the experience. In psalms of distress the struggle over this ambivalence and ambiguity is unmistakably verbalized. A clear example of this is found in Psalm 13:3. In this instance the psalmist expresses a sense of total disempowerment stating, 'I will sleep the sleep of death' and then quoting the words of the enemy who says, 'I have prevailed'.[46]

The second part of the three-way dialectic occurs between the person and God. God is clearly viewed as the 'significant other' in relationship with the psalmist. A profound question such as, 'My God, my God, why have you abandoned me?' is both an expression of relationship *and* of alienation where the person is trying to make sense of the divine–human relationship amid distress.[47] Feelings of alienation, such as those expressed in this question, are common to human experiences of distress.

When psalmists do not feel in control of the situation they express confidence in God to be in control.[48] An affirmation of this kind often includes an assertion that God is already present and in control of the situation. By implication the person believes that they will be protected. Even this assertion, however, is accompanied by ambivalent feelings at times. Broyles highlights the way in which God's disposition is often described in psalms of distress in terms of wrath, rejection, forgetting and hiding of the face.[49] A confronting example of this is Psalm 17:1–5 where the 'faithfulness' of the distressed person is pitted against the implied 'unfaithfulness' of God.[50] The relationship exists but the psalmist is struggling to speak of a god who is perceived as both the solution *and* the problem.

Despite this difficulty, the depth of relationship between the psalmist and God leads to brutal honesty. There is no tacit recognition of God's presence in the situation; the psalmist is not speechless in their predicament. The distressed person sometimes asserts innocence and, on that basis, offers a substantial plea for divine action. This assertive position displays great courage and self-assuredness in speaking *to* God, which has its foundation in the freedom to express oneself *before* God *about* oneself and *about* God.

Farmer encapsulates the picture well by observing that, '[The psalmists] do not wait passively for God to notice their pain and come to their aid. Rather, they cry out as an act of faith in the steadfast love of the one they confidently trust will not reject them for what they feel or say.'[51] This expression by the psalmist shows the freedom to be open and genuine in voicing the story of personal distress.

The third aspect of the three-way relationship is that which exists between the person and their enemy. However, before considering the image of the enemy, it is important to note that there is also evidence within psalms of distress suggesting the presence of others who are sympathetic towards, rather than opposed to, the psalmist. For example, Gerstenberger highlights the presence of the community and a figure he refers to as a 'ritual expert' who aids the person in distress.[52] This is important as it shows that, perhaps ideally, a lament process is best entered with some sense of community rather than alone. In this way the community acts in a supportive role.

While supportive community is fleetingly referred to in psalms of distress, the image of the enemy is pervasive.[53] Although a physical confrontation or direct conversation between them is not described, it is clear from the language that the relationship is fractured. Part of the narrative of distress is recognizing that initially, at least, the enemy is empowered against the psalmist. Often this thought is expressed in terms of what the enemy has done, or may do, to the psalmist and the powerlessness the he or she feels in the situation. This sense of disempowerment can also be seen in the person's relationship with God, usually at the beginning of a psalm of distress. Neither God nor the enemy is responding in the way desired or perhaps expected by the psalmist.

Much internal evidence from the psalms describes the source of distress in terms of the enemy's activities.[54] The anonymity of the enemy contributes to the flexible nature of psalms of distress, so it could be concluded that, 'the enemies are in fact whoever the enemies are for the singers of the Psalms'.[55] Sometimes, the enemy may even be perceived to be the distressed person themselves, or God.[56] Perhaps penitential psalms are the clearest examples of the former where the psalmists view themselves as their own enemies because of personal sin. It seems that a process of lament *requires* an enemy as an object upon which emotion can be vented; the identity of the enemy is a subordinate issue.

So, to this point we have explored the notion of psalms of distress being used in a ritual and how the language used fits with this context. Poetic narrative is a helpful way to think about the language found in these psalms because the text tells a story, while employing metaphor, repetition and various other poetic devices, to express the experience set in motion by personal distress. The power of the poetic narrative style is in its capacity to express both mythic and parabolic thinking. Most psalms of distress offer a mythic image where distress is successfully resolved. However, in doing so, they also embrace the parabolic reality, where distress may not have immediate or even eventual resolution, accommodating residual ambiguity in the distressed person's mind. The dialectic as a three-way communication contributes to expressing these complexities.

When considering the importance of ritual and the function of poetic narrative it becomes clear that the fusing of poetic language and performance can contribute to the forging of a powerful form for expressing thoughts and feelings. This fusion, found in the text and through the practice of praying psalms of distress, provides a resource which cannot be simply examined, analyzed or explained from an objective standpoint. It must, by definition, be experienced. While the poetic narrative provides the medium, it is the dialectic quality which provides the impetus for transformation in the text. These features, embedded in the psalms of distress, provide a structured literary space which, married with ritual, can promote a genuine voicing of distress leading to an opportunity for transformation. The poetic narrative has a particular shape, or form, and understanding this shape provides the next signpost on our journey.

5.

Signpost 4 – Shape and Function

The shape, or form, of psalms of distress provides the framework for expressions of various kinds. The form-critical approach to psalms provided the foundational ideas for identifying and describing the form of all types of psalms, including psalms of distress.[1] Gerstenberger embellished the formative work of Gunkel and others, arguably producing the most comprehensive and helpful description of the form. He identified in the Psalter the presence of up to ten discrete elements making up what he called the classic individual lament form.[2] The elements are as follows:

1. Invocation
2. Complaint
3. Confession of sin/affirmation of innocence
4. Plea/petition for help
5. Imprecation against enemies
6. Affirmation of confidence
7. Acknowledgement of divine response
8. Vow/pledge
9. Hymnic blessing
10. Anticipated thanks

While identifying these elements is helpful in describing the content of the form it does more than this. The elements also imply a possible function for each one as expressions of prayer. Can the ten elements identified by Gerstenberger articulate typical responses of a person in distress? If so, does the existence of these elements in the form of a psalm of distress suggest a model for intentionally engaging with distress? To respond to these questions I have further distilled these elements into four constellations which incorporate all the elements identified in Gerstenberger's typical lament form. The four constellations are:

- *Expressing*
  - Invocation
  - Complaint
- *Asserting*
  - Confession of sin
  - Affirmation of innocence
  - Plea
- *Investing*
  - Imprecation
  - Affirmation of confidence
  - Acknowledgement of divine response
- *Imagining*
  - Vow
  - Pledge
  - Hymnic blessing
  - Anticipation of thanks

The Shape of Psalms of Distress

The distillation above tries to capture the theoretical form of these psalms as well as the capacity of them to be functional. Each response constellation (expressing – asserting – investing – imagining) connotes different functional aspects when the psalm is prayed. Viewed together the constellations make up the Matrix of Lament, a lens through which psalms of distress can be better understood.

Although expressed in a diversity of ways and orders within the text of psalms of distress, essentially these four constellations reflect a dynamic process of engagement with distress. We will explore the Matrix of Lament in detail in the following chapter. However, for now, it is important to understand the shape of these psalms in more detail.

Classifying psalms of distress as a distinct form within the Psalter, and the presence of clearly identifiable elements in the form, again raises questions. Why would experiences such as distress, which could be characterized as evoking feelings of a lack of control, anxiety and hopelessness, be shaped into a stable literary form? It might also be asked, 'Why have they been enshrined in Judeo-Christian ritual?' There are two ways of responding to these questions, both of which provide a deeper understanding of the potential psychodynamic effects these psalms may have on a distressed person who uses them as a form of prayer.

Earlier it was acknowledged that not all psalms of distress contain each of the ten elements identified by Gerstenberger. However, when these psalms are viewed as a collection of four constellations[3] (expressing – asserting – investing – imagining) it is evident that each psalm consistently incorporates most elements of all four constellations. Therefore, the constellations, viewed together, highlight the typical shape of psalms of distress and their consistency of content, even though ordering of the constellations can vary. Brueggemann has called this shaping 'structure-legitimating'.[4] Interestingly, he goes on to argue specifically that psalms of distress legitimate one who 'struggle[s] to be free [and] is open to *the embrace of pain*'.[5] His observations reinforce the idea that these psalms have a functional purpose.

The shape, or structure, of psalms of distress can be viewed as juxtaposed to the lack of structure, or containment, often resulting from personal distress. In this way these psalms offer an engagement which paradoxically invites the distressed person to embrace the chaos caused by distress *through* a structure.[6] Not only is the experience then structure-legitimating but Lewis adds that the structure also contributes to a continuity of experience which he describes as, 'a collective set of experiences that in the best of circumstances results in a feeling that one's life has purpose and meaning, and in the worst of circumstances provides a container for despair and loss'.[7]

To further refine this idea of structure it may be helpful to view it as a divine dance or *perichoresis*. Robbins uses this imagery saying that, 'We want to stick to the dance steps we know and the dance partners we choose'.[8] Psalms of distress provide the steps and the potential partners in distress. The overall shape of the psalms, and any associated ritual, provides a contained space for self-expression and the boundaries within which the dance can be performed. It also offers an opportunity to experience a liminal space for exploring and even making sense out of the distress being experienced.

Shape and Meaning-Making

In considering the process of meaning-making, the underlying assumption is that psalms of distress are in fact an attempt to do just that; make meaning. I would argue that the value of lamenting distress, as an attempt to make meaning, is self-evident in the continuing use of psalms throughout much of Judeo-Christian history. Swinton and Mowat support this notion in a general sense arguing that, 'We cannot be anything other than interpretive beings'.[9] Coining the phrase 'hermeneutic phenomenology' they say that participation in various phenomenological experiences *assumes* the process of meaning-making.[10] Praying psalms of distress is one such experience.

An important part of engaging with distress, then, is the person coming to an understanding of what is happening *for* them and *to* them. This understanding could be characterized as comprehension, in the sense of 'grasping together', prompting Hughes to suggest that, 'when we strain for the meaning of something, we are attempting to find the ways in which its parts form some kind of significant whole and then the ways in which that whole hangs together with whatever else we know of the world'.[11]

A significant part of this process is engaging with oneself in a way which can lead to a deepening self-awareness in light of the distress experienced. Dialogue, or dialectic in the form of psalms of distress, can be an effective structure in which this deepening of self-awareness might occur.[12]

Another way of appreciating the potential for meaning-making through comprehension is to see it as a way of discovering 'worldframes'. Sutherland uses this phrase suggesting that, 'The problem comes when something happens in life and a person is unable to find a sense of meaning and purpose that incorporates that event'. She goes on to suggest that a change of 'worldframe' may be needed to promote meaning-making.[13] If this kind of change is needed in response to distress, then psalms of distress may offer a liminal space to promote such a movement.

For a process like this, it is significant that psalms of distress, while potentially being used with non-verbal ritual processes, are first and foremost verbal expressions. Hence, they can put a new worldframe into words and create a language through which to view personal experience. Byrne describes it this way: 'when the crisis occurs, the person is pushed to the edges of the previous way of being. To push through to the next space, language is essential. This speech will be more than an articulation of one's circumstances, but will have actual creative function. Heidegger says it beautifully, "the poet is the shepherd of being." '[14]

Before moving on from discovering meaning-making a cautionary note is in order. It could be imagined from these ideas that the goal of meaning-making is to make complete sense of experiences of personal distress. However, this is to focus solely on the goal rather than the process. Potentially a goal, such as resolution or making complete sense of an experience, may over-shadow the *form of engagement* and a *focus on the process*. A journey in meaning-making and growth may, or may not, culminate in making complete sense of the distress experienced or in complete resolution. However, it can nonetheless still be viewed as a process of transformation.

So, we have been able to see that psalms of distress repre-sent a structured shape for engaging with personal experience by recounting the story using the metaphorical power of poetic language. The shape of these psalms is fairly stable across the Psalter in that they almost all contain the four constellations (expressing – asserting – investing – imagining). When they are used as a form of prayer they provide an opportunity for reflec-tion and meaning-making.

While the poetic language has certain mimetic qualities attached to it there is also space for a hopeful imagination, both *within* and *beyond* the experience of immediate distress. In this way the shape of the psalms of distress contributes to a process of meaning-making.

Psalms of Distress and Prayer

While we can clearly see that these psalms are poetic narrative language it is also important to recognize that this language is one of prayer. These words are not to be confined to the page. If musical notes were left on the score and never sung or played they would not truly be music. In the same way, if the words of these psalms are left on the page and never spoken, or sung, they never fully become prayers. One way of understanding how words on a page become prayers that actually *do* something is to view them as a collection of speech acts which are collectively characterized as prayer.

So, with this in mind, we need to explore briefly the nature of speech acts to understand what happens when a person prays psalms of distress. The formative work by J.L. Austin entitled *How to Do Things with Words*[15] set the foundation for most later studies in speech act theory and, as Wheelock puts it, 'His [Austin's] key insight was to recognize that utterances could be not only statements of fact but also the *doing* of something . . . Austin came to the realization that all utterances have a performative aspect. To make any utterance is to perform an act.'[16]

Taking this idea as his beginning point Austin highlighted various types of speech and the effects they have on both the speaker and the hearer.[17] Implicit in such a view of language is that words, when spoken, are substantially different from words that are bound to a page. The second observation Austin made was that speech acts imply a relationship between the speaker and the hearer.[18]

Though a consensus has been reached regarding the idea that speaking words does something to speaker and hearer that is where the agreement ends. However, considering the general idea that speaking words *does* do something, it is helpful to bear this in mind when evaluating the function of psalms as they are prayed aloud. Searle's categories offer a useful distinction between types of speech acts when analysing psalms of distress. His categories are as follows:[19]

- *Assertives* – telling people how things are
- *Directives* – trying to get them to do things

- *Commissives* – committing ourselves to do things
- *Expressives* – expressing our feelings and attitudes[20]
- *Declarations* – bringing about changes through our utterances.

Each category highlights the *effect* that the particular speech act achieves[21] and it is interesting that examples of all these speech acts can be found in psalms of distress.

Assertive – Psalm 10:2, 'In arrogance the wicked persecute the poor.'

Directive – Psalm 22:19, 'But you, O Lord, do not be far away! O my help, come quickly to my aid!'

Commissive – Psalm 35:18, 'I will thank you in the great congregation; in the mighty throng I will praise you.'

Expressive – Psalm 55:4, 5, 'My heart is in anguish within me, the terrors of death have fallen upon me. Fear and trembling come upon me, and horror overwhelms me.'

Declaration – Psalm 55:16, 'I call upon God, and the Lord will save me.'[22]

It is evident from Searle's categories, applied to psalms of distress, that when prayed, these psalms become a collection of speech acts and that these speech acts can function for the speaker in a number of ways.

Before we proceed though, it is important to bear in mind that Austin and later theorists, such as John Searle,[23] focused on speech acts as normal speech. They did not examine ritual speech as such. There are differences and similarities between the two types of speech. Wheelock is helpful in drawing a distinction between 'normal' and 'ritual' speech while also seeing the connection, stating:

> My proposal is that one must make a broad distinction between all those speech acts whose fundamental intent is communicating information between a speaker and a hearer, and those speech acts whose intention is to create and allow the participation in a known repeatable situation. This thesis implies that the language of any ritual must be primarily understood and described as 'situating' rather than 'informing' speech.[24]

When speech is incorporated into a ritual process, which implies repetition, the 'informing' nature of the speech acts, although still present, becomes secondary as the information is already known. It is then that the 'situating' of the speech acts becomes the prim-ary focus each time the psalm is spoken or prayed in the ritual. The ideas of informing and situating could be further expanded by viewing them as also being 'appropriating'. Day argues that, 'to speak means both to be spoken into being and to transform what it is that being and speaking can mean'.[25]

The *active* nature of speech cannot be overemphasized. This idea is captured most simply in the title of Austin's book already mentioned: *How to Do Things with Words*. Doing things with words, in some respects, undergirds the process of mean-ing-making previously explored. As experiences are *articulated and reflected on* in a safe, contained environment the words 'do' meaning-making. Kubicki suggests that, 'performative language theory is a helpful tool in liturgical studies because it provides a method which examines the relationship of *meaning* and *text* in the context of ritual. In addition, the theory is relevant to the study of liturgy because it views language more as "doing" than simply communicating *about* a state of affairs.'[26]

Speech can inform, situate and appropriate change but it is the connection between speech and ritual (stressing that it is not speech alone) with physical action that holds significant power.[27] This connection means there is potential to move beyond simply describing events to viewing speech as bringing about meaning for the speaker.

These observations raise critical questions about the implica-tions of speech acts for a person who prays. At a fundamental level speech act theory is a way of talking about the nature of the 'voice' which the speaker possesses.[28] The voice is, by definition, a voice of self-involvement which can be discovered when the text is expressed as a speech act.[29] Finding one's voice amid distress through praying psalms means that it '*presents* the situation [and] facilitates recognition of the situation [and] it expresses this recog-nition'.[30]

Again the emphasis here is on process rather that a particular result. The situation recognized may well simply be a more realistic understanding of the experience rather than a sense of resolution. However, whatever the position arrived at, the speech act has performed the function of at least situating the speaker in their circumstances and presenting the possibility of change.

These spoken words can also be viewed as signs which are, in a sense, incomplete. They are what we encountered earlier and what Le Roux calls 'a partial reflection of the inner word'.[31] He argues that this inner word is ineffable.[32] In this sense the psalms of distress could also be viewed as an opportunity to voice the experience of distress in speech acts, even though such speech acts are only partially representative of the person's 'inner word'. However, when speech acts are expressed through ritual, the ineffability is offered a mode of expression which transcends speech. As the speech acts in ritual are learned by the participant they become 'more a reality to be experienced'.[33]

As highlighted above, each discrete type of speech act identified by Searle can be seen in the psalms of distress. From a speech act theory perspective then, their presence suggests that the function of these words, at least in their original context, was to *do something*. This idea of words *doing something* is in sharp contrast to viewing words simply as a record, informing a reader of events in the past and reflections on those events. It also suggests that a person praying psalms of distress, and by it verbalizing their 'inner voice' as speech acts, can find a ready-made entry point for engagement with personal distress.

The speech acts in psalms, viewed together, form a prayer. So, finally, it is important to consider what effect speech acts have when they are voiced as prayers. In focusing on psalms of distress as prayer it will be first helpful to consider briefly the efficacy of prayer in a more general sense. Finney and Maloney provide a comprehensive literature review of empirical studies of prayer over the past few decades.[34] As the basis of their review they provide a working definition of prayer being 'every kind of inward communion or conversation with the power recognized as divine'.[35] Their definition is general enough to encompass verbal and non-verbal forms of prayer, highlights the existence of relationship between the human and the divine and suggests some intentional self-involvement in the process.

During their research on prayer two themes became increasingly obvious to Finney and Maloney. First, that prayer is often viewed as petition. That is, it seems from observing people's attitudes towards prayer, researchers have discovered that people pray either to express a desire to change the situation they face or for a change in their own subjective response.[36] The second theme was that prayer helped people engage with experiences of distress and aided them in expressing their desire for comfort and communion with God amid that experience.[37] Both these desires are clear in psalms of distress.

As well as this, there is something even more fundamental to the reasons people in fact pray at all. While not denying the petitionary aspect of prayer, or the desire for comfort and communion, Cynthia B. Cohen and others argue that, 'They come to meet their most fundamental need . . . the need for God'.[38] The observation suggests that at the core of any prayer is a perceived need for a sense of relationship with the divine *because of* life rather than *despite* life.

Relationship is the unifying factor in the themes described above and the desire for this could be described as 'inward, outward and upward'.[39] From difficulties faced in various types of relationships, prayer emerges because of a felt need for a cognitive and spiritual structure as a pathway for coping.[40] Interestingly, Cynthia B. Cohen, and Ladd and Spilka do not see the appeal to the divine necessarily because the divine is viewed as more powerful, or all-powerful, but, rather, an appeal simply because the divine is God.[41] The efficacy, for the person praying, is in the existence of the relationship, apart from what God may or may not do in response to the prayer offered.

Further, prayer is a process by which relational connections are made as 'an invitation to partnership, activity, and growth'.[42] In fact other research has suggested that for some who pray regularly, the content is of little importance but 'it [is] as if the words and the rhythm [combine] as a vehicle of contact with God'.[43] Gay adds some clarity to the intrapsychic dynamics at work here, noting the paradoxical nature of prayer as an expression of relationship, stating,

> On an intrapsychic level, the prayerful attitude itself, the salutation of a greater being, and the acceptance of his [*sic*] will, both impinge upon the state of primary narcissism and yet reinforce self-esteem by establishing, if only temporarily, a kind of idealizing transference in which

the self that seeks abasement can also share in the glory transferred to the entity which is hallowed.'[44] This intrapsychic movement comes about not simply because prayer is a collection of speech acts and a process of doing things with words but because it is viewed in terms of the divine–human relationship.

Beyond the idea of prayer as an expression of relationship, Margaret Paloma found that of all types of prayer analyzed in her study (colloquial, petitionary, ritual and meditation), ritual and meditation prayers were rated by the participants as aiding them to feel closer to God.[45] Interestingly, she also discovered that while all types were found to be of value, ritual prayer was most helpful in building a strong sense of positive relationship with God.[46] In a previous study of a similar kind it was concluded that, 'ritual prayer was the lone type of prayer [a]ffecting negative affect'. If ritual prayer is the mode which most effectively connects with 'negative affect',[47] and psalms of distress are largely occupied with 'negative affect', then this is again indicative of the psycho-dynamic potential of these psalms to be transformative.[48]

People often pray with some goal in mind even if they are not fully aware of it. However, from the research, it seems that the primary reason for prayer is as an expression of relationship and, in terms of distress, to be a coping mechanism with the potential for resolution. Therefore, the overall goal of prayer, if there is one, could be viewed as a desire to consolidate relationship with God which may, or may not, result in personal change of some kind. However, regardless of any possible change, praying expresses a desire for deepened intimacy with the divine. This deepened intimacy in the psalms was experienced when, 'God responded to the prayers, and the suppliant's need, in some fashion, was met. A movement has taken place, from plea to praise, from weeping to laughter.'[49]

These observations remind us that the desire for, and the possibility of, resolution of distress was not precluded from the psalmist's expectations as they prayed these psalms.

Therefore, even though there is no real consensus on the goal of prayer, apart from the fact that there is probably more than one, clearly prayer is viewed by most as an expression of self-involvement and relationship. It is, to reiterate the words of Ladd and Spilka, an expression of connection inward, outward and upward.[50] The empirical research undertaken on the effects of prayer supports the idea that prayer deepens the sense of relationship with God for those who pray.

Because of this relational understanding of prayer, and since prayer can be an avenue for expressing personal distress, Kelcourse suggests that, 'Suffering deliberately faced, through the dialogues of the soul in prayer, makes us co-creators with God. Like Wisdom herself, we hover over the primordial face of the deep, trusting that creation, and the light it brings, will be good.'[51] This view holds together the mystery of experiencing personal distress, in the context of relationship with God, and the value of that distress being voiced through the language of prayer. This type of prayer is therefore inherently powerful.

So far we have encountered four signposts which point to important ways of understanding the nature and potential function of psalms of distress in a person's life. To this end we have described psalms of distress in the following ways:

- As text which has been historically connected with ritual and can continue to be connected to ritual today;
- As a particular type of language, which could be more accurately described as poetic narrative consisting of dialectic;
- As being present in the biblical text in a particular shape which can provide legitimacy to, and containment for, the experience as well as a being catalyst for meaning-making; and
- As being a collection of diverse speech acts which *do something* as they are articulated in prayer.

The psalms of distress, being communicated through a medium of poetic narrative, could be described as an opportunity to tell the story of distress and as opening the possibility of re-authoring the narrative with a view to the future. This narrative encompasses both the person's distress and a sense of hope.

The use of poetic narrative language provides an ideal medium for expressing emotions and vivid imaginings. In doing this it incorporates an expression of past, present and future. This means that psalms of distress are not simply raw complaint about a particular set of circumstances, or platitudes, with no significant substance. Any imagining of a hopeful future is based firmly on a recounting of the past and an authentic expression of the present resulting in an anticipation of a hopeful future.

The shape of psalms of distress suggests that the literary mode for articulating distress through cult and ritual was far from haphazard. Rather, it consisted of particular elements which are obvious in the form of most psalms of distress. The stable form of these psalms, as illustrated in the four constellations (expressing – asserting – investing – imagining), also contributes to the process of meaning-making by offering a familiar pattern of prayer to make some sense out of the distress experienced.

Many or perhaps all the features of psalms of distress, which appear real for those who authored and used these psalms, resonate with our present-day experience of distress. While each person's distress is decidedly unique there are aspects common to all experiences simply because the forum is real life and the participants are human. Kraus expresses it well, saying, 'What is typical and paradigmatic in the statements of suffering and praise in their recourse to conventional means of speech and conception, catches hold of something that is archetypal and supraindividual'.[52]

If present-day experiences of distress do hold this commonality with the authors of the biblical psalms, then the model of lament found in these psalms can provide us with a healthy way of engaging with personal distress. If they do offer a pathway for healthy engagement with distress then we must ask: how can this be done most effectively by individuals today and what effect is it likely to have for them? These questions take us into new territory. We begin our quest by exploring, in depth, the Matrix of Lament, as a helpful lens through which to view psalms of distress.

6.

The Matrix of Lament: A Model

It is clear from our journey so far that, at a theoretical level, the psalms of distress are multifaceted and have been useful as prayer for many who have gone before us. However, if these psalms are to be useful in the practice of lament today, an integrated way of viewing their content *and* function will be needed. The Matrix of Lament, first introduced in Chapter 5, is a helpful model which seeks to incorporate an understanding of the content of psalms of distress, discussed thus far, but then also offers a working model of lament using these psalms. The goal of developing this model was simple: to identify the significant features of psalms of distress comprehensively, naming and describing them in a way which assumes a functional purpose.

Matrix of Lament

I have chosen 'Matrix of Lament' to identify the model for several reasons. The word 'matrix' suggests three images, all of which have implications for someone who prays these psalms. A matrix can be a container for something. Psalms of distress, when prayed, can be viewed as a container which holds a person's experience. A second image is that of a mould. The implication here is that distress can not only be contained, or held, by praying a psalm, but also allows for shaping the experience into something different. A final image of a matrix is that of a womb. This image suggests that the matrix is not just a container which holds or even moulds distress but is also a living space which can give birth to something new.[1] Viewed together, these three images capture the variety of functions which praying psalms of distress can perform.

Beyond this it is also helpful to think of the matrix as one of *lament*, which emphasizes the idea that engaging with distress is more a process rather than an event. If psalms of distress, as part of a lament process, are to fulfil the function of being a container, mould and womb, then the distressed person needs to be familiar with their use as prayers. Using the term 'lament' also recognizes that psalms of distress are not the sum total of what it means to lament. In fact the four constellations of the matrix, explained below, could be found in other literature and rituals associated with distress. However, here I am proposing that, when praying these psalms is combined with appropriate rituals, a unique richness of expression can be intentionally embraced by a person in distress.

The Matrix of Lament consists of four unique and yet complementary constellations (expressing – asserting – investing – imagining). Each of the four constellations contains a set of ideas, conditions, symptoms or traits that fall into a pattern. When placed together in the matrix, the four constellations can be seen to represent different aspects of a lament process.

So the Matrix of Lament, with its constellations, provides a contained space within which thoughts and feelings related to distress can be expressed safely. As psalms of distress arise from a faith context, clearly God is explicitly considered to be the significant other for the distressed person within the matrix and is represented by 'I–Thou' language.

However, to reflect the changes in a distressed person's sense of relationship with God throughout the process, I include clarifying prepositions between the 'I' and the 'Thou'.[2] It is also important to stress that the constellations can be encountered more than once as a person engages with distress and this is often reflected in the text of the psalms themselves. It is not so much a linear or sequential experience of the Matrix of Lament that provides the impetus for moving through distress but, rather, the engagement with, and interaction between, all four constellations.

As a way of understanding what constitutes each constellation, and how we encounter them in the psalms of distress, each one is described in detail below with examples drawn from Psalm 22. This psalm clearly contains the four constellations of the matrix, even though there is no clear order. It underlines the fact that the constellations need not be, and often are not, sequential.[3] The diversity of expression in this psalm and the sharp movements within the text are helpful reminders of what genuine human response to distress can be like. The juxtaposing of distress and praise in the psalm highlights an intensity of distress but, at the same time, an unexpected fusion with the possibility of hope. This psalm has been described as 'exploding the limits' of how people can express their feelings to God.[4] Clearly there is a sense of alienation from the start but the exact source, or nature, of the distress is not described.

The presence of all these features means that Psalm 22 brings into sharp focus the usefulness of the Matrix of Lament as a lens through which all psalms of distress can be viewed. Below is the full text of the psalm so that the examples of each constellation in the following sections can also be considered in the context of the psalm as a whole.

An Example: Psalm 22

My God, my God, why have you forsaken me?
  Why are you so far from helping me, from the words of my
    groaning?
O my God, I cry by day, but you do not answer;
  and by night, but find no rest.
Yet you are holy,
  enthroned on the praises of Israel.
In you our ancestors trusted;
  they trusted, and you delivered them.
To you they cried, and were saved;
  in you they trusted, and were not put to shame.
But I am a worm, and not human;
  scorned by others, and despised by the people.
All who see me mock at me;
  they make mouths at me, they shake their heads;
'Commit your cause to the Lord; let him deliver –
  let him rescue the one in whom he delights!'
Yet it was you who took me from the womb;
  you kept me safe on my mother's breast.

On you I was cast from my birth,
 and since my mother bore me you have been my God.
Do not be far from me,
 for trouble is near
 and there is no one to help.
Many bulls encircle me,
 strong bulls of Bashan surround me;
they open wide their mouths at me,
 like a ravening and roaring lion.
I am poured out like water,
 and all my bones are out of joint;
my heart is like wax;
 it is melted within my breast;
my mouth is dried up like a potsherd,
 and my tongue sticks to my jaws;
 you lay me in the dust of death.
For dogs are all around me;
 a company of evildoers encircles me.
My hands and feet have shriveled;
I can count all my bones.
They stare and gloat over me;
they divide my clothes among themselves,
 and for my clothing they cast lots.
But you, O Lord, do not be far away!
 O my help, come quickly to my aid!
Deliver my soul from the sword,
 my life from the power of the dog!
 Save me from the mouth of the lion!
From the horns of the wild oxen you have rescued me.
I will tell of your name to my brothers and sisters;
 in the midst of the congregation I will praise you:
You who fear the Lord, praise him!
 All you offspring of Jacob, glorify him;
 stand in awe of him, all you offspring of Israel!
For he did not despise or abhor
 the affliction of the afflicted;
he did not hide his face from me,
 but heard when I cried to him.
From you comes my praise in the great congregation;

my vows I will pay before those who fear him.
The poor shall eat and be satisfied;
    those who seek him shall praise the LORD.
    May your hearts live for ever!
All the ends of the earth shall remember
    and turn to the LORD;
and all the families of the nations
    shall worship before him.
For dominion belongs to the LORD,
    and he rules over the nations.
To him, indeed, shall all who sleep in the earth bow down;
    before him shall bow all who go down to the dust,
    and I shall live for him.
Posterity will serve him;
    future generations will be told about the Lord,
and proclaim his deliverance to a people yet unborn,
    saying that he has done it.

We will now look at the elements of each constellation in turn and then consider how they are expressed in Psalm 22. First, however, it will be useful to be reminded of the elements that constitute the four constellations in the Matrix of Lament:

- *Expressing*
  - Invocation
  - Complaint
- *Asserting*
  - Confession of sin
  - Affirmation of innocence
  - Plea
- *Investing*
  - Imprecation
  - Affirmation of confidence
  - Acknowledgement of divine response
- *Imagining*
  - Vow
  - Pledge
  - Hymnic blessing
  - Anticipation of thanks

In Figures 1–4 that follow you will observe the three key areas of potential change for the psalmist in each of the constellations. They are identified as levels of distress, consisting of the particular elements listed above which are typical of each constellation; locus of control, which consists of the three characters found in psalms of distress –the asterisk (*) indicating the character with whom control is perceived to be, the cross (x) indicating the character perceived as lacking control and the question mark (?) indicating the character whose degree of control is not clearly defined; and sense of relationship, which is expressed in terms of I–Thou. As the Matrix of Lament takes shape, with the addition of each constellation, the movements present will become clearer.

Expressing Constellation

The expressing constellation is usually formed with an invocation and complaint. Both these elements are present in most psalms of distress and often the invocation leads naturally into the complaint as the psalmist expresses distress. In Figure 1 you can see what the expressing constellation and its elements looks like in relationship to the whole Matrix of Lament.

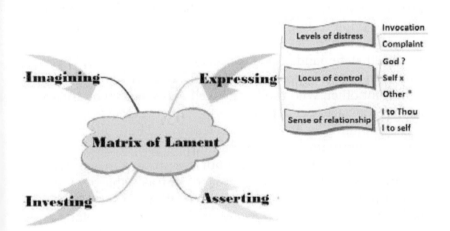

Figure 1. The Matrix of Lament, elaborating Expressing

An invocation sets the tone for this psalm of distress and is integral to the dialectic that the psalmist is initiating. As in Psalm 22, it is often expressed at the beginning of the psalm as a question[5] or a request.[6] Immediately, three features of invocation are clear. First, we are confronted by the expressing of emotions, evoked by distress. Second, we can see the struggle for some sense of control in the face of distress and, third, the invocation is clearly an expression of strained relationship between the psalmist and God.

Despite a sense of isolation, there is a strong sense of 'I' (the psalmist) expressing feelings and thoughts *to* 'Thou' (God). This is the starting point of so many psalms of distress and demonstrates that, in spite of feeling isolation, the psalmist expresses thoughts and feelings in terms of 'I *to* Thou' *because* of a belief in their relationship with God. Westermann makes an interesting observation that the psalmist often uses the more formal address to God in the invocation. He infers that such a manner of address not only recognizes the existence of the divine-human relationship but, also, that God is the focus rather than the psalmist.[7] As a result, he proposes the more formal English word 'Thou' better represents the Hebrew form, which accords honour to the addressee. Despite this affirming of relationship there is no question that the invocation also clearly voices the fractured, or tenuous, sense of that relationship with brutal honesty. The invocation acknowledges, but also questions the divine–human relationship at the same time.

It is also interesting that the invocation can take either a positive or negative form.[8] Both forms often produced a transition into the plea that demands God take action for the psalmist.[9] The invocation is a way of expressing the psalmist's belief that God is their significant other, who can be invoked and who can be trusted to act in response to personal distress.

A complaint has two obvious features. There is a raw boldness in complaining accompanied by graphic descriptions of the situation. Emotions are not suppressed in any way by the psalmist and the harsh language contrasts sharply with the honorific address found in the invocation. It seems that the address can be graphic *because* of the psalmist's relationship rather than *despite* it. What is being hoped for by the psalmist? It could be an attempt to move God to compassion, elicit action or, alternatively, to simply use the sense of relationship with God as a conduit through which emotions can be safely expressed.

In psalms of distress the complaint is often shaped as a question, or series of questions. Although these could be viewed as rhetorical they also imply the desire for a response.[10] The common interrogative, 'Why?' seems to transcend time, culture and theological perspective when prompted by distress. In these psalms it emerges from the presence of distress and the absence of peace.[11] The questions posed are ones which must be asked, even if an adequate response is not forthcoming or possible.

The complaint is one of the more challenging features of a lament process. It provides empowerment for a person to ask the provocative questions which inevitably emerge when people are distressed. Psalms of distress show that these questions *can be asked within* the context of relationship with God, even though there may not be a satisfactory answer. The questions also recognize that, if there is an answer, the most significant, or perhaps the only, source of such a response can be God. With the invocation and complaint the psalmist is expressing a belief that God has control and a hope that, consequently, God will exercise power which the psalmist does not have.

So, the expressing constellation voices the psalmist's predicament, as perceived from a human perspective. It is expressed from a place of deep emotional torment and questioning – a place where the questions need to be asked even if they cannot be answered. Beyond this, however, the constellation also reveals the struggle for personal empowerment amid distress. Although the psalmist wants to see God as the one in control they still seek for a sense of personal empowerment. Clearly at this point the perception is that control lies with the enemy. The psalmist is feeling powerless and God appears to be, at best, inactive or at worst impotent.

Expressing is found in the form of a natural dialectic directed towards God. As mentioned above we can see that God is a significant other in relationship to the psalmist.[12] Here the psalmist is free to express feelings *to* God even though there is a felt alienation in that relationship. However, expressing doesn't end here. The psalmist, through invocation and complaint, is recognizing their own feelings about themselves ('I *to* self'). In other words the psalmist displays a mindfulness of the distress itself, their reactions to it and the effects of it.

There can be as much implicit questioning of oneself as there is questioning of God, but why might this be so? In part, the psalmist is desperately striving to make sense of relationship with God although another facet of this is making sense of one's relationship with oneself. It is significant that the psalmist's expressing marks the beginning in the growth in self-awareness.

Let's see how the elements of the expressing constellation are present in Psalm 22:1–2:

> My God, my God, why have you forsaken me?
>> Why are you so far from helping me, from the words of my groaning?
> O my God, I cry by day, but you do not answer;
>> and by night, but find no rest.

A clear example of both an invocation and a complaint can be found in these opening verses. Here the invocation quickly breaks out into a complaint against God and clearly the relationship is expressed through dialectic with God. Amid distress the psalmist, perhaps rather surprisingly, speaks directly *to* God about God's perceived absence from the situation. Ironically, it is an expression of both doubt and faith together. We will discover later in some of the personal stories of prayer that this was one of the most difficult tensions to hold.

Another way of considering what is happening here is to see it as cognitive dissonance where the experience and theology of the psalmist fail to match. At the same time as the psalmist experiences a sense of abandonment *by* God, their words are directed to God. The existential question becomes a theological question for the person of faith. Is God present amid distress? Does God hear my cry? Does God care? At this point in the matrix, ambivalence overshadows any sense of hope.

The protracted nature of the distress is implied by the use of 'day and night' imagery in Psalm 22:2. God's absence is also described here in two distinct ways: lacking in action to help the psalmist and abandoning the psalmist. Despite this, feelings and thoughts are still expressed within the context of a faith relationship demonstrating a belief that communication with God, as a significant other, continues to prevail. Paradoxically then, the relationship is evident despite these feelings of alienation and isolation being disclosed. All the questions and statements are expressed *to* God and there is an implied questioning of self-belief and self-confidence.

> But I am a worm, and not human;
>> scorned by others, and despised by the people.
> All who see me mock at me;
>> they make mouths at me, they shake their heads;
> 'Commit your cause to the LORD; let him deliver –
>> let him rescue the one in whom he delights!'

Verses 6 to 8 mark a return to the expressing constellation with the psalmist voicing feelings of worthlessness, being an object of scorn and being despised. Interestingly here the words of the enemy are also directly quoted by the psalmist, underlining the reasons for the distress being experienced. Terse language high-lights the often chaotic experience of confronting distress and it also juxtaposes the potential potency of God (immediately prior to this in vv. 3–5) with the impotency of human beings (vv. 6–8). The dialectic at this point includes enemies, even though they are not directly addressed in the psalm. They are characterized as a group actively working against the psalmist and this exacerbates the sense of isolation the distressed person feels from both God and their community.

Expressing complaint then, as found in these verses, repre-sents an outpouring of the emotions resulting from persecution, alienation, isolation and self-doubt. The 'worm' image, as a meta-phor, provides a vivid picture which encapsulates the feelings of lowliness and/or humiliation experienced by the psalmist. These feelings of isolation and powerlessness combine to produce a further struggle for self-understanding and a desire for clarity about the efficacy of the divine–human relationship. The psalmist here views themself as unable to cope alone and no more than fair game for the enemy's attack.

Asserting Constellation

The asserting constellation is a combination of confession of sin or affirmation of innocence,[13] and a plea for divine help in the situation.[14] The first two elements are not always present but the third is always asserted. In fact the plea for divine help is situated at the core of psalms of distress. You can see how the asserting constellation with its elements fits into the Matrix of Lament in Figure 2.

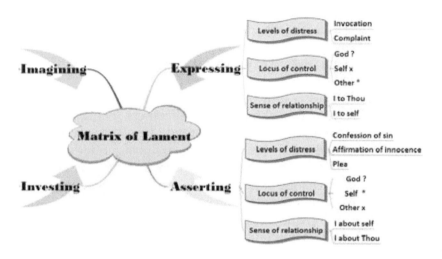

Figure 2. The Matrix of Lament, elaborating Expressing and Asserting

A confession of sin, or affirmation of innocence, is often disproportionately small compared with the other elements but, nonetheless, noteworthy. These elements function within psalms of distress in some significant ways. They show both dis-ease at the lack of control the distressed person feels and an attempt to take some control back through these assertions. They also highlight particular assertions *about* the psalmist's self and *about* God's potential role in the psalmist's predicament. These elements can also be viewed as an attempt to establish a case as to why God should respond positively to the psalmist's distress.

The act of confession is most commonly found in penitential psalms, where the cause of distress is understood as a result of an offence against God.[15] Conversely, affirming innocence argues that the offence is not the reason for distress, therefore the psalmist is an innocent sufferer needing protection, whose distress is caused by enemies[16] and, perhaps indirectly by God.[17] Regardless of the perceived origins of the injustice, and resulting distress, the asserting constellation's elements form a persuasive argument addressed to God. This is a direct appeal to the just and compassionate nature of God based on the psalmist's belief and on God's past action.

The plea for help can be otherwise described as petition and is deeply evocative. It carries the painful emotions of disorientation, or dislocation, in relationship to God and the intense desire for the distress to be relieved and the situation to be resolved. This element raises a question about the potential effect an assertion of this kind may have for the distressed person. At the very least, the expressing and asserting constellations together suggest that the psalmist can ask God for help and face distress with God.

The plea recognizes a latent divine power which is, nonetheless, available to the psalmist. The power imbalance between the psalmist and the enemy is not one the psalmist alone has the ability to redress. By means of a plea, the seeds of hope for divine action are planted. The pivotal nature of the plea is its recognition that the situation can potentially be changed by God, if God should act. In asserting through a plea the psalmist is voicing a particular belief *about* God which, it is hoped, will bring about a response.[18]

It is helpful to characterize the relational aspect of the asserting constellation as 'I *about* Thou' and 'I *about* myself'. In other words, the elements suggest that engaging effectively with distress involves asserting beliefs *about* oneself and *about* God. This may be an attempt, by the distressed person, to feel justified in seeking divine action but it also appears to be an attempt to wrest control from the enemy by asserting some belief in personal empowerment. These assertions stress both the inherent need for personal empowerment[19] and, yet, an accompanying dependence on God through a divine–human relationship.

As already suggested, the element of plea sits at the core of these psalms and, as part of the asserting constellation, marks a significant transition in the Matrix of Lament. This transition occurs as the psalmist attempts to take control of the situation by showing a willingness to recognize the potential for self-empowerment, regained through a collaborative effort with God. As an explicit attempt by the person to motivate God to action, it provides the impetus for moving from asserting concepts *about* oneself and God to an investing *in* oneself and *in* God. Any ability to invest in this way is almost always foreshadowed by asserting a plea.

While there is no example of an affirmation of innocence or confession of sin in Psalm 22:11 and verses 19 to 21, there is a plea for help.

> Do not be far from me, for trouble is near and there is no one
> to help.
>
> But you, O Lord, do not be far away!
> O my help, come quickly to my aid!
> Deliver my soul from the sword,
> my life from the power of the dog!
> Save me from the mouth of the lion!
> From the horns of the wild oxen you have rescued me.

Verse 11 marks the first evidence of this plea and it is re-emphasized and expanded in verses 19 through to the first part of verse 21, providing a clear example of the asserting constellation ('I *about* Thou'). It is clearly a concerted plea for action on God's part. The divine name is used here for the first time in the psalm which, perhaps, suggests a greater sense of intimacy, either real or desired. A renewed confidence in God's capacity to act is clearly asserted as the psalmist sees *Yahweh* as the only hope for resolution in the situation.[20] The asserting constellation reaches a peak of confidence at the close of verse 21 where the psalmist states, 'you have rescued me'. The deliverance is 'experienced' despite the circumstances.

Investing Constellation

The investing constellation combines imprecation, affirmation of confidence and the acknowledgement of a divine response as different ways of voicing the belief that investing *in* God is efficacious. It also implies an investing *in* oneself as a burgeoning sense of self-empowerment emerges. The investing constellation elements found in the Matrix of Lament, are illustrated in Figure 3.

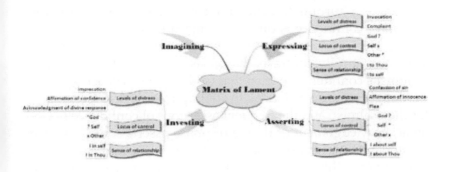

Figure 3. The Matrix of Lament, elaborating Expressing, Asserting and Investing

Often collocated with the plea in psalms of distress is the element of imprecation which is used freely and not infrequently.[21] Imprecation is an impassioned hyperbole, by which the psalmist demands that God take revenge on the distressed person's behalf. It is interesting that imprecation never implies that the psalmists themselves will take violent action against their enemy. Rather, it is a call for divine action. Imprecation is then best defined as a necessary emotional outpouring for the psalmist rather than an indication of intended action.

It seems, from its almost ubiquitous presence in these psalms, that imprecation voices a significant dynamic within the Matrix of Lament. Appreciation of its presence, as indicative of the changing power dynamics in a lament process, is critical. As described above, the plea marks a psychodynamic movement within the psalmist towards recognition of partnership with God amid distress. In imprecation this partnership is not just recognized but also viewed as one which needs to result in action. The psalmist's sense of personal empowerment is vested *in* themselves to seek divine action, and in God to act in response. Through investing *in* God, in this way, the graphic and confronting nature of imprecation exposes the raw emotions of a distressed person.

Imprecation implies the possibility that God *can* act for the psalmist and an affirmation of confidence, when present, supports the belief within psalms of distress. Westermann describes this element as a 'turning to God' or a 'confession of trust'.[22] An affirmation of confidence is often introduced by use of a disjunctive *waw* in Hebrew[23] usually translated into English as 'but' or 'yet'. This dramatically contrasts the sensed inaction of God with the psalmist's confidence to trust that God can and will act.

Alongside imprecation, with its implication that God *can* act for the psalmist, and the frequent assertions of confidence in God, an acknowledgement of divine response asserts something even greater; an *actual* divine response, even if it is anticipatory at this point.[24] While this kind of acknowledgement is not always a statement describing the psalmist's lived experience it does, nevertheless, mark an emerging hopeful vision of relief from distress and can also be accompanied by thanksgiving to God for divine action.[25] The acknowledgement of God's response is forceful, as it emerges from the depths of despair and offers a hope-filled vision in response to the earlier plea. In a sudden change of direction the distressed person invests *in* God, believing in the possibility of imminent response. It represents an attitude which appears to express the person's ability to prevail through the experience of distress *because of* this hope, even though the hope may in fact remain unrealized.

The investing constellation marks a significant shift in both locus of control *and* relationship. This shift could be characterized as 'I *in* self' and 'I *in* Thou'. The psalmist invests *in* God by entrusting God with both the ability and the willingness to respond to the situation of distress. Investing displays a renewed trust which enables the psalmist to rest in the confidence that God will act *for* and not *against* the distressed person. With this in view the enemy does not appear any longer to hold the same position of power in the three-way relationship. In fact a power reversal is implied by the language of the elements in this constellation.

While imprecation is not a feature present in Psalm 22, verses 9 to 10 and verse 21b do voice an affirmation of confidence, which marks a dramatic shift from the asserting constellation to the investing constellation.

> Yet it was you who took me from the womb;
>> you kept me safe on my mother's breast.
> On you I was cast from my birth,
>> and since my mother bore me you have been my God.

> From the horns of the wild oxen you *have* rescued me (italics mine).

Verses 9 to 10 stand in stark contrast to verses 6 to 8 which have been identified above as part of the expressing constellation and describe the impotency of human beings. In light of the impotency just expressed, verses 9 to 10 contain an affirmation of confidence which voices a powerful investment in God for a sense of hope. The relational emphasis, at this point, could be described as 'I *in* Thou', shifting the onus back to God and God's action.

These verses have a narrative quality within the broader story of the whole psalm. Here the story of the past is framed in terms of total dependence on, and connectedness with, God from birth onwards. For the psalmist, it seems that personal safety and solidarity with God are equally important. Addressing God in the second person reinforces this sense of relational connection as the psalmist reframes the story in the light of current experience.

The phrase 'my God', used as part of the affirmation of confidence, provides a contrasting echo to verse 1. The emphasis here is now one of growing intimacy, rather than the alienation expressed in verses 1 and 2. Remembering adds substance to the image of this god being 'my God', for the psalmist. Through the dialectic directed towards God the psalmist can now voice confidence in a god who cannot fail to deliver in the present, based on experience of the past.

Although the acknowledgment of divine response is short in this example it is, nevertheless, significant. In the Hebrew, use of the perfect conjugation for the verb 'rescue' marks the paradox of an event. The form of the verb suggests an action which has already been accomplished, even though it may not yet have eventuated. In other words the psalmist believes in the reality of God's rescuing action *despite* the presenting situation.

Imagining Constellation

The imagining constellation consists of a vow, or what is sometimes referred to as a pledge, together with a hymnic blessing and/or an anticipation of thanks. This constellation clearly imagines a future free from distress and confidence in God's ability to deliver such a situation. The elements of the imagining constellation in the Matrix of Lament are illustrated in Figure 4.

Figure 4. The Matrix of Lament, elaborating Expressing, Asserting, Investing and Imagining

The shift to a hope-filled vision and sense of partnership with God, in the face of distress, is often first heard in the form of a vow or pledge. The psalmist powerfully voices loyalty to God and often expresses this with a personal testimony of what God has 'already' done. While accepting that in reality there may not have been an *actual* response from God, the vow displays two important characteristics now forming a critical part of the psalmist's perspective on distress. It shows the person's inherent desire to believe that God *can* change the situation and also, a personal dec-ision to act on the basis that this belief has already, or will shortly, become reality.[26]

Westermann argues that the presence of praise, such as that found in the vow or pledge, can only be understood within a context of lament.[27] This is what leads him to suggest that the goal of lament is praise. Perhaps it could be viewed as the ultimate goal. However, the immediate goal, for the psalmist, appears to be a desire to reinforce the expectation of a response from God so that the present situation can be endured. Also, often accompanying a vow or pledge is the expression of a desire for God to do, or not to do, particular things in the future.[28] In the form of a hymnic blessing, the desire manifests itself as an outpouring of praise and thanks that continues to seek for divine action. This again shows a shift in the psalmist's state of mind.

The imagining constellation, more than any other part of the Matrix of Lament, marks a return to viewing the relationship between the psalmist and God as one of connection and intimacy. The psalmist imagines a new position of 'I *with* Thou' with an accompanying sense of contentment with themselves ('I *with* self'). The elements of this constellation present a vision of hopeful possibility where the distress has been faced, engaged with and endured *with* God and the sense of alienation has dissipated. It also suggests that the divine–human relationship is now stronger and deeper *because of* the process reflected in the Matrix of Lament. It is interesting to note that the imagining constellation seems to emerge as a direct result of the psalmist confronting their distress *with* God. Personal empowerment is gleaned from this sense of togetherness with God. There is no suggestion, within the Matrix of Lament, that God is requested to take matters completely out of the psalmist's hands. Rather, engaging with distress is an experience to be faced through divine–human cooperation and collaboration.

From verse 22, through to the end of the psalm, perhaps, rather unexpectedly, a hopeful imagining emerges from the melting-pot of thoughts and feelings produced by distress. The relationship between the psalmist and God is best expressed as 'I *with* Thou' and is voiced through a hymn of thanks directed to God. The vision imagines a sense of solidarity, not alienation, between the psalmist and God and they are no longer influenced by the opposition of the enemy. Locus of control is with both the person and God, since the distressed person is now feeling a sense of self-empowerment not previously possessed. The psalmist is praising God, surrounded by a community with whom solidarity is possible.

> I will tell of your name to my brothers and sisters;
>> in the midst of the congregation I will praise you:
> You who fear the LORD, praise him!
>> All you offspring of Jacob, glorify him;
>> stand in awe of him, all you offspring of Israel!

For he did not despise or abhor
  the affliction of the afflicted;
he did not hide his face from me,
  but heard when I cried to him.
From you comes my praise in the great congregation;
  my vows I will pay before those who fear him.
The poor shall eat and be satisfied;
  those who seek him shall praise the LORD.
  May your hearts live for ever!
All the ends of the earth shall remember
  and turn to the LORD;
and all the families of the nations
  shall worship before him.
For dominion belongs to the LORD,
  and he rules over the nations.
To him, indeed, shall all who sleep in the earth bow down;
  before him shall bow all who go down to the dust,
  and I shall live for him.
Posterity will serve him;
  future generations will be told about the Lord,
and proclaim his deliverance to a people yet unborn,
  saying that he has done it.

It is also noteworthy that the hymn contains two vows in verses 22 and 26. The first is one of personal commitment to share with others what God has done and the second describes in more detail the expected response from people who have been satisfied with God's actions. This personal commitment again demonstrates the principle that empowerment is found jointly between the psalmist and God. The hymn of thanks then broadens into a hymn of praise encompassing all creation in verses 27 to 31. This forms the final part of the imagining for the psalmist in Psalm 22. It provides the opportunity for an altered and expanded perspective on both the present and the future. The imagining elements culminate with an unambiguous, hope-filled pronouncement about the future, transcending both the individual and the community to encompass the whole of humankind.

So, we can see an emerging picture of how distress is engaged with by the psalmist, through the lens of the Matrix of Lament and its constellations. The matrix depicts a decrease in the psalmist's level of distress and a movement towards having a greater sense of personal empowerment. Accompanying these movements is a deeper intimacy and strength in the divine–human relationship which could be characterized as a partnership in the imagining constellation. It is important to reiterate that the experience of distress may not have passed at this point; however, a movement towards integration and resolution has begun.

The Characters in Psalms of Distress

Having considered the elements which make up the four constellations we will now briefly explore in more depth the relationships between the characters in psalms of distress. The characters which engage in the three-way dialectic, as explored in Chapter 4, are included in Figure 4. The presence of the dialectic in the four constellations provides the impetus for psychodynamic movement to occur.

The three major characters present within psalms of distress are the psalmist, God and the enemy. Beyond identifying the characters, it is important to ask how we might best describe the relationships between them. Westermann provides a helpful beginning point by describing the relationships as psychological (the psalmist's relationship with self),[29] social (the psalmist's relationship with enemies) and theological (the psalmist's relationship with God).[30] The dialectic itself consists of direct speech (of the psalmist) and quoted speech (of God and/or of the enemy) together with the intrapsychic reflections of the psalmist present in each type of speech.

The psychological relationship

The first consideration is what could be called the psychological relationship, which highlights how psalmists view themselves in relation to others. The language used in psalms of distress is revealing in this regard. One example is the frequent use of a Hebrew word usually translated as 'poor, needy, afflicted or weak'.[31] This type of description is indicative of the distressed person's disempowered predicament.[32]

A confession of sin, which we have already discussed, indicates an awareness of the psalmists in relation to themselves and their perceived personal shortcomings or failures. In contrast to this, the psalmists sometimes describe themselves as being faithful. All these views of self provide insight into the type of self-awareness experiences of distress create.

As psalms of distress unfold it becomes evident that the psalmists' views of themselves can change throughout the process of engagement.[33] It is the voicing of thoughts and feelings about oneself, in relation to distress, that contributes to the impetus for change in the person's concept of self. This change begins with increasing self-awareness and culminates in greater self-understanding.

The theological relationship

The second relationship, evident within these psalms, is between the psalmist and God, or what could be called the theological relationship.[34] Despite the continuous cries of suffering from the psalmist there is still an acknowledgement of divine presence with the person *in* the distress.[35] However, even given this belief in divine presence, psalms of distress express a broad variety of perspectives on what that actually looks like for the psalmist. Divine presence, or lack of it, is variously described as wrathful, rejecting, forgetting and hiding.[36] There is a striking dissonance between these fragmented, negative perceptions of God and the clear plea for a response from a god who the psalmist at least *wants to believe* can do something helpful.

In an attempt to understand this incongruity, Farmer explains the psalmist's calling out to God as proactive, saying, '[The psalmists] do not wait passively for God to notice their pain and come to their aid. Rather, they cry out as an act of faith in the steadfast love of the one they confidently trust will not reject them for what they feel or say.'[37]

She makes a critical observation about psalms of distress, particularly with her final observation. From the psalmist's perspective the relationship with God is such that nothing seems to be outside the bounds of expression towards God. The dialectic is free to contain whatever thoughts and emotions emerge from the distressed person's reflection on their experience. It is also important to notice that the dialectic voices real emotions that need to be expressed somewhere and it is in the context of the divine–human relationship that the psalmist chooses to express them most freely.[38] In the process of doing this, the dialectic voices thoughts and emotions that, at some point, assign power to God as the primary change agent.

To prompt God to act as a change agent the psalmists sometimes use the dialectic to juxtapose the actions of God with the actions of themselves. For example, the faithful life of the psalmist is sometimes contrasted with an implicit cry that God is not being faithful.[39] This could be viewed as an attempt to leverage change resulting in a favourable response from God. Despite all these approaches, even a cursory reading of the psalms of distress suggests the psalmist persists steadfastly looking towards God as the only hope for resolution of the situation.

The social relationship

The third facet of relationship in the dialectic is with those who surround the psalmist. On the positive side of this, Gerstenberger argues convincingly for the significance of the community to the person who is engaging with distress.[40] Although his idea of the presence of a 'ritual expert' with a salvation-type oracle and 'kinsfolk' is speculative, it does highlight two important principles. First, it underlines the traditional place of ritual using psalms of distress and, second, the presence of others highlights the importance of the community to a person who is distressed. The person is not distressed alone even though their feelings of distress may include a sense of isolation.

Although those around the psalmist can be supportive, there are also those who clearly oppose the distressed person and their existence is made obvious in the text of these psalms. These people are, more often than not, characterized as enemies. Though the confrontation, which results in distress, is not clearly defined, the enemy is usually viewed as the cause of the psalmist's distress. So, in these psalms, the person's relationship with God is clearly strained while the relationship with their enemy is palpably detrimental to their well-being. When the enemy is referred to, it is clear that the power is perceived to be with them.

It is interesting that the enemy is not always characterized as other people; sometimes God can also be viewed in this way as well.[41] Despite the regular reference to enemies, their identity is never disclosed, prompting Day to suggest that, 'This is just what we should expect of psalms that were constantly being used in the liturgy of a variety of people'.[42] Day highlights an important issue. These psalms, used as part of liturgical ritual, recognize the presence of some kind of enemy for all people in distress. However, the enemy being anonymous allows for their identity to be metaphorical or real; oneself, God, someone or something else.

What then is the role of the enemy within psalms of distress? Even if a person, who is experiencing distress, cannot identify exactly who their enemy is, the enemy's anonymity shifts the focus from identity to *function*. It seems that the ability of a distressed person to identify the source of distress, irrespective of whether the source is a person or not, creates the possibility of this third direction for the dialectic and contributes to the self-awareness and self-understanding referred to earlier. All this suggests that part of a growth in self-awareness and self-understanding comes through viewing oneself over against the 'other'.

A troubling aspect of the dialectic against the enemy is the use of imprecation, already mentioned. Although this element is sometimes placed in the theological 'too hard basket', it nevertheless performs a critical function within the Matrix of Lament.[43] While imprecation is a calling on God to act for the psalmist, rather than the person taking avenging action into their own hands, it does empower the person by allowing them to acknowledge their struggle with those who are the cause of their distress, even if they are not present. It is also another way in which confidence can be expressed in a god who is perceived to be able to help, contributing to the person's sense of empowerment. Most importantly, however, imprecation provides an avenue for venting vengeful feelings in a non-physical, and yet emotionally cathartic, manner.

The dialectic, found in the form of the three-way relationship in these psalms, is a significant aspect to the transformative potential they possess. In each of the constellations of the matrix, at least one of these relationships is in play as the dialectic unfolds. In a way the dialectic drives the process resulting in a profound psychological effect on the person praying these psalms. This leads Brueggemann to suggest that, 'While the experience shaped the pattern of expression, it is also true that the pattern of expression helped shape the experience, so it could be received, understood and coped with'.[44]

As a person praying psalms of distress actually enters into the dialectic they can discover an effective pathway towards engaging with their experiences of distress. Then the psalms of distress can be viewed as a matrix which not only contains but also moulds experiences of distress, eventually giving birth to something new.

7.

The Practice of Lament

To further understand the birthing potential of the psalms of distress, viewed through the Matrix of Lament lens, it is important to consider the relationship between the shape and content of these psalms for the practice of lament. To do this we will take a short detour into pastoral theology and its exploration of how people in distress best engage with their experiences. Our focus here is best sharpened with three questions:

- Who is lament for?
- What does lament provide?
- How can lament be engaged?

Responding to these questions will, in part, also involve addressing some prominent theological themes found in psalms of distress: the nature of God, the nature of humankind and the nature of the relationship between God and humankind.

Who is Lament for?

As highlighted in Chapter 2, it can be convincingly argued that the Psalter, as a whole, has historically been a critical part of Judeo-Christian worship. This use of the Psalter included regular engagement with psalms of distress. It can be assumed then that, in the past, psalms of distress were accepted as a normative and, in fact, necessary part of expressing human experience in the liturgy. This experience, of course, included situations of distress.

While it might be imagined that a lament process is only appro-priate for those who are facing a particular distress at a particular time, the traditional use would suggest otherwise. It has already been acknowledged that psalms of distress originated from particular people and emerged from particular experiences of distress. However, their inclusion within the canon of Scripture and within the liturgy of both synagogue and church assumes the validity of their *continual use*.[1] That is, not only were they employed when a person faced specific distress but also during times when they were *not* facing specific distress.

On this basis Billman and Migliore argue convincingly that a lament process is in fact divinely sanctioned. They state that, 'for the community of faith it is the living God attested to by the biblical witness who grants the decisive permission to lament'.[2] While I agree with their view it is, perhaps, not strong enough. The prominent place of psalms of distress within the Psalter, together with their historical use, suggests not only *permission* but also perhaps a *requirement* to lament. It is important, then, to consider what such a process facilitates. Again Billman and Migliore are insightful saying that, 'the capacity to grieve deeply is a mark of psychological maturity, rooted in processes that are essential for human life and development. The inability to mourn diminishes human life.'[3]

This being so, a lament process ought to be seen as a necessity rather than an option, if people are to grow in maturity. Of course, their observations also suggest that a lack of such a process may inhibit the maturation process and perhaps, implicitly, suggests a deficient view of the value of human beings externalizing their distress.

Although psalms of distress assume a context of faith, where the existence of God is acknowledged, this should not preclude the possibility that these psalms may also be useful for people of no particular faith. Nor should it suggest that a process of lament apart from an expression of faith in a divine other might not also be beneficial.[4] In other words the *process* has an integrity which can be independent of its *content*. So, lament is for anyone, but the content of the process will vary according to a person's convic-tions about God, humankind and any relationship that exists between the two.

As emphasized in various ways previously, we find, in psalms of distress, a lament process articulated in terms of relationship. One aspect of relationship is an assumed connection between the psalmist and God. Craghan says, 'What the laments really presuppose is that my/our problem necessarily becomes God's problem . . . That there is a God of my/our problem means the death of solitude and isolation. We are linked to Another.'[5]

In a biblical lament process then, the relationship with God and the potential efficacy of such a relationship are supremely important. Although an articulation of distress, directed towards God, could be viewed as originating with the psalmist, Levine argues that it is, in fact, always a response to the 'divine word' which has already been spoken. God's speaking and the person's relationship with God always precedes the cry of distress. Not only this but Levine then adds that, 'The world [also] addresses us, and we must answer from our unique place of existence'.[6] So, in a lament process, the person in distress, being addressed by God and their world, discovers a greater understanding of themselves *through* their experience of these relationships.[7] This discovery is then able to produce something further.[8]

Another way of saying this is that the potential for deeper self-awareness and self-understanding is inextricably linked to one's capacity to engage with a view outside oneself.[9] This practice of engaging with a view outside of oneself is facilitated by the dialectic, already examined.[10] Taking part in the dialectic, through prayer, offers those who are lamenting an opportunity to see themselves and their world from a different perspective. Consequently, broadening self-awareness and self-understanding emerge from reflecting on the critical relationships in which the distressed person is involved. Reflection on oneself, *in* relationship, then presents an opportunity for making sense *of* relationship. Miller highlights the paradox of relationship for the distressed person saying, 'As cries for help, and thus as prayers, the laments belong to us in our aloneness and become the voice of that *isolation*. This is not the voice of solitude.'[11]

These feelings may be so for those who are experiencing particular distress, at a particular time, but what about those are experiencing more generalized distress in everyday life? As already suggested, the use of psalms of distress in Judeo-Christian liturgy implicitly signals that it *is* relevant. Jacobsen even argues that a process of lament is not only relevant for those experiencing generalized distress, but can have value for a person by being intentionally introduced to them 'in order to effect a change in behaviour, a change in attitude, or force the addition of a new thought'.[12]

This could be viewed merely as a contrivance of something which is not a current reality in the person's experience or, alternatively, as an acknowledgement and validation of the fact that specific personal distress is an unavoidable part of real life for all human beings at one time or another. So, an intentional introduction of a process of lament offers a valuable rehearsal for people not in distress to learn how to engage with their distress when they do encounter it. Given then, that a lament process is useful for this, it now leads us to our second question, 'What does lament provide?'

What does Lament Provide?

It is possible that ancient communities recognized the preparatory function of ritual for the unavoidable experiences of distress to come. Tanner stresses this function, proposing that it is easier to pray these psalms *apart from* experiences of specific distress, consequently making it easier to pray them *in* the experience of distress. She adds that, 'It provides a place to go, a biblical place to stand in the dark valleys of life'.[13] Beyond this it also offers a place where transformation can take place; from despair to hope. Billman and Migliore also affirm such a process saying that: 'people are helped when they are encouraged, indeed given biblical authorization, to give voice to the full expression of their experience, and . . . there is a profound connection between healing and participation in the life and worship of a community of faith'.[14]

Their final observations also remind us that individuals cannot be viewed as completely separate from the communities in which they exist. Even if a person expresses and engages with their distressing experiences as an individual, the relationships they have with others will inevitably influence their reflections and responses and vice versa. A healthy lament process, then, will offer a 'full expression . . . of experience' within the person's faith community.[15] So the Matrix of

Lament, with its four constellations, provides the language for such a process and, in doing this, 'evidence[s] at once both the depth of radical suffering and the resiliency of human hope'.[16]

In answering the question, 'What does a lament process provide?' it must also be understood that form and content cannot be viewed as mutually exclusive. As Brueggemann points out, an appreciation of the interplay between form and function within these psalms is important for understanding what they actually provide. He argues that the form '*enhances* the experience and brings to it articulation and also limits the experience'.[17] The idea of 'limits' here alludes to the image of the Matrix of Lament as a container within which distress can be safely held.

The importance of identifying the interplay between form and function is highlighted in Capps' comparison of Kübler-Ross' model of grief and loss with Brueggemann's views of psalms of distress. Capps says, 'The differences are due primarily to the fact that the lament expresses confidence in God's ability to intervene in the lives of the sufferers. Thus the major dissimilarity in the two structures is that *confession of trust* leads to *petition* . . . at precisely the point where, in Kübler-Ross' structure, *bargaining* is followed by *depression*.'[18]

While Capps obviously notes some likenesses in the two 'forms', the content of each opens quite different pathways. The recognition of God in the psalms leads a distressed person to different conclusions about their situation. In the psalms of distress, while the person may not find resolution to their distress there is, nonetheless, a sense of connection with God and an empowerment which comes from this connection. This is in stark contrast to a passive resignation, resulting in what Kübler-Ross calls 'depression'.

In focusing on content, form and function it could be inferred that a process of lament is ordered, controlled or even contrived.[19] On the one hand this is true. Any use of psalms of distress promotes some level of all three, particularly when specific distress is not currently being experienced by the person praying the psalm. On the other hand, however, Hughes points out that lamenting can be spontaneous, originating in the depths of our existential experience recognizing that, 'Lament is a double-meaning term, presenting at the overt level complaint or accusation, but at a deeper level intending to protest the unfairness of the crisis and to seek relief from God'.[20]

He later suggests that lamenting is a very natural response to distress.[21] If lamenting distress can be spontaneous then a learned process helps shape the intuitive form of response. Without a learned response to distress such an experience can 'destroy language' making the experience difficult, or even impossible, to verbalize.[22] Billman and Migliore suggest that, 'since the capacity to name and to speak is a distinctive mark of human life, being without voice only compounds the anguish of the sufferer'.[23] The practice of lament means that experiencing distress need not be voiceless.[24] Hughes expands the idea of voicing lament, saying that, 'as a cry, lament originates in sound, whether incoherent groaning or intelligible speech. The varieties of sound make lament polyphonic and susceptible to differing interpretations.'

The content of these psalms provides 'the capacity to name and to speak' and the words of the psalms, and even the groans, are valid languaging of the experience. This leads Tanner to conclude that, 'It is easier for people who have heard these prayers before they pray them in times of pain'.[25] Her observation highlights that familiarity can lead to a natural and healthy expression of distress, which a person might otherwise find difficult or impossible. Psalms of distress model this kind of expression and reflection by a real person, voiced in a specific way.[26] So paradoxically, while distress itself can be 'language-shattering', an effective process of lament, including psalms of distress, offers a diversity of language for that space.

Billman and Migliore summarize the function of lament with a consensus view on what these psalms provide for the person in distress:

- 'the conviction that bringing the particularity of one's suffering to voice is vital to healing and hope'[27]
- 'a form or structure for expressing acute suffering that facilitates the turn to hope'[28]
- 'that community is indispensable to healing'.[29]

As a lament process becomes part of a person's way of worshipping it also has a pedagogical function so that, '[the psalms of distress] motivate you to learn more about yourself'.[30] So, given this kind of provision, how does a person engage in a process of lament?

How can Lament be Engaged?

Using the image of a dance, introduced earlier, to describe a practice of lament is a helpful starting point. Robbins says ritual is 'the
Divine dance through which we are invited and empowered to be
partners in remembering, revisioning, and reweaving'.[31] As with
many forms of dance, a ritual of lament may be prescriptive and,
if it is, needs to be taught so it can be taken up again and again in
partnership with God. Repeated use of psalms of distress in a ritual
form also places greater emphasis on the *process* of lament rather
than any particular *result* which may, or may not, emerge from the
experience. Continuing engagement through ritual also suggests, in
a sense, that some experiences of distress are never totally cast off or
resolved. They are experiences with which the person may uncon-
sciously continue to live, and so a learned ritual gives permission
to intentionally revisit them regularly. It also embraces the importance of intentionally introducing people to cognitive dissonance.[32]
Jacobsen expands the idea of intentional introduction of cognitive
dissonance suggesting that we should put 'words of disorientation
in the mouth of the congregation by using a lament psalm liturgically. The pastoral goal here would be to introduce a dissonant
cognition of disorientation into the oriented person's mind in the
hopes that this new thought would eventually be a catalyst that
would cause the person to add new cognitions and new attitudes.'[33]

We can see then that a ritual of lament may be engaged within
three separate and yet related real-life scenarios:

- Where a person is seeking to engage with specific, identified,
  current distress.
- Where a person is encouraged to engage with generalized distress even if a specific instance is not identifiable.
- Where a person is encouraged to revisit and engage with a specific and identifiable but past experience of distress.

The experience of the person in each scenario will, of course,
differ. However, the commonality in all cases is twofold. It recognizes the normalcy *and* necessity of responses to distress, while
not limiting the depth or duration of lament. In fact, if the psalms
of distress are used regularly, as part of a personal or community

ritual, it *assumes* that the duration of lament is not only inexact but perhaps, in some cases, never coming to a complete end. Second, it also validates the importance of intentionally, and periodically, revisiting and reflecting on past distress.

It could be argued that this revisiting may become simply an excuse for the person never leaving the place of distress or, to use common language, creates the possibility of getting stuck. However, this is to misunderstand the underlying function of a ritualized process. If the exclusive goal of praying these psalms is viewed as resolving distress, then getting stuck is a real possibility and the most significant function of the psalms will be bypassed. Alternatively, if praying these psalms provides a pathway for making greater sense of oneself, in light of particular distress, then revisiting it can provide the impetus for movement and eventual growth.

Hughes is helpful to our understanding here by emphasizing the need for distress to be narrated as an act of 'restorative retelling'.[34] His observations raise further questions about how this 'restorative retelling' plays out through ritual. As a psalm of distress transitions from text on a page to become spoken, sung or chanted prayers, and as it is connected with other symbols such as body movement and/or icons, it can transform into a dramatic 'retelling' of the psalmist's distress. As a result the one praying can become engaged in intentional role-taking, which enables them to retell and act out their own distress in a safe and contained environment. In role-taking one cannot remain detached. While it can provide an opportunity to narrate distress, it can also enable a person to act out hope which past generations experienced.[35] One way of explaining this phenomenon is to say that, 'A role-taking or co-orientation paradigm of prayer thus draws upon a past situation or promise, enabling a person to anticipate the divine response in the present'.[36]

Ritual role-taking can also 'give deliberate structure to our lives. Structure gives us as sense of security. And that sense of security is *the ground of meaning*' (italics mine).[37] Ritual, which involves role-taking, can be a *one-off* revisiting of an experience of distress resulting in reflection. This, in turn can be a forerunner to significant meaning-making. However, when this revisiting and retelling is a repeated activity, through a ritual, it facilitates the powerful possibility of a continual evolving of meaning. In other words, each time the event is revisited and retold a new insight can arise or a fresh reflection can be experienced.[38] Even if this does not occur on every occasion it at least allows for the possibility. Hughes summarizes in this way saying that 'the retelling becomes a life-long task with on-going reformulations of the narrative'.[39] The ritual itself becomes a 'crucible of meanings'.[40]

Stopping at this point could leave us viewing psalms of distress as simply a place to find meaning without offering any final opportunity for resolution of the distress. Although clearly psalms of distress focus on *process* rather than *result* it must be recognized that there is a patent expectation, on the part of the psalmist, of some kind of resolution. At times, an indignant response results when resolution is not forthcoming.[41] This brings us to the final observation of a lament process in practice: the goal of meaning-making, in which people of faith can engage as they respond to personal distress.

Lament and Meaning-Making

The fact that psalms of distress are included in the Scriptures of the Judeo-Christian tradition cannot be ignored when considering their value in meaning-making. Definitions for the term 'Scripture' will no doubt vary, but they at least allude to a recognition that these psalms are uniquely, and inherently, theological in contrast to non-sacred literature.[42] Psalms of distress represent, at least in part, attempts to make sense out of distressing situations in light of a relationship with God. A lament process, using psalms of distress, can contribute to meaning-making by enabling reflection on the three key issues mentioned above: the nature of God, humankind and the relationship between the two.

As one reads through the psalms of distress, acknowledgement of God's existence is obvious and pervasive, even when the divine presence is not immediately obvious to the psalmist. However, it must be recognized that these psalms do not present propositional statements about God. Rather, they are human attempts to make sense of who God is and God's role in the situation of the distressed person. They also assume that there is a willingness, on God's part, to be involved *with* the person in distress.

Given these underlying assumptions on the part of the psalmist, there is the freedom to question the presence of God at the time of distress and to seek a divine response to these situations with an air of confidence. This theological need could be described as, 'present[ing] an image of a God who prefers opening oneself unashamedly in relationship to God rather than keeping polite distance, and they convey the sense that others have travelled the road of terror and rage thereby mitigating some of the isolation of grief'.[43]

So the Psalter's presentation of God is as one who *allows for* rather than *discourages* expression when a person feels disaffected from God through distress. This kind of expression, set in the sacred text, validates its expression for people of Judeo-Christian faith from both the human *and* the divine perspectives. The process, then, provides a catalyst and vehicle for the distressed person to try to make sense of God's response in the situation.

Of course the psalms of distress go beyond validation and making sense of the situation. They also voice specific requests for a divine response, which raises questions about the effect that these prayers may have on the god who hears them. Does God *in fact* respond in requested ways to the distressed person? Or, is the process of lament more about their attempts at meaning-making, irrespective of the ultimate outcome? Theologically speaking the text of the psalms shows that, for those who prayed to God in their distress, there was a strong sense that God could, and God would, respond favourably.[44]

Billman and Migliore are again perceptive at this point, arguing for the passibility and mutability of God because the psalmists 'trust that God has the power to save them even as they ask why God has not yet acted'.[45] They conclude that 'God's power is different to unilateral/absolute power but is seen as something engaged by the lament prayer'.[46]

Two observations are important here. The psalmist assumes that a distressed person's prayer can affect God's response in some way and that the transformative power of a lament process is not God's sole responsibility. Rather there is a need for personal responsibility to be taken. While the first of these may potentially resolve distress it is the second which leads to transformative meaning-making. However, before we can examine the transforming dynamic of the divine–human partnership in facing distress we will look briefly at how these psalms portray the nature of humankind.

As we have already discovered the psalms of distress are essentially anonymous and lacking historical information. However, there is no doubt they emerge from the crucible of real human experience. We have also concluded that the presence of psalms of distress in the Psalter suggests that it is normal, and natural, for human beings to express these experiences in the form of prayer. The fact that psalms of distress exist reinforce that, 'What we believe, acknowledge, and become by praying are deep features of what we profess about God'.[47] In this sense then, these psalms say much, not just about God, from a human standpoint, but also about how we understand ourselves and our experiences as human beings.

In a fundamental way the psalms of distress voice the possibility of faith and doubt co-existing for a person. It is the coexistence of faith and doubt in tension, often produced by the distress itself, which results in the distressing cry from the person of faith. The cry emerges as a reflection on this tension which then, in turn, gives impetus to the meaning-making process as the person attempts to make sense of their theology in the light of their experience. Distress has a unique ability to create these opportunities for reflection.

In an existential sense this tension is also produced by a clash between what a person thinks life *ought to be like* and what it *is actually like*. Hughes puts it this way, saying, 'moral emotions are the practical vehicles of lament. As an example, anger is not simply an outburst of hostility for its own sake but a sign of an ethical gap between what is (e.g. unfairness) and what ought to be (e.g. fairness). Anger bears a moral intentionality of protest and search, and this fits the function of biblical lament.'[48]

Tension of this kind, between faith and doubt, and the clash between what is and what ought to be, could be viewed as a normal response to situations of personal distress. It also recognizes that part of being human is that we are rarely in a situation where distress, of some kind, is absent and the tension between faith and doubt is resolved. Saliers calls this a 'crucible of testing', arguing that it 'brings us to face the truth about ourselves'.[49] In this sense, psalms of distress could be characterized as a subversive form of prayer which may reveal facets of our human nature that we might otherwise seek to ignore or even unintentionally conceal. As this aspect of our humanity is voiced in the context of relationship with God it becomes personally confronting but, at the same time, facilitates the possibility of personal transformation through reflection.

These perspectives on the nature of God and the nature of humankind of course play out in the context of the divine–human relationship and this is especially evident in the text of these psalms. Much of what we see in the biblical psalms of distress is also present in all religious traditions throughout the generations and widespread in secular settings.[50] However, these psalms are unique in that they are prayers, to a particular god, based on the belief that this god has had a continuing and intimate involvement with the community of faith throughout its history.

This belief presents a challenge to the person of faith. In the face of distress, how does one reconcile the idea of divine involvement with people of faith and God's perceived lack of response? Clearly the psalmist is not calling out to an anonymous, or detached, god. Viewed within the broader context of the Psalter and the Hebrew Bible the god is *Yahweh*, God of the Israelite people. In the same way, Christians also call out, through the Psalms, to this god, consummately manifested in the flesh as the person of Christ. Self- evidently, God has been, and Christians believe continues to be, involved in our world and our lives.

In analyzing the nature of this relationship, Reid reminds us of the pre-eminence of covenant in thinking about ancient Israelite people, suggesting that the practice of questioning and challenging God is inherent to this kind of relationship.[51] His stance accords with what we observe in the story of Israel throughout the Hebrew Bible. Rather than a relationship moving towards the poles of either passive resignation or total rebellion, we see the ebb and flow of a relationship often based on question and challenge.[52]

In this way the Psalter, as a whole, does provide a helpful articulation of what the relationship between God and humankind is like. It also offers a pedagogical tool which aids in discovering how the relationship might work amid distress.[53] However, total clarity in understanding the divine–human relationship is probably unrealistic. Billman and Migliore offer the caution that,

'Prayers of lament honestly acknowledge that we may now experience God as hidden, absent or silent. In such prayer God is not experienced as familiar, predictable, or comforting but as shattering, different and "other".'[54]

So the relationship between God and humankind, as portrayed in psalms of distress, presents another theological tension not uncommon throughout the rest of Scripture. God can, in prayer, be protested against and called on to act but is concurrently portrayed as unable to be manipulated yet open to respond compassionately to the people. In the light of this paradox, God can be viewed as both the potential solution to the problem of human distress and the problem itself.[55] It is possible that the action of prayer is something which explores the idea of 'how we perceive God working in the world'.[56] The prayers we pray, in this instance, psalms of distress, ' "restructure" the situation by creating an interaction with God'.[57] This interaction enables a person to wrestle in conversation with God about God's action in the world. The conversation opens an avenue for reflection and meaning-making, in contrast to silence which could lead to the distressed person becoming stuck in their situation.

We began this chapter by exploring the importance of lament as a process in response to experiences of personal distress. A process of this kind is not only relevant to people of faith but to all human beings. If such a process is engaged with, particularly as part of a ritual, the value of revisiting distress in reflection can lead to productive meaning-making and this meaning-making can take place even if the distress is never fully resolved.

Psalms of distress are particularly relevant and helpful in this kind of process. While these psalms originated from deeply personal encounters with distress, they have been shaped afterwards into deep expressions of wrestling with the divine–human relationship. Despite the mystery of the relationship, from a human perspective, psalms of distress assist in articulating various perspectives on God, humankind and the relationship between the two, seeking to make sense of life as it is lived.

These perspectives are formed *because of* engaging with personal distress rather than avoiding it. Psalms of distress also suggest that making sense out of one's experience and gaining a deeper theological understanding of God can actually *only* come through an engagement with distress *because* the experience's inherent tensions and mysteries are articulated.

So, what are the potential psychodynamic movements that can occur when a process like the one described above is entered? Our exploration now moves to a more detailed discussion of three particular psychodynamics embedded in the Matrix of Lament and draws out some implications for those who use these psalms as a form of prayer.

8.

The Psychodynamics of Lament

So far we have gained an understanding of the function and nature of psalms of distress and an appreciation of the Matrix of Lament as a lens through which to appreciate both the psalms' form and function. Beyond these insights we have also explored the importance of psalms of distress as part of a lament process. Before hearing some stories of people who have explored their distress through praying these psalms we will consider the potential psychodynamic changes for those who use them as prayer.[1] Three psychodynamic movements present in the Matrix of Lament are:

- Levels of distress
- Locus of control
- Sense of relationship.

These movements are reflected in the matrix, being observed in the way the psalmists voice their struggles with their distress in the text. As a context in which to consider each psychodynamic we will briefly explore the holistic nature of human beings and some of the ways in which people think, feel and behave in response to life events. These perspectives will help us to recognize the psychodynamic movements evident in psalms of distress.

Despite various ways of describing human beings in discrete terms as cognitive, emotional and physical, a foundational perspective here is an appreciation of the holistic nature of human beings. This is in keeping with a Hebraic world-view which does not appear to compartmentalize human beings as one thing or another but treats each person as a whole in, and of, themselves. One way of thinking about this holistic idea is to use the term 'psychophysical organism' to describe human beings.[2] An important aspect of this holistic view is the inclusion of a spiritual dimension and the significance of faith. Those who choose to pray the psalms are presumably alert to the existence of a divine other and a sense of relationship with that entity. So, for a person of faith, the nature of a human being cannot be defined by considering the person in isolation. A sense of our humanity, for people of faith, is found in relationship with a divine other and other people.

A view such as this, which recognizes the holistic nature of human beings, raises a question about how psalms of distress help us to understand and express this wholeness. We have already explored, to some degree, the idea that perspectives on oneself can be formed in three ways. First, by viewing oneself through one's own eyes; second, viewing oneself through God's eyes; and third, viewing oneself through the eyes of others, most often characterized in the psalms as enemies. Rollo May convincingly argues that a growing concept of oneself can ultimately lead to 'the capacity of the human organism to have conscious awareness of its activities and, through this awareness, to exercise a measure of freedom in directing these activities'.[3]

The concept of oneself in a faith context is necessitated when praying psalms of distress. McDargh stresses the importance of interpersonal relationships in the forming of self but, at the same time, emphasizes that the person need not be totally subsumed by the other; divine or human. This is an important observation when considering a person's engagement with distress. It ought to result in a *discovery of self* rather than a *loss of self* in the context of relationship. He makes the interesting observation that, 'many Christian spiritual writers have been insistent that while God is the ultimate reality, that in which we "live and move and have our being," the graced awareness of our *participation in God* is one that does not dissolve the *otherness of God or ourselves*' (italics mine).[4]

These observations suggest that the healthy self, while engaging with the divine other, preserves the integrity of the self without abrogating a sense of personal responsibility. Inherent in this view, however, is recognition of a person's inadequacy to cope with distress alone. A distinction between *individuation* and *relationship* with God, recognizing the significance of a human–divine relationship, is the context for understanding the psychodynamic movements set in the Matrix of Lament.

Within this context the need for a fine balance emerges between the discovery of the self within oneself, and discovering the self within God. Merton refines this idea further, suggesting that any such discovery of oneself must begin first with God, prioritizing the person's relationship with God over that with oneself or other people, saying, 'In the "prayer of the heart" we seek first of all the deepest ground of our identity in God . . . We seek . . . to gain a direct existential grasp, a personal experience of the deepest truths of the life and faith, finding ourselves in God's truth.'[5]

Clearly, whatever position is taken, the importance of recognizing oneself and God as distinct and, yet, co-existing entities in an interdependent relationship provides the relational framework within which distress can be expressed. When a person in distress has this perspective on their relationship with God, distress can not only be expressed but also engaged with to gain a deepening intimacy between oneself and God.

Of course the specifics of what each one experiences, when engaging with distress in a faith context, will necessarily vary from person to person. However, as a general observation, May makes an interesting point, saying that, 'For a long time people thought of spiritual experience as the achievement of a new and different perspective on reality. Something to be achieved. Something which takes us *beyond* the usual world. But in fact it seems that spiritual experience is more a vision *of* the usual world; a clearing away of the distortions and confusions which normally cloud our vision of the world.'[6]

From his perspective, then, the goal of a spiritual experience, such as praying psalms of distress, could be characterized as a kind of 'reality check' through an engagement with the disavowed self. The person's distress is accepted as normal and something to be embraced rather than avoided. Therefore, the experience of distress, and an engagement with it, can be viewed as an opportunity for growth, rather than an obstacle in the way; an opportunity for learning, rather than a problem to be resolved. So, bearing in mind this holistic view of human beings we will now consider three facets of that wholeness: thinking, feeling and behaving.

Thinking

The language of psalms of distress expresses a world-view which embraces thinking about God, oneself and others. On the one hand these psalms can be viewed simply as the expression of distress by a person bearing no relevance to one who might pray such a psalm today. In this view the thinking of the psalmist bears no relationship to the thinking of a person praying today. On the other hand, if a person, today, *engages* with the text, allowing it to resonate with their own experience, then this can lead to greater self-awareness of their own thinking about distress.

When ritual is added to praying these psalms, thinking can be significantly influenced. For example, D'Aquili, in examining the cognitive effects of ritual, observed three types of transformation that can take place:

- 'possible alteration or substitution of one element for another'
- 'addition of new elements of content which were not previously present'
- 'specific rules of reorganization of all the elements of content'.[7]

Adding ritual, then, to the text of a psalm of distress will necessarily affect the way a person thinks about it and the distress it recounts. This appears to be, at least in part, because while ritual incorporates thinking it also transcends thinking to engage the whole person. As mentioned earlier, one of the prominent features of the thinking found in psalms of distress is cognitive dissonance. That is, the psalmist's experience of distress does not match their beliefs about themselves, God and others. One way cognitive dissonant thinking can be accommodated is 'by *expressing* the myth in the form of ceremonial ritual' (italics mine).[8]

So thinking about distress is developed by expressing it through ritual action. However, the realm of thinking here is not limited to what one thinks about oneself, but also includes thinking about God and other people. As one example of cognitive dissonance, in regard to thinking about God, Ritzema notes that, 'Christians, most of whom perceive God as having considerable control over their lives, are probably uncomfortable with the notion that he [*sic*] can produce negative outcomes. They might thus avoid attributing causality for negative events to God.'[9]

It cannot be denied that people do sometimes attribute the cause of their distress to God. Praying of psalms of distress, by virtue of their content, encourages thinking around the validity of this view but in a boundaried way. An absence of the boundaries of Scripture (in this case, psalms of distress) could leave a person in distress wondering whether there is any containment for their thoughts and, if there is, what that might be.

Feeling

Despite the importance of thinking about distress, this alone is not sufficient. Ritual can also be valuable in making the connection between a person's thoughts and feelings. D'Aquili says that, 'a powerfully affective resolution arises primarily from ritual and rarely from a cognitive fusion of antinomies alone, although such cognitive fusion may be a necessary precursor to human religious ritual'.[10]

So, what does it mean for a person to *feel* their distress? The content of psalms of distress supports the view that the psalmist engages with God in the realms of both thinking and feeling. Acknowledgement and ownership of feelings can also occur when thinking about cognitive dissonances is voiced. There is an openness and honesty by the psalmist and yet no sense of this merely being a thinking exercise or a 'going through the motions' activity.[11] In noting this, I am not suggesting a progression from thinking to feeling. In fact the poetic language of these psalms captures the visceral blending of thoughts and feelings in a seamless way. The two aspects of our holistic nature are woven together as they recount the story of distress.

In psalms of distress, clearly language provides the mode through which both thoughts and feelings can be acknowledged. Hall and Gorman are helpful, when they highlight that giving language to cognitive and affective experience is, in fact, made possible largely through 'language, or explicit, conceptual knowledge . . . [which] gives us more control over the emotional information that is processed'.[12] Psalms of distress provide the language and, used as prayer with a ritual, present an opportunity for connecting thoughts and feelings to actions. The outcome is establishing a pathway towards transformation of both thoughts and feelings. Feelings can be articulated through the language and action of ritual and, as a result, people become 'assertive participants in [their] future'.[13]

Given this perspective, it would be reasonable to suggest that, in a presenting situation of personal distress, a one-off use of language and ritual will be helpful. However, embedding distress within a repeated ritual presents the possibility that, 'repeated new experiences create new implicit memories; at the neurobiological level [with] the increased likelihood for a particular neural network to fire in the future'.[14]

So, the ritualizing of a person's engagement with distress can be a rehearsed response to such events and this can then become a normative response pattern for acknowledging thoughts and feelings associated with future distress.

Behaving

Ritual implies a particular set of behaviours through which thoughts and feelings are represented by actions. Hall and Gorman propose that a connection between the 'subsymbolic' and the 'symbolic', as they call it, can be made through ritual behaviour. A lack of this kind of process in their view 'prevents integrating and processing negative aspects of spirituality'.[15]

As noted earlier, ritual can occur spontaneously in response to distress but the practice of ritual makes it more intentional. Either way 'there is a powerful inbuilt mechanism encouraging us to act out our thoughts'.[16] If this inevitability is so, then creating rituals to engage with distress becomes of critical importance. The Matrix of Lament is one model which can form the basis of our intentional, ritual response to distress. Proactively it invites our positive engagement with the experience. The lack of a planned ritual response to distress leaves us open to the real possibility that our thoughts and feelings may be internalized or externalized through various behaviours; at best inadequate or, at worst, destructive.

Ritual behaviour not only provides the context for our thoughts and feelings, associated with distress, to be embraced and integrated into our experience, but also an opportunity for growth in the relationship between ourselves and God. This integration could be called 'implicit knowledge' which is perhaps 'better described as a process of knowing'.[17] Action and reflection is necessary for this kind of integration to occur. Ritual behaviour can shape our experience by offering a space for reflection and an opportunity to make sense of what we are ritualizing. Hall and Gorman conclude that, 'we have very little *direct* control over implicit spiritual processes; however, we do have *indirect* control over them through spiritual practices. The purpose of a spiritual discipline is to do something we can do . . . in order to develop the capacity to do something that we are currently unable to do.'[18]

In this sense, using psalms of distress enables us to express and explore our thoughts and feelings through the spiritual discipline of ritual in a way that reflects our holistic nature. By doing this we can engage with our experiences of distress in ways which would have otherwise been impossible, opening the way for transformation of the whole person.

So, bearing in mind the way in which psalms of distress can engage our thinking, feelings and behaviours, we will now explore the three specific psychodynamic movements evident in the text of these psalms.

Levels of Distress

We have been using the name 'psalms of distress' as our preferred way of referring to the psalms we are considering. However, it is important to examine more closely what distress is and the various levels of distress expressed in the text. Distress refers to an experience which has been caused by forces that are either external or internal to the person, and the thinking, feelings and behaviour resulting from a particular event. The responses could be summarized as stress and anxiety.

These psalms display a movement through levels of distress which biblical scholars often describe as a movement from lament to praise.[19] Although I have already cautioned against seeing the Matrix of Lament as a sequential process, it is apparent that the four constellations of the matrix do generally reflect this movement in the text. So, taken on face value, the progression of the text suggests a decrease in the psalmist's level of distress. Some have then concluded that praying psalms of distress could be characterized as a mode of 'religious coping . . . associated with reduced stress and other forms of improved mental health'.[20] One way of understanding how this happens is that a 'turning to religious faith brings an omnipotent and ever-present Partner to one's life, lending a greater sense of control, which is a critical element to decreasing posttraumatic stress'.[21]

While we are not considering posttraumatic distress here it would seem reasonable that this argument also holds for those expressing less acute levels of distress.

In the Matrix of Lament the expressing and asserting constellations depict acute levels of distress. The invocation and complaint are evidence of deeply felt distress, as are the confession of sin/affirmation of innocence and the plea. However, the plea, which is always present, that God would do something in response to the situation does signal the beginning of a diminishing level of personal distress, with an accompanying increase in hope for divine action. The investing constellation marks a continuing decrease in distress and the imagining constellation presents a vision of a dramatically decreased sense of distress. Overall then, a general movement towards the lower levels of distress is apparent.

Locus of Control

Observations by Meisenhelder and Marcum alert us to a second aspect of psychodynamic movement; that of empowerment (in their terms, locus of control).[22] This aspect is reflected in the Matrix of Lament as locus of control, capturing the idea that different characters possess control of the situation at various times. The questions are, 'With whom does empowerment lie?' and, 'Can a sense of personal empowerment emerge from the midst of distress?' These are central to the psalmist's struggle. As stressed earlier, the ideal balance of empowerment is one which acknowledges divine action but does not abrogate personal responsibility. It is interesting to note that, 'A common secular perspective on religion assumes that believing God is an active agent in one's life requires relinquishing a sense of personal or internal control'.[23]

The reality, however, is that the 'findings . . . indicate the exact opposite of the traditional psychological position that God control is equivalent to an external locus of control'.[24] In contrast to the view that religious people relinquish personal locus of control, in response to distress, this reinforces the function of prayer in discovering a sense of joint empowerment with God. In a later study, Douglas Richards provided an additional insight saying that, 'individuals reporting a deeper sense of change of state in prayer are particularly low in this [external locus of control] trait'.[25] So those who pray psalms of distress, in fact, access an opportunity to acknowledge and experience a collaborative approach to their situation.

Praying psalms of distress enables the person praying to recognize where the locus of control currently resides amid distress and where it might potentially move to as distress is engaged with more fully. The result, potentially, is a movement towards greater personal empowerment. In the expressing constellation, locus of control lies with the psalmist's enemy. God and the person appear powerless in dealing with the causes of distress. However, the asserting constellation displays a shift, voicing a plea, in particular, which suggests that the person begins to feel empowered enough to voice what they want from God. This culminates in asserting the belief that God may in fact be able to respond in a tangible way.

The investing constellation demonstrates a further movement with the distressed person now sensing some self-empowerment to rely on God, who is now viewed as the one in control, having wrested control from the enemy. Finally, the imagining constellation reveals a level of personal empowerment with a sense of divine empowerment where the person and God jointly engage with the distress.

Jackson and Coursey capture the desired outcome concluding that, 'effective coping is achieved via personal control *through* God'.[26] When considered in connection with ritual, this is a helpful observation about the locus of control and the nature of empowerment. Mitchell notes that empowerment (or 'locus of control' as she calls it) 'is a learned approach to assigning cause to outcomes'.[27] This being the case, it suggests that a process of lament, incorporating praying psalms of distress, could reinforce a healthy balance between personal empowerment and the confidence in God to act.

Sense of Relationship

The final psychodynamic movement is in a person's sense of relationship with themselves, others and God. While the divine–human relationship could be viewed as different from any human-to-human relationship, there are some likenesses. Hall et al. along with others agree that, 'psychological and spiritual functioning are inextricably related because people relate to God through the same psychological mechanisms that mediate relationships with other people. If spiritual and psychological functioning, understood from an object relations perspective, are intricately related as suggested above, the positive relationship between the level of object relations development and spiritual maturity would be theoretically expected.'[28]

In essence these observations emphasize something we have encountered earlier; that both psychological and spiritual maturity are embedded in the experience of relationships. In addition they point out the interconnectedness between human relationships and relationship which might be found with God. So, 'the quality of one's relationship with God is . . . highly related to quality of relationship with others'.[29]

These observations and conclusions offer important perspectives on relationships. While divine–human and human-to-human relationships can be distinguished substantially, they cannot be separated in terms of their implications for the person of faith in distress. Given this conclusion, it also implies that any process which addresses *both* the divine–human and the human-to-human relationship will ultimately strengthen a person's relationship with both God and with others.[30]

A heightening sense of relationship may also lead to increased meaning-making and a deepening of spirituality. One way of growing spirituality is through recognizing 'a conflictual drive which threaten[s] self-identity'.[31] The conflictual drive is evident in psalms of distress and opens a pathway for greater self-awareness and an exploration of issues of self-identity. It achieves this through an 'integrated spiritual experience [which] tends to move an individual away from the importance of need-satisfaction'.[32]

The Matrix of Lament captures the changing perception of relationship for the psalmist as psalms of distress express thoughts and feelings about the divine–human and the human-to-human relationship. The one praying these psalms is alerted to their connection with themselves, God and the enemy. The authoring of these psalms and their first use may in fact have been a reactionary cry for divine intervention. However, once ensconced in ritual they took on another, more profound, trajectory providing a pathway for greater reflection and meaning-making which moved beyond a primal cry of distress to a more sophisticated response.

A further aspect of relationship, addressed in these psalms, is that of the psalmist and their enemy. This relationship also contributes to a sense of the 'conflictual self'. The ubiquitous presence of the enemy throughout psalms of distress has already been acknowledged. It seems that, amid distress, it is critical for the distressed person not to ignore those who support *or* those who oppose, but it is those who oppose that expose the conflictual self. Perhaps the presence of those who oppose prompts the deeper questions of life such as, 'Who am I?' In this way conflict with the enemy creates conflict within the psalmists themselves and, if grappled with, becomes a catalyst for spiritual growth.

So we can say that an engagement with distress, by praying psalms of distress in a ritual manner, makes it a holistic approach. The significance of the need for a holistic approach is based on valuing the person as a holistic being. There seems little doubt, therefore, that use of psalms of distress, as a form of prayer, can influence the whole person in their thoughts, feelings and behaviours as they engage with their experiences of distress.

9.

The Journey of a Few

So far, on our journey, we have paused to consider some important signposts, which help us to understand the nature of psalms of distress. As we have taken in the view that these signposts point to and looked at the journey ahead through the lens of the Matrix of Lament, we have seen something of the territory which stretches out before us. This view calls us to a new leg of the journey, exploring the transformative potential of praying psalms of distress and, through a lament process, moving to a place of hopeful praise. Before I invite you to explore the psalms' transformative potential for yourselves we will listen to the stories of some who have trodden the road before us.

The focus of the stories will be mostly on the experiences of individuals within a group. However, it is also interesting to appreciate the experience of the group itself as they gathered together before and after an extended period of praying psalms of distress and reflecting on their experiences. The ritual pattern of prayer, which the group followed, will form an outline for the final chapter. You will then be invited to join with us in the transformative journey through lament to praise but, for now, our focus is the stories themselves.

The group embarking on this journey consisted of six males and six females, some of whose stories follow.[1] It was interesting to find that there were many others, at that time, who indicated their desire to participate in such a journey and so the numbers needed to be limited. This suggested to me that there are many people who have a desire to engage with the distresses of life in an intentional way. The twelve group members came from various Christian traditions. Some were part of communities with a more formal practice of prayer while others were from settings which valued a more laissez-faire approach. None had specific training in prayer or journaling and so, in this regard, there was a common skill-set.

We met to discuss the reality of personal distress, as a normal part of life, and began to explore how prayer might be beneficial in addressing the issue. In doing this, I introduced the Matrix of Lament as a lens through which to view psalms of distress and the idea of lamenting distress as an intentional process to follow. The group was immediately enlivened with both the matrix itself and the potential psalms of distress might have in helping them to engage with their experience. The matrix generated discussion and questions yet all group members grasped the concept easily. This was important as I didn't want them to be preoccupied with the model so as to miss the dynamic of the process when they began the ritual of prayer.

The pattern I suggested they follow in praying psalms of distress was prescriptive. My intent here was not to restrict or limit them for any other reason than to provide me with the ability to evaluate the different outcomes for different people based on a common experience. No doubt the content and pattern of any ritual can be as creative and varied as a person wants it to be. However, this would be something for each group member to consider in the future as they think about uniquely personal ways of ritualizing their prayers of distress.

I encouraged each person to find a space where they could pray a designated psalm of distress each day, free from distractions, where they felt comfortable to freely respond in prayer in whatever way they desired. I provided them with six psalms of distress and they were asked to pray the first psalm once a day, on six consecutive days, with a break on the seventh day. For each subsequent week they were then asked to pray another psalm, repeating the pattern over a six-week period.[2]

Having explained the ritual in detail, and having introduced each psalm briefly, we then spent considerable time discussing the Matrix of Lament and the pattern for praying the psalms. To give some sense of the group members' situation in life, at that time, they then took part in three psychometric evaluations. These were helpful in establishing a baseline for each person in the three psychodynamic areas highlighted in the previous chapter.[3] These evaluations were also administered at the close of the process and the results were then compared to identify if, or where, any change had occurred. During the intervening weeks I kept in touch with each person to oversee their progress.

The best way to understand what happened for each of them during those six weeks is to listen to their reactions, responses and reflections. Each person's story presented here is in two parts. First, there are selected reflections from their journals, recorded during the period of prayer and second, selections from one-on-one and group discussions where they shared their stories and reflected on their experience in light of the psychometric evaluations. Considering all these facets together offers a well-rounded picture of how effective each one found the process to be and what changes they experienced as they courageously faced their distress.

As we hear these stories it will be helpful to keep in mind the signposts and the Matrix of Lament because they form the backdrop to our observations and responses. In listening, I encourage you to focus on the broader movements within each story, rather than the specific changes that may, or may not, take place for the storytellers. However, if, as you read the stories and reflect on them, there are specifics which resonate for you, then maybe these are thoughts to take away for your own further reflection.

John's Story

It was immediately clear that John had approached the process of praying psalms of distress in a systematic and controlled way from the timing of his periods of prayer to the reflection and writing-up of his observations. He began with an explicit attitude of belief that the process would be of benefit to him personally. This suggested that he was consciously looking for those aspects which were most helpful. He showed from his journaling that he wanted to be honest and genuine in his reflections and responses and his journaling offered ample evidence of this willingness.

John stated at the beginning of the first week that he set out to focus on several distressing experiences from *the past*.[4] It was apparent that, although his attention was initially directed towards these past experiences, he increasingly began to reflect on them in connection with the distress he was currently facing. So, John's focus on past distress seemed to provide an impetus for recognizing generalized distress in the present. This led him to comment that *the source or point of my distress is hard to pinpoint, but I think praying this psalm [Psalm 10] and reflecting on it will bring some of that out.* His journal reflections over the following days supported the validity of this observation.

As he followed the ritual and continued to record his responses John became increasingly able to identify accurately, engage with, and mull over present distress. One outcome early on in the process was that he showed an awareness that *when at the depths I find that there is little self-care in the moment.* This reflection prompted him to explore, through journaling, what self-care might look like as he experienced distress. As John's attention continued to shift from the past to the present he described the efficacy of the process of prayer saying, *What is new is the fact that real truth has to be felt, as it is experienced, and 'known' as a present tool if it is to be of any use in the life of faith.* This shift in thinking was reflected a couple of weeks later as he said *I don't think I felt as much of the pain of distress in praying this time.* The observation reveals a perception that his general feelings of distress had decreased. From these feelings of decreased distress John continued to find an avenue to express his thoughts and feelings through the psalms. He described his sense of decreased distress as a *peace that transcends my own under-standing.* It became apparent through his journal reflections that a precursor to this diminution, before any feelings of peace were experienced, was an increasing awareness of, and ability to name, his emotional reactions to experience of distress. For example, he said *I know at times I feel like this . . . like there [is] a range of emotions or stimuli coming in and I just try to deal with it honestly and rationally – rationality in emotion – now there's an incongruency!*

His reflection here also belied an early prominence in John's perspectives on rational thinking rather than emotional expression. Despite this, as the weeks transpired, he appeared to find a more even balance between thinking and feeling in response to distress. It was clear from John's reflections that the process did not cause him to avoid expressing his sense of distress or deny its existence. Rather, he embraced it further but with a sense of hope, not hopelessness.

As mentioned above, John's journal was presented in a consistent and ordered format[5] and he made his attitude towards the process clear from the beginning. Although, from a practical perspective, it appeared that John was exercising control over the process, his attitude towards experiences of distress was quite the opposite. At one point, for example, he clearly stated, *God is in control. Again I felt this.* The notion of God-control, in relation to distress, was perhaps best encapsulated when he stated that God *takes me to the depths, but He is God.*

A sense of personal empowerment seemed absent for John here and a belief in divine empowerment was voiced in its place. Nevertheless these perceptions were often countered by him revealing some significant questions, and doubts, about the actual reality of God being in control. Despite his questions and doubts, with increasing feelings of loneliness, rejection and the absence of God, he discovered his 'voice' for these thoughts and feelings.

As he continued to reflect in the fourth week, he boldly asserted that *it felt as if the Lord had really left me, that his wrath did lie heavy upon me. I was being truthful about my emotions, and I was so relieved to have such words to use* (emphasis John's). So, rather than leading him away from trust in God, John discovered that prayer led him towards a deeper level of trust in God. In making sense of this experience he concluded that *God is so good to allow this sort of darkness in His Word.*

Accompanying these experiences, John sometimes mentioned physical sensations such as crying, sobbing and quivering of the voice in response to praying the psalms. He recognized these responses as being an appropriate expression of his thoughts and emotions in the situation. Importantly John expressed a sense of being *okay* with his physical reactions and seeing them as a necessary part of his response as he prayed. Feelings of despair amid distress were increasingly embraced as the process unfolded.

This discovery of trusting God, in God's perceived absence, also led to a growing recognition of personal responsibility amid distress for John.[5] Early on he reflected a strong belief in what could be described as a 'rescuing god'. He expressed this by treating prayer as a way of handing the problem over for God to resolve, saying at one point, as mentioned above, *God is in control. Again I felt this.*

However, as he continued to pray psalms of distress over the weeks, John increasingly recognized the significance of what he could do. The beginnings of this attitude could be heard in statements like, *I feel that God is silent regarding the distress and wonder what He thinks of me defending myself like I'd like to*. Interestingly the challenges facing John about God's omnipotence, and his struggle to assert some self-control, appeared to lead him towards, rather than away from, recognizing the importance of partnership between himself and God in engaging with distress.

John's journal responses ranged from expressing a very strong sense of God's presence with statements such as *knowing that God was actually there was the life-giving component I experienced today* (emphasis John's). However, at times he also voiced a sense of divine absence with observations such as *I felt this way; that I could say it validly, that at times, many times, God does not answer*. His journaling became progressively more focused on the emotions related to God's presence and absence, suggesting a movement from the 'head' to the 'heart'. He used language such as *disappointment, isolation* and *sense of injustice* to describe his emotional responses.

John also freely described his relationship with himself and his perceived enemies. While he did not describe God as an enemy at any point, the sentiment expressed at times suggests this may have been his perception (for example, *his wrath [was] heavy upon me* [emphasis John's]). There were, however, explicit references to feelings he had of being an enemy to himself (*the self betrays*) and also feeling as if other people were sometimes his enemies.

Again the psalms of distress provided a voice for these thoughts and feelings. John resonated strongly with the three-way relationship identified in these psalms. The language of imprecation in some of the psalms was a particular challenge for him. However, he seemed to reconcile this kind of expression with the insight that at times he *feels* destructive attitudes towards someone when he is distressed. He also acknowledged that it was helpful to feel that these could be expressed safely through prayer to God.

John's journal stressed his belief in the efficacy of the process in affirming his relationship with God. To this end he noticed quite early on that *the prayer, reflection and response process is actually helping me to express myself better* and that *I think this process is actually affirming my faith in God.* As a caution though, he also felt that the exclusive focus on distress was perhaps unrealistic.

The ritual, with which he became increasingly comfortable, provided a helpful structure and added a deeper sense of meaning to the activity for him while praying aloud. Combining this with physical movements often reinforced what he was thinking and feeling. John also found that he prayed about issues in ways that he would not normally choose, concluding that this had great value for his reflection and meaning-making. Reflecting on the whole experience he felt that he had achieved *a greater sense of well-being* by the end of the process.

It was evident that throughout his journaling John consistently attempted to make sense of his distress in both the past and the present. Knowledge of the matrix helped him become more aware of his emotional and physical responses and this contributed to his attempts at meaning-making. The journal reflections recorded attempts at this kind of meaning-making often suggesting that significant attitudinal changes took place.

As explained above, it seemed important to consider both the person's written reflections and also offer them the opportunity to talk about their experiences. In talking through John's experience of praying psalms of distress he reinforced many of his journal reflections but also added some interesting insights as he had continued to reflect in the time following his participation.

John found the discipline of praying a psalm each day helpful even though he was not used to this kind of regular use. He did find it taxing towards the end of each week, together with the   other activities in his daily life, but persevered. He said that praying aloud helped him to *hear the words* in a fresh way and he made the interesting observation that by doing this they *became mine.* In this way John encountered a resonant connection between what the psalmist wrote and how he wanted to 'language' his experience.

John discovered that using psalms of distress, as the major content of the ritual over an extended time, helped him to *get into it* more fully rather than engage superficially with it. Repeating the same psalm each day for six days was helpful in this respect. He did find Psalm 88 to be a struggle with the absence of the imagining constellation. The lack of imagining was at first troubling for him but, despite this, he *pushed through* using the psalm and eventually it did cause him to revisit specific, past distress which was unresolved. A lack of total resolution of distress, as reflected in Psalm 88, became obvious to John through the process.

John said that he also found the expression vented towards enemies to be problematic, struggling to reconcile these words with his Christian world-view. However, he did ultimately see the words as emotionally cathartic. They became a necessary, if unsavoury, part of his emotional expression as he recognized strong feelings against those whom he felt to be opposing him in some way.

The ritual was a powerful extrinsic motivation which caused him to continue praying the psalms. While John recognized the value in this he also felt that an intrinsic motivation in the longer term would be most valuable. Having said this, he did observe that the ritual was helpful for perseverance when the emotional willingness was not there. John also showed awareness that, even though it began as external motivation, the ritual did in fact become an intrinsic motivator as it became a regular practice for him.

The ritual provided John with a vehicle which enabled him to look backwards into the past and forwards into the future, in the light of personal distress. The vehicle was perceived to be safe and secure, reinforcing his sense of relationship with himself and God.

Anne's Story

Anne's journal reflections showed a healthy balance between awareness of her thoughts and feelings and various attempts at trying to make sense out of these responses. She had little difficulty identifying unresolved past distress with which to begin her prayer and reflection. It was only later in the process that she moved to more immediate distress after engaging with her past opened a pathway for dealing with the present.

Anne's journal reflections revealed an increasing willingness to continue in the process, even though this sometimes exacerbated her sense of distress for a time. Early on she observed that *the way the pain was brought to the surface was very powerful*. However, perseverance led to her grasping a greater sense of meaning in her distress and a greater capacity to work through it rather than retreating into denial. Anne pointed out that denial had, in the past, been her typical response to distress. Some of this meaning-making aided her in discovering a greater understanding of God's role in her distress. For example, on reflection, she took the view that *God did and does see* and that *God does care for the wounded* when distress is experienced. She made greater sense of her own responses at times asking herself at one point, *Have I discovered any new sense of meaning in my distress?* What followed was a thoughtful reflection on Psalm 35 and an intentional connection between the words of the psalm and her present experience of distress.

It became obvious in Anne's journal reflections that she was facing significant issues of distress at the time, but that her level of distress decreased because of her prayer. She described her ability to *relinquish* her distress[6] and embellished this idea saying that now *I have a peace that I didn't have before*. It is interesting that a marked awareness of her distress preceded her decreasing feelings of distress. For Anne it appears that the first step towards a decrease in feelings of distress was recognition of its reality and then an intentional labelling or articulation of thoughts and feelings.

Her journal reflections also suggested that she increasingly discovered the voice of the psalmist *becoming my own voice*. This voice resonated with her feelings of distress. The practice of praying aloud also assisted her in discovering her voice. Repeating the ritual process aided her self-awareness because, after a few days, she discovered that she did not need to focus on what she was doing but, rather, on what was happening for her.

A major theme throughout Anne's journal reflections was the observation that *God is in control* and that *God does see and know*. To begin with these ideas seemed to be expressed as more of a hope than a felt reality but as the weeks transpired, this hope appeared to become more of a firm conviction. In describing her experience, she characterized it as a *rebalancing* of her perception of what it means to have self-control in the face of personal distress and what God's control might look like.

In the last week Anne said, *I am so small in the face of almighty God and yet he chooses to hear my prayer*. Her observation reinforced a belief that God was in control as she handed her distress over to God. She did this because she perceived God to be the one able to deliver her from her difficulty. However, it also reflected an awareness of the importance of personal empowerment to her finding a voice amid distress.

Anne refers to two particular experiences of distress which she believed she had already *handed over to God*. In revisiting these experiences she discovered that she was now able to work through a process which began with a belief of personal powerlessness, hoping God could do something. This was followed by a shift in attitude towards believing God would in fact do something together with her. So she discovered an empowered partnership working with God towards resolution rather than resorting to her previous abrogation of personal responsibility.

Anne's sense of relationship with God, at the beginning of the process, was expressed in terms of abandonment and the paradox which existed for her between what she thought theologically and her felt experience. She described her feelings of *resentment* and *almost drowning* and the challenge for her was to find a way of grappling with these feelings and finding some sense of resolution. Anne's struggle was reflected in her journal through a continual conflict between her thoughts and feelings.

Ultimately, praying the psalms did reinforce the significance of God's presence *in* her distress since the psalms became *affirmations of what I know to be true; that God does see and know*. She came to a fresh realization of the presence of God in her situation. One result of this was Anne's emerging acceptance of the paradoxes between her thoughts and her feelings, realizing that ultimate resolution to her distress may not become a reality. However, she did experience a movement towards hope for the future, observing in the last week that *the issues of lament have been drained of their urgency and power.*

Anne's praying of the psalms shifted gradually from a focus on the expressing and asserting constellations to acknowledging the investing and imagining constellations, saying that she had discovered a well-rounded articulation of both distress and hope. Her final journal reflection recounted how she now found herself able to *relinquish* her experience of distress.

Anne said that the discipline of the ritual wash very helpful. The process *led me to expression* and she was surprised that there was *so much stuff*. In her normal practice of praying she said that she would vary between praying quietly and aloud but, in this situation, discovered that praying aloud enabled her to *participate meaningfully* in the psalms. She also discovered that praying aloud *slowed me down* from her normal pace of reading and praying which enabled her to feel that the psalms were her own.

From the beginning Anne felt that the psalms, as a whole, were *written for me*. However, she struggled with the idea of enemies and wondered whether it was appropriate for Christians to wish destruction on an enemy. Eventually she rationalized this by saying that it is prayer and poetry, so it is a venting of emotion rather than a description of her wish to act violently.

In the last couple of weeks Anne did not find the content as useful, saying she felt as if *I'm done* in regard to distress. It was not that she sensed she would never be distressed again but the concentrated focus meant that for the moment she had gone as far as necessary. Anne noted that Psalm 88, without an imagining constellation, was a struggle to pray but, nonetheless, *awesome* as she recognized distress in her life that had not been, and may never be, fully resolved. She was looking for the imagining constellation and was challenged by the fact that she could not find it!

Overall, she found the ritual was helpful, but felt that it could become meaningless if it never changed. She described the preparation time as *very* helpful in centring herself and acknowledging the fragility of life but also in sensing the security and safety in knowing *her place and God's place in the universe*.

Anne also identified the Matrix of Lament as a very helpful way to view psalms of distress. She felt that the ordering/revisiting/repeating of the four constellations in different psalms reflected the *ebb and flow* (*wave effect* is another term she used) nature of the experience of distress very well. It created a resonance, for her, with ordinary human experience and an accompanying sense of *validation*.

As a final observation Anne indicated that psalms of distress had challenged her ideas about God's omnipotence and omnipresence amid distress. In doing this they highlighted a dissonance between what she thought about God and what she felt about God. She did not fully resolve her views on these theological issues but felt that the psalms provided a catalyst for thinking around them.

Sandra's Story

Sandra approached her journal reflections in a systematic and consistent manner, so much so that the first two weeks' responses were confined to a question-and-answer process. However, beyond that the responses became much more enriched in describing her thinking, feelings and experience. The content also broadened mainly through Sandra expressing her responses to the reflection questions by writing her own prayer to God. This provided greater insight into her experience of praying the psalms of distress. What was initially perceived to be a restricting structure (that is, in terms of the reflection questions provided) actually provided a catalyst for deeper reflection.

Sandra engaged with experiences of personal distress in both the present and the past. This in turn led to her gaining an increased ability to make some sense of her experience. There was evidence throughout her journal of attempts to do this. In one example from week three she observed that, *I felt a degree of pain of the inner child and then the love of that child by God . . . I felt encouraged that my future decisions and communication with others will be more from a place of strength in God.* Though distressed, she discovered a sense of solidarity with God as she prayed the psalm.

Sandra's journaling began by identifying several experiences of distress and as she engaged with these her primary emotion was one of disappointment with God. While she recognized its reality for her in the past, she now overtly expressed it to God. Reflecting on her new-found courage to express disappointment to God she said *I felt like I needed to look after myself, to stand up and do what I could in my . . . situation.* Interestingly, in our final discussion Sandra described this shift as *a blockage which became an avenue.*

A little further along in the process Sandra discovered that psalms of distress *enabled me to express pain, hurt, regret and release unresolved issues of the past.* As she attempted to make sense of this experience she came to the realization that complete resolution may not be possible and that engagement is painful but, nevertheless, valuable in shaping her as a person. She recognized that *I have more peaceful thoughts towards myself, God and others* which revealed itself as a *deeper trust and delight [in God].* These reflections suggested that she came to terms with her feelings towards

God by expressing herself to God. The psalms of distress provided a pathway for her to achieve this level of expression.

Throughout her journaling Sandra expressed a clear understanding of the Matrix of Lament as a lens, finding that it helped her to reframe her experience of distress. It was evident from the frequent use of terms such as *safety* and *security* in regard to the matrix that these were important issues for her. The matrix, with the ritual and the psalms, provided a pathway for freedom of expression which Sandra had not experienced before in prayer.

The content of the psalms resonated with an inner desire Sandra had to be more expressive. They encouraged her to take a more assertive approach towards God. Statements such as *I felt like I needed to look after myself* reflect this assertiveness. It was evident from Sandra's journaling that her assertiveness before God continued to become stronger to the point where her responses became prayers of her own. These prayers combined the expression of distress, attempts at making sense of her experience and recognition of where she had the ability to assert personal empowerment. By week three Sandra said that she now had *a greater sense of self-control for the future*.

Her sense of *self-control* developed progressively. In the first week Sandra expressed a desire for God to rescue her from the distress she was experiencing and yet a sense of isolation where *God is standing far off*. However, from week two onwards she gained a greater sense of her own responsibility to deal with distress through an increased reliance on God. This culminated with her reflecting on what it meant to be reliant on God saying, *I recognized that I had a degree of responsibility for my thoughts and how I perceived the events of life* and also, *I expressed to myself it was ok to sit in the mud because God is God and He is bigger than any other circumstances, any feeling of loss.* So, while initially Sandra polarized strongly between God in total control and herself in total self-control, ultimately she displayed growth towards engaging distress jointly with God.

Feeling self-empowered, and yet acknowledging the need to engage distress with God, meant that Sandra gained a stronger sense of relationship with God. Early in the process she expressed feelings of isolation and alienation from God saying, *I saw God standing afar off like an overseer.* However, as the weeks proceeded a stronger connection with God became evident. This stronger connection is seen most obviously in her formulation of prayer responses to the reflection questions such as the following: *I felt a real connection with myself, God and others and how I related to people. God helped expose deep hidden hurts and needs that were unmet and co-dependent coping habits that had formed and there was a beginning of healing and release.*

A constant feature of Sandra's writing was the prominence of relationships. While the focus on her relationship with God was significant, it was also evident that Sandra placed great value on her relationship with herself. By engaging with her distress, through praying psalms, she was able to reflect on how she related to herself and became more aware of a broader range of emotions and thoughts within herself.

Sandra also reflected deeply on how she related to others in her life. This was particularly obvious with those she perceived as enemies who were causing her distress. It seems that praying these psalms enabled her to view her distress more from the perspective of God and others which, in turn, led to a deeper self-awareness of what was happening for her in the process. It caused her to focus more on what she could control, rather than on what she could not control in her situation.

The discipline of praying a psalm each day was helpful for Sandra. She said that a different aspect of the psalm tended to *stand out* at *different times* for her and the repetitive process gave this the space to happen. Praying the psalms aloud helped her to be able to hear herself more and be personally involved with the words on the page.

Initially she said that it was difficult for her to return to Psalm 22, recognizing that she was angry with God, let down by God and blocked in expressing her emotions. However, she discovered that in staying with the ritual and returning to Psalm 22, it eventually became an avenue for expressing these emotions.[7] Sandra also discovered that using these psalms as prayer made her aware of a broad range of emotions and situations. They helped her to think a lot about God, and others, and how she related to them when distressed. Sandra felt that this was possible because the psalms helped her to make more sense of life and express her distress *privately* allowing her the *freedom to say what I feel.*

The Matrix of Lament was helpful for her as a way of looking at the content and structure of these psalms and she affirmed that, for her, it reflected the normative human response to distress. The matrix aided Sandra in realizing that she had been *internalizing my distress for so long* and that it was helpful to *see it and deal with it* through praying these psalms. She also realized, through praying them, that there was more work to be done on some experiences in her past but that now, she sensed a closer relationship with God and greater personal empowerment to do the work.

Anton's Story

Anton showed in his journaling that he was willing and open to learn and grow through prayer. His journal entries clearly described what he observed in each psalm as he prayed them, and a significant level of reflection and meaning-making.

In contrast to others in the group it became clear throughout Anton's journal that his distress increased as he reflected on his situation in life. Very early on he described what he was noticing as *a shock*. These feelings were particularly confronting for Anton as he concluded that *I found myself on the side of the oppressor*. He clearly gained an increased awareness of his distress and it resulted in exacerbated feelings of dis-ease about, and within, himself. Despite this early reaction Anton continued in the process. In his theological reflection on identification with his oppressor, he decided that *God is not scared away* from a person like this. So, he persevered through his initial reactions leading to a deeper exploration of his thoughts and feelings.

Ultimately the early increase in distress was not a negative experience for Anton. His confronting self-identification with the oppressor led him to a greater depth of honesty with God. However, as time passed, this increasing honesty did become problematic as he struggled with a desire for honesty and an accompanying ambivalence about its appropriateness. This ambivalence was never fully resolved. However, he did conclude that it was a valuable growth for him. An example of his new-found freedom of expression came in week two. He said that, *I can express the isolation I feel and the experience of suffering I am feeling* and that he was discovering a growing *understanding of the love that God has for people*. As Anton continued to reflect on his feelings of dis-ease with himself he eventually described God as one *who reaches into the lives of the afflicted.*

It is evident from Anton's journaling that the feelings of dis-ease he experienced were not only uncomfortable but also uncontrollable for him. In continuing to identify himself with the enemy in the psalms, he described what he characterized as *powerlessness* in others and found himself reflecting on taking advantage of others' weakness as *the oppressor*. Rather ironically, he then admitted his own feelings of powerlessness before God.

One response to these perceptions was for Anton to ask for forgiveness from God for his attitudes and actions. As a result, he felt personally empowered to take responsibility for what he perceived as sin but also recognized that his personal empowerment was not an omnipotent power. God, he believed, would play a significant role in his struggle with his self-perception. He acknowledged God's role by intentionally giving control of the situation over to God to offer forgiveness and, presumably, relief from the distress.

The place of confession and forgiveness and their relationship to distress, which persisted in Anton's journal reflections for some time, was unique to his experience within the group. The key here seemed to be not only recognizing that he needed God's forgiveness but, also, forgiving himself for his own attitudes so that his distress could be relieved. Despite a growing sense of self-empowerment Anton still asserted that *God is king* suggesting that, for him, ultimately God is in control of the situation. However, while he strongly affirmed God's control throughout his journal he also showed a growing recognition of personal culpability, responsibility and self-empowerment.

A view of low self-worth emerged as Anton continued to pray psalms of distress and was contrasted with a sense of God's high worth. Although characterizing himself as a *worm* and *worthless* he did not see his relationship damaged because of this perception. In fact expressing this lack of self-worth through the psalms of distress seems to have led Anton to greater confidence in his relationship with God.

So, despite these feelings of low self-worth, Anton experienced comfort in the relationship he has with God amid his personal distress. He described God's response to his distress in terms of rescuing but clearly does not see this as God simply removing his distress. On the contrary he acknowledged his role in dealing with distress by working positively in the relationships he has with God and those around him.

The Matrix of Lament helped Anton by providing a useful lens through which to view his distress. His grasping of the principle behind the practice resonated with Anton's increased desire for a sense of personal empowerment. Having gained this perspective Anton felt safe in expressing thoughts and emotions that were previously left unexpressed. The discovery for him was twofold. He recognized that his relationship with God was not affected by any poor perceptions he had of himself. From this he gained a renewed sense of God's presence as empowering his self-expression rather than silencing his voice.

Anton said that he *loved the content of the lament psalms*. He discovered that they reflected his thoughts and feelings and that he resonated with them very deeply even after finding himself *shocked and challenged* at times by what he was praying. Finding himself *often on the side of the oppressor* challenged his *view of my relationship with others* leading him to conclude that the process became *redefining* in how he could better relate to God and others. This then led to him considering how these relationships could function more effectively.

Samuel's Story

To begin with Samuel had great difficulty in identifying any issues of personal distress. Very early he concluded that *I really don't know of much distress in my life at the moment* and observed that *I am either blessed or in denial*. As he reflected on the possibility that he might be in denial this became a major struggle for him as he saw no element of denial in psalms of distress. Therefore, he was *caused* to look for his personal distress by praying these psalms each day.

Persisting with prayer though, Samuel's journal entries began to show an increasing engagement with personal distress from both his past and the present experience. The first week revealed a progression from struggling to find distress to, *we all have li'l struggles* and

then to describing a situation of *dread*. This suggested a growing
mindfulness about distress and a developing self-awareness about
how distress affected his life. Samuel pointed out that the process
did eventually help him to begin to *remember* experiences of distress
rather than ignoring or denying them, which is what he then realized he had done in the past.

The prayer and reflective process, in prompting memory, began
to open an opportunity for meaning-making to take place. Samuel's
journal recorded meaning-making in several places. In describing
one past experience he saw himself as *surviving* at the time. In
remembering the circumstances and his reactions he then reflected
on why he felt empowered to survive at that time. This led him to
a greater awareness of the significance of the divine–human relationship for him in situations of distress. As Samuel began to reflect
in this way he recognized that the imagining constellation of each
psalm meant *I felt empowered every time I read this aloud*. Again, meaning-making was evident as he discovered a sense of hope in a seem-
ingly hopeless situation. Because of his reflection, Samuel's distress
did not increase as he revisited the past situation, and in doing so, he
could make greater sense of his experience.

His journal reflections expressed a growing sense of empowerment as he took the opportunity to voice his experiences. While
he recognized his personal responsibility for voicing distress, his
engagement with distress was viewed in terms of divine–human
cooperation. By speaking about this as *team*, he remarked that
distress is best met with God. He did not sense he was alone; God
was an empowering presence who would *fight with me* and the
distress was not *too big* for the *team* to overcome.

Despite viewing God's presence as empowering, Samuel did
not abrogate his personal responsibility for voicing his distress in
prayer to God. He came to value articulating distress and personal empowerment in terms of interdependence. This reflects the
imagining constellation's locus of control shared between oneself
and God. The discovery of interdependence seems to have come
about in part because of the frequent clash between what Samuel
knew and what he felt amid distress. Growth was obvious in
his journal reflections as he reconciled sometimes paradoxical
thoughts and feelings to a point of being at ease with both, even if
the paradox remained.

Samuel did not express any sense of isolation from God in his reflections. The issue was more a question of how God's presence was actually evident for him in times of distress. By deciding that perceptions of both isolation from and togetherness with God can co-exist, he formed the belief that God was present with his uncertainty. Samuel discovered great freedom and validation in being able to express this relationship paradox through prayer. One way he described his experience was in *being able to see beyond the issue* even though the paradox was not easy to fully accept. In sum-mary then, over the whole journey, Samuel moved from denying that personal distress existed for him to acknowledging its presence and beginning a process of engagement and integration.

Samuel said that the discipline of praying a psalm each day was helpful even though he had not experienced this kind of prayer before. The practice of praying the psalms aloud was *weird* at first but then he felt that it helped him to engage his heart in the process, to *slow down* and *connect with the words.*

The content of the psalms, as an expression of distress, was not unique to Samuel. He made the interesting observation that in his *pre-Christian experience* he engaged in a process of honest expression of distress even if his distress had not been expressed to God at that time. He did feel that the psalms of distress *gave permission* for this kind of expression to God within a faith context and that it provided a new perspective to his faith experience. Samuel also felt that the process was a very positive experience and found it rather strange when he became aware that some Christians might find the content of these psalms difficult to use. He did not face the theological conundrum with which others in the group grappled.

Journaling proved *interesting* for Samuel but he felt that, at times, he simply *didn't have stuff* and *wondered what to do.* Rather than try to answer the questions he found it better to simply be honest in how he felt at the time. He *felt stifled* in expressing his feelings through writing because he does not see himself as a writer and has not reflected in this way for some time. He preferred to walk, and process the psalms as he did so. Samuel's response suggested that journal reflection may not be the most helpful way for all people to reflect on what happens for them in a process like this.

He did feel that he clearly understood the nature of the Matrix of Lament and that it helped to *clarify* what he was encountering in the psalms of distress as he prayed them. He also noticed that, for him, the matrix constellations represented a reflection of real-life experience today when people engage with distress. Samuel also discovered that *denial* was not encountered in these psalms, realizing that this was something he had done regularly in the past. From this recognition he had decided that he would continue to pray these psalms as a way of engaging with distress because he now saw them as a *true* reflection of real-life experience for a person of faith.

Fran's Story

Fran began praying with an open mind and an awareness of both past and present distress. Even though ritualizing prayer, and   reflecting on it, was not something very familiar to her, both the journal entries and our final discussion suggested that she found the experience worthwhile on the whole. Fran followed the suggested pattern of prayer, reflection and response systematically. However, as the weeks unfolded, she began to alter the ritual at times to fit with her situation and to complement the words of the psalms with her own. The change in her behaviour suggested that the structure of the ritual provided Fran with the impetus to engage with it, but then continue to become creative through it as she personalized the process.

She noticed that there were several times when the process exacerbated her experience of distress but overall it eventually led her to a place of greater calm and deeper contemplation. One reflection on this appeared at the end of week three with Fran stating: *Clearly a movement between yesterday and today – emotions much calmer today even though the situation remains unchanged.* This, in turn, resulted in her finding a fresh perspective on her distress as she sought to make sense of her experience.

Anger towards God emerged for Fran at various times. The way she expressed this was reflected in the observation that *huge anger rose up at his lack of care and protection of me* (emphasis Fran's). Out of these kinds of responses and reflections she was then often able to identify several specific emotions, such as *helplessness*. This emerged in response to the content of the psalm being prayed and linked to the situation of distress upon which she was focusing. In both her journal, at various points, and again in our final discussion she pointed out that the process was a major factor in her feeling less distressed.

Fran never identified a distressing situation as being resolved but that the result of the reflection aided her in coping with the experience more effectively. Supporting this observation, she noticed that the imagining constellation became more prominent and meaningful in her praying as she moved through each week. To begin with, she seemed to see no point in praying this constellation because she sensed no hope. However, as she continued to pray it anyway, the hope expressed in the constellation of each psalm became more real in her experience. An increasing desire to be honest in prayer emerged over the course of the process. By week three she stated that, *I can't pretend I don't care* about distress. She then proceeded to express why she did care, how she had responded to the situation and what she wanted God to do in response. This movement in her sense of empowerment enabled her to embrace the imagining constellation in a greater way than at the start of the process.

While Fran's sense of personal empowerment increased, the process uncovered theological challenges for her. She entertained questions about the nature of God's control in the situation and this became increasingly troubling for her. The first hint of the tension came early on when she observed that *divine intervention has seemed slow to come for me.* Her expectations of God gave rise to an emerging anger at God because of God's perceived inaction. It seemed that underlying Fran's observation was the belief that, at least theologically, she could expect God to intervene. Therefore, anxiety was produced when this had not occurred. Nevertheless expecting divine intervention persisted in Fran's journaling with perspectives such as *only God can organize that* and *a sense of confidence that God will intervene.*

As her reflection developed, Fran gravitated between expressing anger with God for not acting and a belief that God should act. This was never resolved for her during the process, though the two perspectives did seem to come to an uneasy co-existence in her mind. It could be that Fran's felt lack of control, and her sense that perhaps God did not control her distress, was countered to some degree by the empowerment she felt in performing the ritual. However, in resignation, she concluded with quite a profound reflection: *I am helpless . . . only God can help me.*

In thinking about her enemies, the issue of personal empowerment again figured significantly and, again, raised a theological concern. In both her journal and our final discussion she expressed the dissonance she felt between words expressing a wish for the enemy's destruction and her perspective on this as a Christian. For Fran these words were taken as literal, not figurative, and she appeared to believe that if these words of destruction were prayed they might in fact become reality. This created another layer of angst for her as a Christian person.

Fran identified the three-way relationship between herself, God and her enemy early in the process. She made insightful observations of the dynamics in the relationships and reflected on them in meaningful ways. Despite her concerns about words of destruction towards her enemy becoming reality, she did espouse a theological certainty that God would deal with them in the end saying, God *will call us all to accountability.* The psalms of distress affirmed this for her and the view aided her to cope with a lack of resolution to her distress.

During the prayer she discovered that the psalms often affirmed her belief that God's presence was with her in the here and now. Even Psalm 88, which lacks an imagining constellation, became a helpful prayer for Fran. Though she struggled with the psalm suggesting God caused the distress, it at least affirmed her belief about God's presence with her in the distress.

A growing awareness of the three-way relationship in psalms of distress meant that Fran could understand the value of these relationships more highly. This led her to a greater acceptance of her attitudes to God and her enemy. She also concluded that, while a sense of God's presence was significant, her trust that her relationship with God existed was paramount in coping with distress. To this end Fran displayed an increasing capacity to view the divine–human relationship as a partnership when distress was encountered. She concluded, towards the end of the process, with a prayer that God would provide *energy, agility, enthusiasm, sound sleep and good concentration* so that she could cope with distress. She also reiterated that praying the psalm provided an opportunity to *let the emotions out* but not for resolution. The resources to cope with distressing situations were her focus.

Fran said that the discipline of the process was a challenge, in that she did not see this as an area of personal strength. Praying in this way for a protracted period was difficult and she often found herself praying the psalm twice a day following a day's break. She did not find praying aloud unusual but did find that the process helped to *externalize the inside*.

Fran explained that it was difficult to cope with certain psalms in some sections because of the depth of emotion expressed. She also struggled with the relevance of some words to those who have a Christian faith. However, this meant that she felt prompted to reflect on significant questions about whether Christians could, or should, pray some of these words. She did find that it helped her to resonate with other people in distress and cited one particular close personal relationship where she discovered empathy with one she felt was *the enemy*.

In using the psalms, Fran added that she sometimes emended the words to fit her own situation. She also sometimes inserted the exact issue of distress being experienced and changed the language which did not reflect what she wanted to say. Doing this she felt was part of making the psalm of distress her own.

Journaling was not difficult for Fran to do and she felt it was useful. The writing was helpful as a further means of expression and the questions enabled her to focus her reflections. Fran added that, after journaling, she knew that there was *still stuff here* and so sensed that this process was incomplete in and of itself. With this she did feel the journaling process promoted expressing emotion and that there was great value in *being able to say it and get it out there*.

The Matrix of Lament made sense to her and was helpful in understanding the content and structure of psalms of distress. Fran felt that without the matrix lens it would have been difficult for her to understand, or engage with, the content. She also concluded that the psalms reflected personal distress very well and helped in *feeling my feelings*. Fran also felt that *words in the psalms and words out of the psalms* connected strongly with her. She explained this idea by saying that the words of someone else could be reworked or reworded into one's own words.

Each person in the group embarked on their own journey with remarkable courage and told their stories with openness and honesty. The stories they shared confirmed many of the discoveries we have made in the first few chapters of this book. This encourages us to consider how our discoveries and the stories we have heard might help us to join with those who have prayed their sorrows before us.

10.

The Final Destination

To consider what our responses might be we will now return to
where we began our journey and consider the original signposts
in light of the stories we have just heard. We will also relate the
stories to the Matrix of Lament, the practice of lament and the
potential for psychodynamic change. To do this, we will revisit
each aspect briefly and, as in the previous chapter, include some
related vignettes from the personal stories. These vignettes will
illustrate how the various aspects could be observed in the group
members' experiences.[1] I hope that in doing this a clearer picture
will emerge of the importance of the theory in forming a foundation for our practice of praying our sorrows. You will remember
that the four signposts are:

Signpost 1   What is Lament?
Signpost 2   Lament and Ritual
Signpost 3   The Language of Lament
Signpost 4   Shape and Function

What is Lament?

Signpost 1 alerted us to the question of how we might best
label what have typically been referred to as lament psalms. We
concluded with my proposal that 'psalms of distress' is a more apt
way of naming the content of the particular psalms in focus here.

   In discussing the term 'lament' during the first group meeting, it
quickly became obvious that group members had little or no understanding of what this term suggested about content or process when

used to describe particular psalms. Suggesting that the psalms we were focusing on could be understood as psalms of complaint and disorientation elicited a more understanding response. However, describing them as psalms of distress proved to be most enlightening with quite a few acknowledging that they were unaware of the presence of this kind of material in the Psalter. Despite their unawareness of these psalms, all group members warmed to the description and resonated with the content as I shared an example with them.

The journal entries from each person clearly showed that by labelling these psalms as psalms of distress they were able to grasp the content, perhaps more easily than if another term had been used. Interestingly though, once the connection between the ideas of distress, as an experience, and lament, as a process, had been explained, most in the group used the term 'lament'. For them, this term could encompass *both* the type of psalm in focus and the process in which they were involved.

John recorded in his journal at one point that he *woke with a <u>desire</u> to pray a lament psalm!* (Emphasis his). He continued to use this term in preference to the word 'distress'. Anne, referring to her experience in the final group discussion, used the term to describe the process saying that at one point she found it *odd to be lamenting in this way* (a prescribed way). Both these comments, together with many others, suggested that 'lament' was a useful label for both a type of psalm and a process in which they were engaged, once they understood what the word meant. It was their encounter with these psalms in the ritual process that had provided them with a fuller understanding of an otherwise loosely defined concept.

So in summary, it seems helpful to understand these psalms as psalms of distress, particularly if they have not been encountered before. This aids in grasping the content of the psalms and then in understanding how a lament process incorporates them as a way of voicing and engaging with personal distress.

Lament and Ritual

Signpost 2 pointed to the historical use of the psalms of distress as a part of liturgy. It also highlighted the potential function of ritual as a valuable pathway for expression and the possibility of it being transformative. Ritual was also recognized as a way of identifying God's involvement with the person in distress. Based on the evidence of historical use, I suggested that this provided the impetus to explore what might happen for those who connect ritual and praying psalms of distress.

Before this experience, members of the group had encountered various ways of praying from more formal or ritualized approaches to more extemporary forms of prayer. Interestingly, none was experienced in using psalms for prayer although all had read the Psalter at various times in the past. Their responses to the ritual were varied but nevertheless contained some common strands of reflection. None reacted negatively to the requirements of the ritual, in a general sense. However, different aspects appeared to be more significant for some than for others.

The preparation phase, which focused on breathing, was an aspect of the ritual which a few noticed was helpful. Tanya observed that after doing this she *felt calm*. Her observation is indicative of comments by others about its value for them. It is also significant that Anton reported in our final discussion a greater sense of *focus* following the breathing and Tanya felt that it *slowed her down* in preparation for praying. So, the breathing focus is important as a preparatory action in settling a person's emotions and centring their thoughts, as they prepare to pray the psalms.

Most affirmed the use of the 'I am ready to begin' prayer as a significant starting point for the process each day.[2] For Anton it was *central to the experience*, while Sandra discovered that it gave her a stronger *sense of God*. Sandra's observation was reinforced by her feeling that the prayer also provided a sense of *safety and security*. These sentiments were also expressed by others using similar language. Of all the aspects of the ritual used, this prayer contributed most positively to most people. It seems that the prayer helped them to prepare to focus on their thoughts, feelings and experience while providing a familiar and safe foundation. John encapsulated the group's feelings when he said that the prayer *started the ritual off on the right footing*. While the suggested prayer may not be the one chosen in your practice of praying your sorrows, we can conclude that use of a familiar preparation prayer is beneficial.

The physical movements accompanying praying the psalms met with a mixed reaction.[3] Charles began using the movements with *some anxiety* but, eventually, discovered that they influenced how he thought and felt in positive ways, describing them as *moving me into a different sphere*. Both Anne and Sandra indicated that the movements *reinforced* the ideas of each constellation while Peter went even further in saying that the physical movement *enhanced meaning* for him. Anton and Fran, however, took a different view, noticing that the movements were more *distracting* than helpful.

On the whole then, physical action with prayer was mostly helpful and focusing. The idea of making prayer more physical with breathing preparation and then hand movements reinforced what was being said for most group members. However, it also alerts us to the possibility that physical action, with prayer, may not be helpful for all those who pray. This aspect of the ritual is one which can be explored in various creative ways. If you find that movement reinforces what you want to express in prayer, then it is valuable to find an action that reflects your thoughts and feelings. For praying your sorrows the action you choose could be as simple as a single posture for your time of prayer or something more complex, such as a different hand movement for each constellation of the matrix.

Few comments were made in the journals about repetition of each psalm over a period of days. However, a question about this in the final group discussion prompted many thoughtful reflections. John observed that the repetition helped him to *get into it more* which he clarified as him sensing a greater connection with the content as the words were repeated. Through repetition Anne also noticed that the psalms where the constellations were less sequential helped her to experience the *ebb and flow* of the text. For her this *ebb and flow* resonated with the unevenness of her day-to-day struggle with distress. A number expressed the value of the discipline of repetition, especially when they did not feel like praying the psalm again. Both Jim and Sandra pointed out that because of the repetition they could see things *from a different perspective* (Jim) and *slow down and connect with the words* (Sandra). This, in turn, enabled them to reflect more deeply on the content of the particular psalm and their personal connection with the words.

Praying the psalm aloud is important. It is particularly helpful to slow us down and cause us to reflect more closely on the words we are praying. Repeating a psalm also provides opportunities for the words to sink in and become more resonant with our experiences. No doubt, as some group members found, you may struggle with repetition but it seems that, for most, the effort to persevere is rewarding.

In summary then, the various aspects of the prescribed ritual contributed in mostly positive ways to the use of psalms. The kind of value expressed by many in the group echoed the findings about the power of combining prayer with ritual. The ritual aspects of the process provided a pathway for experiences to be voiced and reinforced the felt need for safety and security when praying about these kinds of issues to God. The ritual provides a pathway in two ways. First, it provides a familiar pattern which contributes to a sense of safety and security and second, it offers tools which will help prepare you to engage with the psalms in a focused and thoughtful manner.

The Language of Lament

Signpost 3 pointed to both the narrative and poetic qualities of these psalms and the potential significance of both these forms of discourse for voicing distress. As well as these features, a three-way dialectic was also identified between the psalmist, God and the enemy. Identifying the dialectic led to the suggestion that the impetus for movement through the Matrix of Lament may come when a person praying enters the dialectic themselves in the place of the psalmist.

In considering group members' responses, it became clear that, for most, both the poetic imagery and the narrative nature of the psalms resonated with their experiences of distress and invited them into the dialectic. The imagery produced by metaphor and simile, particularly in expressing feelings of powerlessness and isolation, was often identified as deeply meaningful. An example of this is John's reflection on the language of betrayal used in Psalm 55. The way this psalm told the story and the picture it produced for him resonated with his experience of personal distress at that time. Sandra found the imagery of a bird, also in Psalm 55, to be a picture of her, in her situation. These are just a couple of examples of responses to the imagery, and the language used to produce that imagery, resonating with the person's sense of self, God and others by becoming expressions of their own thoughts and feelings.

The narrative character of these psalms was also prominent in most people's thinking. Praying these psalms provided permission both to tell the story of a particular situation of distress, and subsequently, to find validation of their experience. The journals, as a whole, recorded many stories, both past and present, being retold because of praying psalms of distress. The narrative power of these psalms was so prominent for Anne that she reworded a psalm to include her story in her own words. In similar ways most felt that their story, and the story of the psalmist, became one in the form of a psalm prayed to God.

The dialectic nature of psalms of distress was not addressed directly by any in their reflections. However, an awareness of the three-way relationship and the conversations between themselves, God and others, was threaded through their reflections. Although quite a few faced a theological challenge as they embraced the dialectic most continued praying it anyway. A clear example of this is when Sandra struggled with being angry at God, wanting to express it, but having been told by some that *being angry is ungodly*. Despite her struggle with the language of the dialectic it ultimately provided the framework for the psalmist's expression of anger to become her own. Sandra then discovered a new-found freedom to express her emotions in response to distress.

The same was also the case for both Julie and Tanya. Tanya, for example, concluded that the language of the psalms *allowed me to express my anger and frustration . . . it gave me permission*. The dialectic also proved powerful in other ways. Charles struggled with anger towards himself creating a dialectic between himself and his own beliefs and attitudes. On the other hand John, Anton and Sandra focused more on the dialectic with their perceived enemies. However, in all these cases the dialectic enabled them to achieve a higher level of self-awareness and self-understanding.

So, the power of the dialectic was affirmed in different ways by different people. The common experience, however, was that they felt able to enter into it with the psalmist or in the place of the psalmist.[4] By doing this, they felt empowered to express a broad range of thinking and emotions, some of which had never previously been expressed. The depth of expression, through personal participation in the dialectic, contributed to a willingness to explore their distress in several significant ways.

Because the discourse uses direct quotes from God and the enemy, the stories suggest to us that the dialectic may challenge some of our theological presuppositions. So, it may be helpful for you to reflect on what you think God and others might be saying about you and your situation as this may help you to gain a clearer perspective on your thoughts and feelings from outside yourself. You might also like to consider the poetic narrative quality of the text as invitational, encouraging you to author your own story in the form of a personal psalm, describing your specific circumstances of distress.

Shape and Function

Signpost 4 pointed to the shape, or form, of a psalm of distress as a matrix with four distinct constellations and how it related to its function as prayer. It was suggested that viewing the psalms of distress through the lens of the Matrix of Lament could promote greater meaning-making for a person seeking to engage with their distress in prayer.

While some in the group had formally studied the psalms in the past, others had not considered them at all. Nevertheless, for the whole group, the idea of viewing the shape of psalms of distress through the lens of the Matrix of Lament was new and helpful. The four constellations (expressing – asserting – investing – imagining), with a description of their elements and function, helped each person to engage with the content more effectively through understanding what was happening in the text of the psalm itself.

Anton's journal reflection on the usefulness of the matrix pointed out that, while it was not helpful *as he pray[ed] the psalm*, it did help his understanding and reflection to see how the prayer was shaped. John felt that understanding the matrix *makes praying this psalm so practical*. His observation suggested that, for him, the knowledge of the matrix had an effect on his attitude towards a psalm of distress and his ability to use it.

Sandra described the matrix as *set[ting] a framework* for noticing and valuing the various aspects of her experience of distress. This 'framework', as she called it, enabled her to realize that she had been *internalizing for so long* and that it was helpful to *see it [her distress] and deal with it* through praying these psalms. These observations suggest that an awareness of the matrix provides reference points for reflections to emerge from your prayer experience. These reflections can then form the basis for you to make sense out of both your experiences of praying and your experiences of personal distress.

The group agreed that the differing constellations were also helpful in reflecting the variety of facets to experiences of distress. Two further observations are also of interest. Julie expressed her growing understanding of the matrix and described how, because of this, she began to restate the constellations by creating her own psalm of distress. She did this to reflect specifically on her own circumstances. Jim noticed that in looking at psalms of distress, other than the ones he had been asked to pray, he could see the pattern of the Matrix of Lament present in them.

So, the matrix clearly offers a helpful approach for you to understand the shape and content of these psalms. Through this lens the relevance of these psalms is more obvious and can be more easily connected to your everyday experiences as you pray. The corollary of this is an increasing engagement for you in trying to make sense of your distress. One example of this is John thinking about a past event of personal distress and considering it in light of the matrix. From this he began to ponder his relationship with God. In his attempts to make sense out of the event and out of his thoughts, he discovered that, *God was present during this initial event of distress.* John's new realization made him aware that, while his distress was painful at the time, it did not mean that God was necessarily absent. His reflection ultimately led him to realize that when he experiences distress now, or in the future, he could envisage a god who is present with him *in* and *through* the situation. The fresh insight provided him with a new resolve to face distress rather than denying or ignoring it.

This final signpost also pointed to the practice of praying our laments. We considered psalms of distress as a collection of speech acts which, when verbalized as a prayer, *do something* to the speaker.

Both the journal reflections and our discussions supported the theory that verbalizing these psalms as prayer affected people in various ways. Most group members said that praying these psalms aloud was unique for them and they found that part of the experience to be meaningful. Hearing the words of the psalms in their own voice helped them to feel that in facing their distress they were doing something about it, even if it were just speaking aloud to God. Speaking in prayer also enabled them to bridge the gap between their own experience and that of the psalmist consequently connecting more deeply with their own experience of distress. Verbalizing the psalm moved the person praying from viewing it as 'informing' to an experience of 'situating' which is a distinction in speech acts, as explored in Chapter 5.

Fran, noticing her feelings of anger, discovered that they *crystallized* for her as she prayed one of the psalms. Both reflecting on her anger, and the praying aloud of angry words, provided an informing function but, following this, she also became aware of how the emotion had situated in her. Sandra prayed words of imprecation in one psalm and reflected on expressing her anger in this way; she said it was *foreign but liberating*. In doing so she was able to situate herself with the psalmist and notice her thoughts and feelings towards her enemies. Jim also discovered praying aloud as both informing and situating. He reported finding that when he quoted others' words, from a psalm, they caused him to identify with the enemy in the psalm, thus realizing that he actually felt like the enemy. Jim concluded that *I found myself on the side of the oppressor*. So, in a subversive way, the verbalizing of the psalm led Jim to a self-awareness that he thought he would otherwise have ignored.

Considering the idea of speech acts as informing and situating in connection with ritual reminds us that repeated action causes them to be reinforced. The reflections by most of the group suggested that verbalizing the psalms in the first two weeks or so were more informing, while in the latter weeks it became more situating. The ritual played a critical role in this transition, enabling speech acts to become acts of *creating* through which reflection and meaning-making emerged. For some, these kinds of speech acts created further distress. An example of this is from John's reflections on Psalm 88 where he observed: *It felt as if the* LORD *had really left me, that his <u>wrath</u> did <u>lie heavy upon me.</u> I have definitely felt something from the asserting sections of the matrix today. I was being truthful about my emotions, and I was so relieved (in my depression??) to have such words to use.* (The emphases here are in the original journal.)

In this reflection John displays a high level of self-involvement in the words of the psalm where the distress of the psalmist resonates strongly with his own. Extended examples of this 'voice' can also be observed in Sandra's journal reflections where her reflective responses to the psalms become prayers of her own, sometimes modelled on the psalms of distress.

Speech acts, as prayer, are also an expression of relationship and, again, this is congruent with the reflections of most group members. Foremost was the understanding that speech acts in prayer are an expression of relationship with God. Because of this some questioned whether it was permissible to verbalize certain attitudes to God or not. One such instance, mentioned already, is Sandra wondering whether *being angry is ungodly.* Although not supplying an answer to this dilemma, the question being posed was nevertheless powerfully thought-provoking for her. Despite some reservations like these, several people observed in their journals, and our discussions, that the *words of the psalms became their own* more than if they had prayed them silently or simply read them as a text.

Promoting the expression of thoughts and feelings aloud to God can be a challenging, yet freeing, experience. Some will feel that emotions such as anger are better kept to oneself. However, if you can move beyond this and pray the psalms as they are, you will find that voicing your emotions in this way will be a validating experience.

Another aspect to praying these psalms aloud was occasional responses to verbalizing God's words and the enemy's words. Most underlined the sense of reality this brought as it caused them to see these characters as a real part of their personal struggle. It then enabled them to reflect on their relationships from different perspectives. For most it reinforced their relationship with God but also produced uneasy feelings as they sometimes blamed their enemy, or even God, for their predicament.[5] There seemed to be reservations about the validity of placing blame. However, it did cause many to reflect more on their own disavowing of responsibility when blaming others.

The journal reflections of most confirmed, as did our discussions, that by verbalizing the words of the psalms, each person had a sense of doing something with their words rather than simply reciting them. These reflections anecdotally support the argument of speech act theorists. Though the outcomes were different for each person, some emerging speech act themes became evident. The majority expressed a growing awareness of their desire for distress to be resolved but decided that simply verbalizing the words of the psalms alone was not going to achieve this result. However, continuing to hold the tension, almost all decided that the greatest value of praying these psalms was the opportunity it gave them to enter a process of engagement.

While the result of this engagement may, or may not, be resolution of distress, most found it an opportunity for transformation of some kind. Anne expressed her experience of transformation, saying that the *process of the week . . . 'drained off' a lot of the intensity* while Sandra expressed it as realizing the importance of *being true to oneself* and *being true to God*. This ultimately led to her adopting a different attitude toward a particular situation of distress.

Finally, the level of honesty evoked by verbalizing these psalms led most to a more intimate sense of relationship with God. Contrary to what some may imagine, it was *because* they could verbalize their deepest thoughts and feelings about personal distress that their relationship with God was enhanced, not damaged. No matter how acute the person's sense of isolation from God, verbalized psalms offered a pathway for reconnection.

As you pray these psalms, there seems little doubt that you are doing things with the words you are praying. As the words become yours, naming and validating your thoughts and emotions, an opportunity is created for you to own them and express them in relationship with God. As a result, the transformation of your thoughts and feelings becomes a possibility.

Of course praying this way will not be without its challenges. As we have heard from some stories, the boundaries of what we think we can, or ought, to express to God will vary from person to person. However, the psalms of distress offer you an opportunity to explore where those boundaries might be for you.

The Matrix of Lament: A Model

Having introduced the Matrix of Lament in Chapter 6 it is important to evaluate how helpful it was as a lens through which to view these psalms. Did it enable a greater appreciation of the content of these psalms and an increased understanding of a lament process?

Before attempting to answer this it is worth reminding ourselves of exactly what elements constitute the matrix (see Figure 4).

Figure 5. The Matrix of Lament, elaborating expressing, asserting, investing and imagining

Expressing constellation

Taken together, the journals contained expressions of an expansive range of emotions in response to various experiences of distress. John affirmed strongly that *the prayer, reflection and response process . . . actually help[ed] me to express myself better* and his observation captured the sentiments of several others. Despite an intentional focus on distressing experiences, it is interesting that expressing, for various group members, was not limited to negative affect. Again, John's comments show how he could articulate hope, saying that the *more that I can think [about] . . . my life thus far, I have peace that transcends my own understanding.*

Even when a particular person possessed limited language for emotional expression, the constellation alerted them, as they prayed, to their deeper feelings and provided a language for them.

Anton began praying with either a reluctance, or perhaps inability, to express how he was feeling about his situation. However, the expressing constellation broadened his reflection to the point where he discovered that he could express *the isolation [he was] feel[ing] and the experience of suffering [he was] feeling.*

The verbalizing of questions in the expressing constellation also offered permission for thoughts and feelings, which otherwise could have been ignored or denied, to be expressed in the context of the divine–human relationship. Both Charles and Sandra expressed anger towards God and, while some felt that this kind of emerging negative affect was initially problematic, it was eventually viewed as both critical and helpful to express by most in the group.

Many focused, at various times, on questions associated with feeling isolation from God, God's perceived absence and doubts that God would, or could, act on their behalf. At one point Jim expressed his sense of isolation by saying, *I miss you.* The words of the expressing constellation resonated very strongly with the emotions being experienced by most in the group. It is clear from the journal reflections that, once they engaged in the practice of invocation, complaint and questioning God about their situation, most experienced a freeing-up of emotional expression. An important outcome of this expression was an increased capacity to sense *how empowered I am as a son of God (Samuel)* and for Anne to express *faith in God's control/provision/care.*

For those of you experiencing negative feelings, the expressing constellation illustrates the way in which psalms of distress are 'permission-giving'. As well as this, the constellation can also be a beginning point for expressing positive affirmations about yourself, God and a hope for the future. So, the expressing constellation can be viewed as an effective gateway to verbalizing your feelings and thoughts associated with distress.

Asserting constellation

Most found the asserting aspects of the psalms to be both eye-opening and empowering. Of the three elements forming this constellation (confession of sin, affirmation of innocence and plea), confession of sin was prominent in several reflections.

Anton provided a clear example of this as he asserted *the need of forgiveness in this area of my life.* While there were no obvious examples of affirmation of innocence, several projected blame for their distress onto others. Two people, in particular, while not directly affirming personal innocence, asserted a belief in a *satanic* figure who was perceived to be the cause of distress.

Clear affirmation of innocence seemed to be a difficult challenge for most. For most the reluctance seemed to relate to their theological world-view which precluded the possibility that any person could claim complete innocence. Another way of expressing this idea is a belief that, at some level, they are 'sinful'.

Although the plea was identified as a significant and deeply evocative feature of the asserting constellation, only rarely did any specifically identify it as most important. In some ways quite a few viewed the act of bringing the whole psalm before God in prayer as forming a plea. When asked to reflect on the idea of plea, and particularly on the request for resolution, most expressed a desire, first and foremost, to find the resources to sustain them *through* distress. This was clearly shown as Sandra appealed directly to God to *sustain* and *help* her. Interestingly, she moved beyond the plea to use several verbs which asserted her action in *asking, giving* and *fulfilling*. The outcome of this for her was a felt sense of emerging hope as she recognized and took up personal responsibility for her actions.

Many were surprised at the assertions made by the psalmist about themselves, God and their enemies. However, when praying the words themselves, they began to discover a resonance with the perspectives they could assert *with* the psalmist. From this Julie felt encouraged to be more self-assertive and, faced with her distress, she responded with assertive statements such *as I talk, I look for, I will continue.*

Despite the lack of focus on the plea by those praying the psalms, it is clear that the opportunity to assert themselves led to an increased investing in God. Tanya noted that the shift from the asserting constellation to the investing constellation was *striking for me.* From expressing a deeply painful experience and then asserting herself before God through praying the psalm, she then found she could express at length her sense of God's love and presence. Finally, Tanya affirmed that she could *trust Him with everything . . . even my heart* and concluded that she *refuse[d] to become a victim.*

The ability to assert oneself before God became significant for each person in the group. The struggle with asserting seemed to be in knowing what one can actually assert. As you reflect on praying your sorrows using psalms of distress you will discover that they provide a variety of ways in which to assert things about yourself and God in prayer. In doing this the way is opened for trusting in God's presence with you, even in the midst of your distress.

Investing constellation

The way in which the asserting constellation opened a pathway towards investing in both God and each group member is congruent with an overall movement towards a higher internal locus of control for the whole group.[6] It is interesting to note, however, that the increase in internal locus of control did not lead to a discounting or dismissing of God's role. A sense of self-empowerment is accompanied by a renewed sense of God's presence with the person in distress.

Clearly imprecation was the greatest challenge in the investing elements, causing about a third of the group members some anxiety. They struggled to reconcile the idea of wishing evil on enemies, particularly because of a New Testament faith. None of those troubled by imprecation fully resolved the issue in their own minds, although most eventually viewed it as an expression of emotion, as opposed to actually doing the evil themselves. The consensus view expressed an appreciation that violent thoughts, directed towards an enemy, are deeply human. Imprecation offered a pathway to express and resolve these feelings without compromising personal values through violent action. Fran reflected at length on imprecation, explaining strongly and consistently her belief that God alone would do the avenging. We noted earlier that at one point she stated that God *will call to account*, and she appeared to take a very literal view of God's ultimate action. Rather paradoxically, her conclusion brought comfort to her even though verbalizing it troubled her deeply.

The opportunity to affirm confidence in God and acknowledge divine response evoked strongly positive reactions. Anne noticed that these were *life-giving* and understood as *affirmations of what I know to be true; that God does see and know, and there will be justice.*

This led to a greater self-awareness when she then stated that *I seem to be less acutely aware of pain in the memory*.[7] The investing constellations elements provided the impetus for John to continue in prayer. He said that it became *a compelling passion*.

Feelings associated with distress shifted from negative to positive perspectives on the situation as the person praying progressed through to investing. It did not signal that the distress was now no longer present but, rather, the presence of a light in the darkness. Sandra put it this way saying, *I am amazed at how hopeful I feel when reflecting on something which could be perceived as gloomy and hopeless.*

Verbalizing an investing in God's presence in the situation of distress, and affirming a confidence in God, formed a significant foundation for facing distress with God. Even though an accompanying ambivalence about God's presence and God's omnipotence was often evident in the reflections, investing in God was still possible. The sense, from many journal reflections, was one of 'At this point, who else can I rely on?' From the uncertainty in the investing constellation, all welcomed the movement to the clarity of the imagining constellation.

Moving from asserting yourself before God to investing in God, even before you experience a divine response, will be challenging but not impossible. As with most in the group you will probably be challenged with questions about whether or not God is able and willing to respond to you in your distress. Yet the impetus of the dialectic of prayer will encourage you to pray through to the final 'imagining' constellation.

Imagining constellation

The sense of hope formed by the imagining constellation was consistently obvious in the reflections. Several described their excited anticipation of this constellation once they were familiar with the particular psalm they were praying. Samuel pointed out that his anticipation helped him to pray through the psalm to the end. Many could express, assert and invest because they knew that the imagining was near. Each person discovered that pledging loyalty to God was both comforting and encouraging. Jim described the imagining in Psalm 22 as an affirmation that *I imagine my world not empty of God.* His capacity to imagine God's presence was significant here given that he did not necessarily *sense any response* from God. However, he did sense *[God's] presence* as he prayed.

The imagining constellation reinforced the shift which began in the asserting and investing constellations. John identified this constellation as the place where he expressed his praise to God and discovered *new meaning in [his] distress.* Fran recounted her experience of the imagining constellation as seeing *a movement between yesterday and today – emotions much calmer today even though the situation remains unchanged.*

The physical action of raising hands with palms upwards as the person prayed this constellation proved profound for many. John noticed on one occasion that his hands were *more emphatically raised, higher, straighter; that straight in fact I could feel my eyes drawn to them . . . a noticeably different pose.* He went on to say that the physical movement was an expression of his emotional state at the time, in response to his distress.

John also recalled that he had actually experienced the imagining described in Psalm 10 during a time of past distress without realizing it then. As he used the psalms now he discovered that he could *relive it* through praying this psalm. John's observation was congruent with three concepts discussed earlier. First, that ritualizing of the imagining constellation performed a situating function for him and second, that speaking the words in prayer appeared to re-create the situation in his mind. The third concept reinforced by John's experience is that the imagining constellation reflects not only a desired response to distress but, also, a healthily normative one.

It is significant that Psalm 88, which did not contain the imagining constellation, proved problematic to most. Both the absence of imagining and the practice of blaming God for personal distress caused great consternation and challenge to some in the group. This was particularly because of their theological presuppositions about God's providence and God's omnipotence. Julie found the psalm *difficult to relate to* and *draining and dismal* and was unwilling to blame God, saying, *God has not caused my distress.* Yet Fran noticed that, for her, the psalm *touched something deep.* John reflected on the psalm finally acknowledging towards the end of that week that there may in fact be hopeless situations like this in life. He could resonate with the sentiment of the psalm and the absence of an imagining constellation as he reflected on some life experien- ces. Because of this connection John remarked, *how good it would have been to be able to pray this psalm in those days.* He felt that Psalm 88 also helped him express his desire to rely on God and that *God is so good to allow this sort of darkness in His Word.*

The rest of the group attempted to reconcile the words of the psalm and their personal experiences with little success. While Psalm 88 proved valuable for some it highlighted the profound importance of imagining for a person in distress. This also rein- forced the value of this constellation in all other psalms of distress.

Arriving at the imagining constellation is an energizing and encouraging experience. Despite the possibility that distress is still your experience this constellation offers you the opportunity to glimpse a hopeful vision from amid your situation. From the group's experience it seems important that, while praying this constellation, you include some kind of physical action, such as the raising of hands, to reinforce the hope-filled vision of the psalm.

It is clear then that the four constellations, and most of their elements, were often recognized in the journal reflections and discussions. The Matrix of Lament, as a whole, provided a helpful lens to understand both the content and process of lament as the psalms were prayed. This in turn led to a heightened awareness of what was happening for each person at an intrapsychic level as they prayed.

Within the constellations we also explored the three relation- ships present within psalms of distress, describing them as follows:

- The psychological relationship.
- The theological relationship.
- The social relationship.

Through praying psalms of distress with an understanding of the Matrix of Lament, most displayed a growing awareness of the three aspects of relationship for themselves. The process was psycholog- ical in that their reflections recorded a growing capacity to be more acutely mindful of themselves, and their responses to their distress, as they prayed. How this mindfulness was expressed, and what it resulted in, varied enormously for each person. Some reacted by recoiling from the process altogether and ceasing to reflect, at least formally. Jim withdrew from the process saying, *I just don't think it is healthy to keep on reflecting on (particularly if you aren't experiencing it).* Conversely, some moved to a deeper level of self-reflection, such as John who pointed out that *it has been safe to just go and check* on past experiences. This led him to deeper reflection on the issues for himself.

The theological relationship within psalms of distress was also prominent throughout the reflections. The group members' sense of relationship with God was paramount for most as they engaged with their distress. In a paradoxical way, the personal reflections often showed that God's presence, while sought after by all, was both comforting and problematic to the distressed person.

One positive theological response can be seen as Anton resolved to seek God's presence *even in debilitating circumstances*. His decision came directly in response to a situation of distress where he wanted to see God, but failed to see God. In contrast to this, Fran experienced a total lack of God's presence in caring for her through distress and it resulted in *huge anger* for her. She felt that recognizing anger was *unbeneficial* and continued to try to move on from it rather than reflect more deeply on it. From these two examples the major hurdle in continuing to pray the psalms was not in the emotions they evoked but, rather, the theological readiness of the person to reflect on what was happening for them.

The social relationship aspect of the psalms was also evident in most reflections. However, the major focus within this broader context was firmly placed on felt enemies rather than those who might be a support. Through focusing on enemies, some found that this enabled them to clarify the causes and solutions to their distress. An example of this is Sandra's observation that *people spoke ill of me to others*. While she admitted that viewing anyone as an enemy was difficult for her, recognizing the nature of the relationship seemed to help her reflect on her reactions and then decide her response to the situation. So, in a sense, identification of an enemy aided some in becoming more mindful of their own attitudes and actions, sharpening their definition of themselves and clarifying their response.

It was also interesting to note that, at various points in the six-week process, several in the group engaged supportive people in their process of praying the psalms of distress. For a few it was a spouse while for others, a friend. The goal of this was different for each person. Some sought affirmation that they were doing something worthwhile; others simply wanted to share some of their discoveries along the way. All reported that the responses from those with whom they shared were both positive and supportive. Some even wanted to join in the process, having seen the effect it was having on the person involved.

The Practice of Lament

All the perspectives explored above are different aspects of a process of lament. In an earlier chapter we highlighted the importance of this kind of process for a person engaging with and navigating through distress. The reflections of those who prayed these psalms provided some valuable insights into the efficacy of the process as they experienced it. Although it has been helpful to break the process of lament down into its major parts there is a sense in which the whole is greater than the sum of its parts.

First, it was obvious from the journal reflections, and our discussions, that each person easily identified specific distress that they were currently experiencing. Whether they identified distress as mild or as severe, the process clearly created both an awareness of the distress and an opportunity for it to be named. A second aspect obvious from the reflections was the way in which the process offered an opportunity to re-engage with past distress. In doing this some began with current distress and moved to reflect on past distress while others moved in the opposite direction. The process itself seemed to be of value irrespective of the direction of movement.

These observations suggest that a process of lament is helpful in various ways and that this helpfulness did not depend on the person beginning with an identifiable current *or* past experience of personal distress. In fact a key for many entering the process was the exposure, and identification, of disavowed personal distress which could then be engaged with through reflection to facilitate its alleviation. If a process of lament can impact in this way it then becomes important to ask what relief might result for you from engaging in such a ritual to identify distress.

Many reflections from the group on the efficacy of praying these psalms emphasized the power of praying about distress *away* from the moment as a pathway to praying about distress in the moment. The fact that some began focusing on distress *in* the past, finding that it then became relevant to present distress and vice versa, suggests that it can help you to intentionally practise a process of lament. Consequently, when you encounter distress in the future, you will be able to more effectively engage with it either at the time of the experience, or by reflecting on it after the experience is over.

Earlier we also considered a process of lament as a way of limiting the experience by offering clear parameters or boundaries. Again this is plainly reflected in the observations of several who described this process as offering them a sense of *safety and security*. The limit of praying each psalm for one week only also suggested an obvious point of closure to each part of the process, as did the daily ritual.

The question of boundaries is not without its challenges though. While for some the boundaries provide a limiting of expression, others felt that the psalms' boundaries extended beyond their personal boundaries. As a result some felt themselves pushed beyond their personal limits as they verbalized their distress. One obvious outcome of this was the early withdrawal of a few. For these group members it seemed that the process was not limiting enough for them and, therefore, did *not* provide the secure containment for distress which was discovered by others. The fact that two people withdrew for this reason does not detract from the value of the process. It seems that the challenge remains with the distressed person as to how far they are prepared to go in trusting the process for languaging their experience.

We also explored the way in which a lament process might encourage connection with God. Many reflections confirmed people's deeper sense of connection with God as they engaged with their distress over the weeks of prayer. Interestingly, rather than struggling with a lack of God's response and a distancing in relationship, most felt a stronger connection with God *as they engaged* with their experiences. The stronger connection was not gained by seeing God's activity but by experiencing a greater sense of God's presence. Sandra's extended reflection perhaps best shows this growing sense of connection with God saying, *I felt a real connection with myself, God and others and how I related to people. God helped expose deep hidden hurts and needs that were unmet and co-dependent coping habits that had formed and there was a beginning of healing and release.*

We also considered the way in which a lament process can provide languaging for a situation which otherwise might be 'language-shattering'. Praying the psalms offered words to voice thoughts and feelings which group members admitted would otherwise have been difficult to verbalize. This is not to suggest that the words were the only mode of expression emerging from the engagement. There were various points where the 'language-shattering' nature of distress, and resulting attempts to pray using a psalm of distress, led the person to cry or simply be silent, among other reactions. In these cases the opportunity for a new language became available for each person as they sought to express their thoughts and feelings in various ways.

We described a person's participation in a process of lament as a 'divine dance'. This image captured the connection between prayer and ritual, and the relationship between the distressed person and God. As already highlighted several times, most group members experienced a deepening relationship with God as ritual and words were used together. In fact voicing these psalms in a ritual was a significant factor leading people to discover and express the divine–human relationship not only in deeper ways but, also, in new ways.

It was also interesting to observe the effect of an intentional introduction of a lament process to a person, regardless of what distress they were or were not experiencing at the time. For all those involved, irrespective of their situation in life, the process evoked responses. Some discovered underlying distress, which was close to the surface, and could therefore be quickly uncovered. For others the process exposed deeply hidden distress, often from the past, which proved more difficult to reveal and embrace. In all cases over time the process uncovered varying levels of distress and, therefore, opportunities for reflection.

Finally, we explored the idea of a lament process as an opportunity for a 'restorative retelling'. Reflections, particularly from those who completed the whole process, indicated that this did take place. It provided an opportunity to revisit past distress safely, with John recalling that it was an *enormous comfort to me to reflect back*. However, as suggested by the idea of 'restorative retelling', it was more than simply reflecting, or going back. The journals retold distress in a way which restored the storyteller and enabled most then to move beyond the experience. Because the retelling was by way of prayer, they embraced a sense of hope for the present and future and felt restored in their relationship with God. To this end Anne reflected in the last week of the process that *I feel like I am 'done' . . . the issues of lament have been drained of the urgency and power.*

Of significance is the capacity of a lament process to offer opportunities for meaning-making. We have already recognized that meaning-making, or making sense of our distress, through a lament process means reflecting on the nature of God, human-kind and the relationship between the two. Any lament process which involves God raises questions about God's capacity to act. The psalmist self-evidently believed that praying could cause God to act *for* them and against their enemy. This belief was regularly reflected in the journaling of all those involved in praying the psalms of distress. A clear example of this is when Anton described a god *who reaches into the lives of the afflicted.*

Neither the journaling nor our discussions revealed beliefs in a powerless God; perhaps one who was unwilling but certainly not unable to act in response to prayer. Even though each person believed God could respond, most were comforted by a sense of God's presence and the provision of resources to endure their distress; any hope of resolution remained secondary. While the plea for, and expectation of, resolution is clear in the text of psalms of distress, it appears that expressing the plea was enough for most in the group. This could also suggest something about the way in which we can read psalms of distress. Could it be that the psalmist also experienced comfort in discovering resources with which to cope, even if resolution were not forthcoming?

A further perspective on God, found in these psalms, is a belief in the relational nature of God and its potentially transformative function. A distressed person's ability to pray to a god with whom relationship is assured, regardless of the outcome, provided a resilience for the person to continue. This resilience is even more pronounced when the distress is *not* resolved and yet the person continues to pray and reflect.

Another key aspect to the lament process was accommodating the co-existence of faith and doubt in psalms of distress. Journal reflections and discussions showed that group members were divided on this issue. Those who withdrew early, such as Jim, suggested that it was because they felt like they were *trying to be distressed*, but a closer examination of the journal reflections suggested that the real struggle was coming to grips with co-existing faith and doubt. Those who persisted to the end of the whole process also wrestled with faith alongside doubt and had similar questions about whether to trust God or not. However, they could persevere through the paradox of faith and doubt as they continued to pray. This paradox was never resolved but those who persisted embraced it, finding that the process enabled them to reach a point of acceptance.

It could be that these psalms act subversively in highlighting this paradox of faith and doubt. In doing so they expose aspects of our human nature which some might otherwise seek to intentionally ignore or conceal. The journal reflections suggested at various points that some discovered thoughts, feelings and attitudes which, before this, they were either denying or ignoring. As we saw in the previous chapter, the subversive nature of the process is evident in Samuel's reflections as they unfold. He began with what could be described as either an ignorance of, or denial of, distress in his life experience. However, as he continued to pray the psalms of distress he recorded many reflections on both present and past distress. In doing this he realized that he *had* tried either to ignore or deny in the past.

Of course psalms of distress also contain reflections on the divine–human relationship for the psalmist. The overarching concept for the psalmist is the covenant relationship with God which we discussed earlier. The psalmist's belief in covenant provided a kind of protective cover under which questions and challenges can be safely put to God. This also seemed to be the case for the group members who persevered in the process. Whatever they asked of, or stated to, God in prayer, whether it be in the words of the psalmist or in their own words, the underlying belief was one of confidence that their relationship with God remained secure. So, in this sense, they discovered freedom of expression without any fear of disbarment from relationship with God.

We also noted earlier that psalms of distress displayed a growth in understanding and appreciation of how God works in the world through a process of interaction. In other words, perceptions of God and God's work are not confined to just observing but, rather, are helped by an interactive process which not only allows for question, protest and challenge but actively encourages these expressions. The reflections showed that people were willing to enter into this kind of interaction and it aided them in forming a fresh perspective on God's work in their life and the world around them.

A helpful example of the possibility of a fresh perspective emerged for several people from the use of Psalm 10. The focus on the words 'But you do see' helped many apprehend afresh a picture of God's role in both their past and present distress. This, in turn, provided a great sense of comfort as they reflected on God's action.[8] So the potential for psalms of distress to open fresh perspectives on the nature of God, humankind and the relationship between the two became a reality for many group members.

We also considered the implications for the whole person in terms of thinking, feelings and behaviour as they prayed psalms of distress. Each person's reflections reinforced the view of human beings as holistic. In various ways these reflections described how engaging with their thoughts, feelings and behaviour throughout the process heightened their experience of prayer. Charles observed at many points that he felt *bodily immersed in this prayer.* As part of his 'bodily immersion' Charles then identified the emotion of anger with associated thoughts and feelings. The resulting reflection included an exploration of his thoughts, feelings and behaviours in response to his new level of self-awareness.

Another aspect of the holistic experience was the opportunity for significant thinking about relationship with God and, yet, individuation from God. Sandra, reflecting on her distress, found herself thinking about the need for individuation from God. She stated, *I saw God as standing afar off like an overseer* and in response remarked, *I felt like I needed to look after myself, to stand up and do what I could in my . . . situation.* This perspective of viewing relationship and individuation together emerged regularly for several, expressed in similar ways to Sandra's reflection.

The lament process also presented opportunities for thinking about the disavowed self. Anton's discovery of himself as the *oppressor* in the psalm he was praying led him to thinking about how he had been *taking advantage of others' powerlessness*. A later reflection on this observation led him to think about how to respond to the situation. In doing this he realized that one possible response was for him to recognize the thoughts he had about the inappropriateness of his attitudes and actions, subsequently confessing and seeking forgiveness. This kind of processing also suggested an engagement with his cognitive dissonance and, through the interaction in prayer, led to a change in thinking about the situation and how to resolve it.

In regard to affect, it was suggested that verbalizing and ritualizing emotions could provide a pathway for 'subsymbolic' feelings to find representations in words and actions. Again this proved to be the case for many who discovered a broadened vocabulary of expression as they continued to pray the psalms. The use of body movement, as part of the ritual, supported the vocabulary for affect by involving the person physically in the ritual. This physical action at times tangibly reinforced, and helped to externalize, the emotions being experienced. John described his response clearly as he observed that, *the hand and arm positions helped greatly to accentuate the actual movement in the prayer from that of desperation to hopefulness.* His feelings, then, were clearly influenced by physical engagement in the ritual and vice versa.

The experiences of those praying were described earlier as a 'process of knowing', which suggests that it engendered a deeper sense of mindfulness about thoughts, feelings and behaviour. From the journal reflections and our final discussions it became evident that each person had, in fact, entered a 'process of knowing'. For some, entry into this process led to a deeper mindfulness of themselves. Deepening mindfulness manifested itself in three psychodynamic aspects of the person's experience introduced in Chapter 8.

The Psychodynamics of Lament

The three psychodynamics, previously discussed, are levels of distress, locus of control and sense of relationship. Listed below are the movements in each of the three areas which were evident within the group:[9]

- Level of distress – decreased
- Locus of control – increased internal[10]
- Sense of relationship – increased.

The journal entries suggested that group members had little or no expectations about how praying these psalms would affect their levels of distress. Initially each person found the engagement with distress particularly confronting. Below is a summary showing initial thinking, feeling and behavioural expressions of increased distress:

- *Thinking*
  - *there is a chasm between me and God.* (Peter)
  - *For me, this brings thoughts of rejection.* (John)
  - *I thought about my emotions as I had been containing them to a large degree.* (Sandra)
- *Feeling*
  - *How is it I feel spiritually strong and reliant on God, yet there is still the odd nagging thought that busts it[s] way in?* (John)
  - *Like coming down a hill having been on top.* (Charles)
  - *Express the isolation I feel.* (Anton)
- *Behaving*
  - *Inability to solve [the situation].* (Julie)
  - *Gave voice to the utter helplessness of the situation back then.* (John)
  - *No natural healing.* (Charles)

For most, the upshot of being able to express thoughts, feelings and behaviours related to initial increased distress was a decrease in stress and anxiety. Despite the decrease, few said that they felt their distress was resolved. This again underlines the significance of lament as a process for *holding* distress rather than, necessarily, *resolving* it.

A significant contributor to these decreasing levels seemed to be the way in which praying the psalms promoted the re-authoring of the story of distress. The re-authoring occurred through praying the words of the psalms. Anne demonstrated this when she noted that *I see this as God's intervention and blessing – that he truly has rescued me from the horns* (emphasis Anne's). Her new story came about as she revisited an experience but was able to recount it from a different perspective using the language of the psalm. The result for Anne was a decrease in her level of distress in relation to that incident.

However, while the re-authoring proved to be a productive way of engaging with distress it was also problematic. Most experienced consternation at various times when they realized that their stories resonated with the psalmist in distress but were not their ideal self-stories. Embracing the consternation and anxiety, however, led to a raw honesty and an authenticity becoming increasingly evident and acceptable. This emerging greater honesty with God also contributed to a decrease in levels of distress.

For those who began praying the psalms with no specific experiences in mind, events surfaced naturally, and quickly, in the first week. These events were often accompanied by significant amounts of pain and anxiety. For instance, Anne found early on that *all the pain . . . just rose to the surface again, even though I thought I had 'done that'*. Some withdrew as a result of the initial emergence of pain. However, two-thirds of the group continued and, though difficult for them, discovered some rewarding opportunities for greater self-awareness, meaning-making and a resultant decrease in levels of distress.

It seems that for the other third remembering the past proved too difficult. Peter's memory and his observation that *there is a chasm between me and God* caused his distress to increase to a point where he withdrew early from the process. Even though he, and others, did withdraw, it was interesting to find that they provided many insightful observations as they grappled with significant questions related to their experiences of distress. It remains unclear how these kinds of observations and questions might have been processed if people like Peter had continued. However, it at least demonstrates that the process played a significant role in exposing the issues.

None seemed to believe, at the outset, that participation in the process would fully resolve their distress, although some may well have implicitly held this hope. The journaling and our discussions indicated that none of them did in fact find complete resolution to their distress. However, while praying over the weeks there were some instances where a person felt temporary, or even prolonged, relief from a specific distressing issue (for example, Sandra's observation of *a greater sense of peace and quiet confidence*); or gained a greater understanding not previously grasped (for example, Samel's observation of how *empowered I felt when I 'survived'*).

The group reached a consensus, when we met the second time, that their participation had helped them realize that both generalized and specific distress would always be a significant part of life experience. While resolution was a reasonable desire, they all agreed that, because of the ubiquitous presence of distress, a process to engage with it was even more desirable. These realizations crystallized, in part, through the intensive and intentional focus on distress during the process.

The group also agreed that honesty about distress in life, and engagement with these experiences, is of supreme importance for their maturation. As all group members had a belief in God, they felt that their engagement with distress through prayer was also of high value. It provided them with an opportunity to situate their experiences within their relationship with God.

So, in summarizing the group's experiences, it became clear that the *process* was of far greater significance than any *resolution*. Most, who completed the whole six-week journey, had a sense that their levels of distress decreased and the psychometric evaluations confirmed this perception. Alongside this, most also suggested that the way they viewed their experience had also altered, affording them the opportunity to embrace fresh perspectives, begin to find a sense of hope and even make greater sense out of their experiences. Anne asked at one point: *Have I discovered any new sense of meaning in my distress?* She then proceeded to reflect on how she had in fact discovered a new sense of meaning and what that looked like for her.

As well as a movement in levels of distress, the Matrix of Lament includes shifts in locus of control as a potential aspect of change. This shift could be characterized as moving from a belief that the distressed person's enemy has locus of control to a sense that control is with God and themselves (a relational dyad). The shift could also be characterized as moving from a lack of personal control (or personal disempowerment) to a greater level of self-control *with* God (self-empowerment).

At first most wanted to think that God was in control of their distress even if they didn't feel it. Anne's clear statement that *God is in control* is indicative of the majority perspective, at least at the beginning. Despite this kind of sentiment, an increasing perception of, and reflection on, the dissonance between thoughts and feelings led to a sense of isolation from God. One consequence of this was a questioning of their belief in divine omnipotence. John expressed it as *disappointment, isolation and sense of injustice* in his relationship with God. The language shows both his sense of powerlessness and a questioning of divine power.

Conversely, some discovered a new sense of God *in* their distress, finding the concept of divine retribution towards their enemies helpful in affirming a belief in God's omnipotence, despite any actual response. Fran expressed, at one point, a *sense of confidence that God will change things*. Later she described her understanding of God's action as calling her enemies to account. While some could call for divine action, the capacity of the distressed person to affirm God's presence *with* them signalled the empowering possibility of divine–human cooperation in facing distress. As highlighted above, Samuel described this sense of joint empowerment as being in a *team* with God. That is, the locus of control is with the relational dyad of Samuel *and* God.

While an exacerbated sense of powerlessness was the early effect of praying psalms of distress for most, this progressively changed as the weeks of prayer continued. As suggested by the matrix, most began to discover two significant movements in their experience. First, in gaining a greater sense of God's presence *in* their situation and second an emerging sense of self-empowerment in facing their distress.

The investing constellation's elements, such as affirmation of confidence in God, imprecation and acknowledgement of divine response, articulate this sense of self-empowerment with God. These elements underline that distress is to be faced *with* God, rather than alone. Sandra expressed her growing empowerment with God as having *a greater sense of peace and quiet confidence* in God's response to her distress. Fran often affirmed her sense that God will *call to account* and the empowerment this provided her over her reactions to distress.

Despite the growing belief that God was not powerless, rarely, in the journaling process, did anyone resign themselves simply to being indolent and waiting for God to act. The increase in personal empowerment, expressed in the reflections, is congruent with the increase in internal locus of control indicated by the psychometric evaluation at the end of the process.

The imagining constellation's representation of empowerment being discovered in the relationship between oneself and God, with the enemy's power finally dissipating, was also reflected in the journaling. Julie described her self-empowerment, together with relationship with God, as *I'm sticking with God*, pointing out that it was the partnership which helped engagement with her distress. Sandra expressed the 'both and' nature of the divine–human relationship saying, I *thought [I would] take charge of my emotions, to cry out to God and depend on God now.* This kind of observation suggests a sense of solidarity with, and yet individuation from, the divine other.

The ritual aspect of the process was also significant for most in relation to self-empowerment. It offered permission to voice distress along with a contained space to hold the experience. The ritual also empowered the person as it birthed something new out of distress; a concept intrinsic to the use of the word 'matrix'.

The final psychodynamic movement included in the Matrix of Lament is the person's sense of relationship with themselves and God. This movement was described earlier by using Martin Buber's idea of the 'I–Thou'. This was expanded to be more explicitly descriptive of the *nature* of the relationship between the distressed person, God and others. To remind you, the constellations and their relational qualities are reiterated below:

- *Expressing*
  - I *to* Thou
  - I *to* self
- *Asserting*
  - I *about* self
  - I *about* Thou

- *Investing*
  - I *in* self
  - I *in* Thou
- *Imagining*
  - I *with* self
  - I *with* Thou

Group members' reflections affirmed that each person achieved a greater openness with God than they had previously experienced ('I *about* Thou'). This freedom displayed itself in expressions of anger, frustration, isolation and fear, just to name a few examples. While freedom of expression was, at least initially, problematic for most, those who persisted to the end of the process discovered that their theological concerns and objections became subordinate to an increasing desire to be honest with God. The clearest, but not the only, example of this was Fran's *anger*, which she identified and, despite some theological reservations about appropriateness, expressed to God as she prayed a psalm.

So, the hesitation in expressing feelings to God was not because of a lack of desire but, rather, concern about the boundaries in prayer language. The boundaries for each person in language expressed to God varied but all group members discovered a new-found freedom in the language of the psalms. Ultimately, they did not feel this language threatened their sense of relationship with God. Despite any reticence, the process actually expanded the depth and breadth of their sense of relationship with God, affirming that such a relationship could bear whatever intensity of expression was felt necessary.

Another feature of the growth in the sense of relationship is displayed in an increasing desire by many to assert themselves before God by retelling their story in the form of a psalm of distress. John, reflecting on an experience from his past, asserted that, *I felt this way; that I could say it validly, that at times, many times, God does not answer.* It became clear in his following thoughts that he had felt enabled, by praying a psalm of distress, to say some things about God, and to God, with a voice that had been previously silenced. Despite his honesty, which even surprised John, there was no reticence in retelling what he felt, believing that his relationship with God could still prevail.

Those who completed the whole process showed an increasing willingness to be honest about their thoughts and feelings rather than trying to silence these voices within themselves. The psalms of distress enabled those voices to find words and sound to accompany the thoughts and feelings experienced from distress. This willingness led to an assertiveness, but it was assertiveness of a particular type. The focus, in reflecting on distress, became one of asserting the continuing existence of the divine–human relationship and for the resources to cope with distress. Ironically the relationship, within which most felt uneasy about expressing their distress, actually became the relationship through which they would seek coping resources. An example of the cry for resources is Anton's recognition of the need for forgiveness and his resulting request that it be granted by God. It was the capacity of those to *assert* their thoughts and feelings about the potential for divine action which resulted in a sense of hope and an increased closeness of relationship between the person and God.

A growing confidence in the self, to be able to endure experiences of personal distress, and in God, to be present, aiding that endurance, became increasingly evident in the journal reflections. God was only rarely characterized as a rescuer yet still worthy to invest in with confidence ('I *in* Thou'). Clearly the most important movement for all group members was one from isolation towards greater intimacy with God in the face of distress. So at one point Anton observed that he was able to *express the isolation I feel and the experience of suffering I am feeling*. Yet later he felt a greater sense of intimacy with God and noted his *growing understanding of the love that God has for people*.

Viewed together these experiences and reflections demonstrate that an engagement with distress opened a pathway from relational isolation to greater intimacy with God. While doubtless each person held in high regard God's ability to respond to their distress the emphasis shifted from a focus on that perceived power to the significance of divine presence. The perception of divine presence *in* distress cannot be underestimated. This single factor contributed the most to people being able to embrace their experiences of distress, reflect on them and make some sense of them.

Each person agreed that praying the imagining constellation proved to be of great solace. The constellation's identification of a sense of relationship *with* self and *with* God is reflected often in the journaling ('I *with* Thou'). Words such as *partner, partnership* and *team* were often used to characterize the relationship that the imagining constellation brought into focus. As well as this, the growing freedom in the journaling, for most, as the weeks transpired, suggested a growing acceptance of their thoughts and feelings, rather than needing to silence these responses.

So we can see from their stories that most in the group experienced a lowering of their levels of distress, a growing sense of self-empowerment in partnership with God and a deepened sense of intimacy in their relationship with God. This was achieved through the discovery of openness and honesty in prayer to God, and a fresh resolve to voice thoughts and feelings as they were. The psalms of distress provided a voice for asking 'Why, O Lord?' and a ritual for praying their sorrows while viewing their experiences through the Matrix of Lament.

11.

Now It's Your Turn

Our journey is almost at an end but, like many journeys, the destination often presents the opportunity for a new one to begin. We have spent considerable time exploring the theory behind psalms of distress in an attempt to discover their significance, as prayer, in the Judeo-Christian tradition. We have also looked at psalms of distress through the lens of the Matrix of Lament. As well as this we have considered the potential psychodynamic movements for those who are courageous enough to pray these psalms. Another important aspect we have incorporated into our thinking is the value of people having a process to follow as a way of lamenting the difficult experiences of life and how psalms of distress might fit into such a process.

In doing this we have discovered the intrinsic value of these psalms as a way of voicing our feelings and thoughts in response to distress. It has been my hope that, as you have joined with us on this journey, you have begun to realize the value of psalms of distress when used as prayer. I also hope that the Matrix of Lament has provided a helpful lens through which to discover more about the potential of praying your sorrows and, as a result, encourages you to embark on the transformative journey through lament to praise for yourself. Praying psalms of distress offers the possibility of experiencing personal transformation from a place of distress to a place of acceptance and intimacy with ourselves and God. This transformation will, in turn, enable our lives to be more fully lived in praise of God's glory. So, there is one final step we must take to complete this part of the journey.

It is one thing to examine theory, and to hear the stories of others who have already begun the journey of praying our sorrows through lament to praise but it is quite another to embark on the journey yourself. That is what I now invite you to do. As with most journeys, it is important to take supplies for the trek ahead and so, in this final chapter, I want to offer you some things that I have found helpful on such a journey. Some might be invaluable and some superfluous; you might even find that there are some other things you want to add. There are no prescriptions, only suggestions, so I invite you to consider what I have taken and then decide for yourself what is useful.

However, before reading on, it would be helpful to remind yourself once more of the Matrix of Lament. Keep it in mind as you explore the invitation to pray. So, once again, see Figure 6 below.

Figure 6. The Matrix of Lament, elaborating expressing, asserting, investing and imagining

The Psalms

To begin with you will need some psalms of distress to pray. While over a third of the Psalter is made up of these psalms the three below are helpful ones with which to begin. I would suggest that you take each psalm below and pray it once a day for a few days to get the feel of it. Once it becomes familiar, you can move onto the next one and so on, and so forth. If the focus on distress becomes difficult you will probably find it helpful to intersperse your praying of these psalms with a psalm of thanksgiving or praise, both of which are also common throughout the Psalter.

Here I have included a short summary of what I think is helpful in each suggested psalm and then the full text of the psalm, coded to indicate the four constellations of the Matrix of Lament:

- Expressing – Plain text
- Asserting – *Italics*
- Investing – <u>Underlined</u>
- Imagining – *<u>Italics underlined</u>*

Psalm 10

Psalm 10 contains all four constellations of the matrix in order (expressing – asserting – investing – imagining) and begins with two questions, which are characteristic of many psalms of distress. It is also one of the shorter psalms of distress and, so, will not take long to pray aloud.

By beginning with this one you will interact with a psalm of distress which contains all the significant elements of the form, presented in a straightforward manner, before tackling some of the more complex ones. I hope that after praying Psalm 10 for some time, you will gain a clear grasp of the four constellations of psalms of distress before engaging with the other psalms.

There are several significant features in this psalm you might want to look out for. Two questions posed at the beginning of the psalm: 'Why, O Lord, do you stand far off? Why do you hide yourself in times of trouble?' articulate feelings of isolation and distress *in the form of questions*. The interrogative immediately places the prayer in the context of a human–divine relationship rather than simply an expression of emotion because of personal distress.

A second feature is the way in which the text directly quotes the words of the enemy. While this does occur in other psalms of distress, it is not present in every one. Psalm 10 offers the opportunity for the person praying to reflect on what it is like to quote the words of an enemy. It also presents an image of what an enemy might look like and act like, and how these descriptions might help to orient oneself towards one's distress. Not only are the enemy's words quoted but an extended description of their actions and attitudes is also provided in verses 2 to 11 and again in verse 13. This description may help you to build a picture of what an enemy might be like for you.

Finally it also incorporates an element of imprecation.[1] Again this is present in some, but not all, other psalms of distress. It is an element which can form part of the investing constellation and may provide you with a reference point for praying through your feelings of anger and a desire for revenge against your enemies.

The plea: 'Rise up, O LORD; O God, lift up your hand; do not forget the oppressed'[2] creates the pivot point for a movement from expressing and asserting to a position of investing. Finally, a climax is reached with the imagining constellation, contrasting both the perceived powerfulness of God and the importance of the relationship between God and the person praying.

Here is the text of Psalm 10 with the four constellations marked:

Why, O LORD, do you stand far off?
Why do you hide yourself in times of trouble?
In arrogance the wicked persecute the poor –
let them be caught in the schemes they have devised.
For the wicked boast of the desires of their heart,
those greedy for gain curse and renounce the LORD.
In the pride of their countenance the wicked say, 'God will not seek
it out';
all their thoughts are, 'There is no God.'
Their ways prosper at all times;
your judgements are on high, out of their sight;
as for their foes, they scoff at them.
They think in their heart, 'We shall not be moved;
throughout all generations we shall not meet adversity.'
Their mouths are filled with cursing and deceit and oppression;
under their tongues are mischief and iniquity.
They sit in ambush in the villages;
in hiding-places they murder the innocent.
Their eyes stealthily watch for the helpless;

> *they lurk in secret like a lion in its covert;*
> *they lurk that they may seize the poor;*
> > *they seize the poor and drag them off in their net.*
> *They stoop, they crouch,*
> > *and the helpless fall by their might.*
> *They think in their heart, 'God has forgotten,*
> > *he has hidden his face, he will never see it.'*
> *Rise up, O Lord; O God, lift up your hand;*
> > *do not forget the oppressed.*
> *Why do the wicked renounce God,*
> > *and say in their hearts, 'You will not call us to account'?*
> <u>But you do see! Indeed you note trouble and grief,</u>
> > <u>that you may take it into your hands;</u>
> <u>the helpless commit themselves to you;</u>
> > <u>you have been the helper of the orphan.</u>
> <u>Break the arm of the wicked and evildoers;</u>
> > <u>seek out their wickedness until you find none.</u>
> <u>*The Lord is king for ever and ever;*</u>
> > <u>*the nations shall perish from his land.*</u>
> <u>*O Lord, you will hear the desire of the meek;*</u>
> > <u>*you will strengthen their heart, you will incline your ear*</u>
> <u>*to do justice for the orphan and the oppressed,*</u>
> > <u>*so that those from earth may strike terror no more.*</u>

Psalm 55

Psalm 55 also begins with the plea. However, it swiftly launches into a heartfelt and prolonged expression of emotions using descriptive words such as 'troubled', 'distraught' and 'anguished', among others. While emotion is often expressed in psalms of distress, the length of this example is quite unusual. It provides you with an   opportunity to linger on some of the emotions which engage you with your distress and to reflect on your possible responses.

Psalm 55 also offers a lyrical quote of the psalmist expressing a desire of hope to be released from the presenting distress. The words are rich in imagery and evoke hope for the future. Interestingly here, hope is not so much in God's action but, rather, in the action of the one who is distressed. The psalmist says,

'O that I had wings like a dove!
    I would fly away and be at rest;
truly, I would flee far away;
    I would lodge in the wilderness;
I would hurry to find a shelter for myself
    from the raging wind and tempest.'[3]

This psalm ends in a rather abrupt fashion with a combination of imprecation (part of the investing constellation) emerging as a vow of trust (part of the imagining constellation). Conflating these two ideas underlines succinctly a confidence in God's ability to deal with the cause of the distress. It also helps to describe the nature of the relationship between the distressed person and God, and the supposed fate of the enemy in the hands of God.

Although all four constellations are represented here in this psalm there is no clear sequence. An oscillation between each constellation is evident throughout, as it is in so many psalms of distress. Here is the text of the whole psalm:

Give ear to my prayer, O God;
    do not hide yourself from my supplication.
Attend to me, and answer me;
    I am troubled in my complaint.
I am distraught by the noise of the enemy,
    because of the clamour of the wicked.
For they bring trouble upon me,
    and in anger they cherish enmity against me.
My heart is in anguish within me,
    the terrors of death have fallen upon me.
Fear and trembling come upon me,
    and horror overwhelms me.
And I say, 'O that I had wings like a dove!
    I would fly away and be at rest;
truly, I would flee far away;
    I would lodge in the wilderness;
I would hurry to find a shelter for myself
    from the raging wind and tempest.'
Confuse, O Lord, confound their speech;
    for I see violence and strife in the city.

Day and night they go around it
 on its walls,
and iniquity and trouble are within it;
 ruin is in its midst;
oppression and fraud
 do not depart from its market-place.
It is not enemies who taunt me –
 I could bear that;
it is not adversaries who deal insolently with me –
 I could hide from them.
But it is you, my equal,
 my companion, my familiar friend,
with whom I kept pleasant company;
 we walked in the house of God with the throng.
<u>Let death come upon them;</u>
 <u>let them go down alive to Sheol;</u>
 <u>for evil is in their homes and in their hearts.</u>
<u>*But I call upon God,*</u>
 <u>*and the* Lord *will save me.*</u>
<u>*Evening and morning and at noon*</u>
 <u>*I utter my complaint and moan,*</u>
 <u>*and he will hear my voice.*</u>
<u>*He will redeem me unharmed*</u>
 <u>*from the battle that I wage,*</u>
 <u>*for many are arrayed against me.*</u>
<u>*God, who is enthroned from of old,*</u>
 <u>*will hear, and will humble them –*</u>
<u>*because they do not change,*</u>
 <u>*and do not fear God.*</u>
My companion laid hands on a friend
 and violated a covenant with me
with speech smoother than butter,
 but with a heart set on war;
with words that were softer than oil,
 but in fact were drawn swords.
<u>Cast your burden on the Lord,</u>
 <u>and he will sustain you;</u>
<u>he will never permit</u>
 <u>the righteous to be moved.</u>

But you, O God, will cast them down
    into the lowest pit;
the bloodthirsty and treacherous
    shall not live out half their days.
But I will trust in you.

Psalm 102

Psalm 102 also begins with a plea and then provides graphic language describing the emotional state of the psalmist.[4] A short affirmation of confidence in verse 12, 'But you, O LORD, are enthroned for ever; your name endures for all generations', provides a pivot into the imagining constellation. Here the position, and character, of God is viewed in contrast to that of the distressed person. However, as with asserting confidence, the imagining is expressed first as the distressed person speaking *to* God (second person)[5] and then shifting quickly to the third person for the rest.[6] This psalm highlights the visceral nature of the relationship with God amid distress.

Psalm 102 also contains a quotation of the self in verse 24 which is quite unique in these psalms. Here the person in distress appears to be either recalling words spoken or prayed at an earlier time, or perhaps attempting to emphasize words currently being prayed by clearly pointing out that they are spoken and not only thoughts. This may help you to reflect on the words that have been spoken by you, or to you, amid your experiences of distress and the effect these words had on you.

As with most of the other psalms of distress this psalm contains all four constellations of the Matrix of Lament. However, here, there is no particular sequence. The psalm moves freely from one constellation to another and back. This provides another opportunity to reflect on the potential for your distress to be disorienting and disordered in both your experience of it and response to it.

Hear my prayer, O LORD
    let my cry come to you.
Do not hide your face from me
    on the day of my distress.

Now It's Your Turn

Incline your ear to me;
  answer me speedily on the day when I call.
For my days pass away like smoke,
  and my bones burn like a furnace.
My heart is stricken and withered like grass;
  I am too wasted to eat my bread.
Because of my loud groaning
  my bones cling to my skin.
I am like an owl of the wilderness,
  like a little owl of the waste places.
I lie awake;
  I am like a lonely bird on the housetop.
All day long my enemies taunt me;
  those who deride me use my name for a curse.
For I eat ashes like bread,
  and mingle tears with my drink,
because of your indignation and anger;
  for you have lifted me up and thrown me aside.
My days are like an evening shadow;
  I wither away like grass.
But you, O Lord, are enthroned for ever;
  your name endures to all generations.
You will rise up and have compassion on Zion,
  for it is time to favour it;
  the appointed time has come.
For your servants hold its stones dear,
  and have pity on its dust.
The nations will fear the name of the Lord,
  and all the kings of the earth your glory.
For the Lord will build up Zion;
  he will appear in his glory.
He will regard the prayer of the destitute,
  and will not despise their prayer.
Let this be recorded for a generation to come,
  so that a people yet unborn may praise the Lord:
that he looked down from his holy height,
  from heaven the Lord looked at the earth,
to hear the groans of the prisoners,
  to set free those who were doomed to die;

so that the name of the Lord may be declared in Zion,
  and his praise in Jerusalem,
when peoples gather together,
  and kingdoms, to worship the Lord.
He has broken my strength in midcourse;
  he has shortened my days.
'O my God,' I say, 'do not take me away
  at the mid-point of my life,
you whose years endure
  throughout all generations.'
Long ago you laid the foundation of the earth,
  and the heavens are the work of your hands.
They will perish, but you endure;
  they will all wear out like a garment.
You change them like clothing, and they pass away;
  but you are the same, and your years have no end.
The children of your servants shall live secure;
  their offspring shall be established in your presence.

The Ritual

In preparing to pray these psalms it is helpful to have a pattern, or ritual. The ritual you follow can be created by you incorporating activities and symbols that are meaningful to you but, if you are not sure where to start, then, you can begin with what I suggest below. You might want to stay with this pattern or it may provide you with ideas for your own ritual. Whatever ritual you create, it is helpful to follow the same pattern each time you pray the psalms.

Prepare

- Light a candle and place it on a table in front of you.
- Sit with your back straight and your feet on the floor.
- Focus on your lower abdomen, breathing through your nose.
- Breathe in; hold for four seconds and then breathe out for six to nine seconds.
- Pause before repeating.

Preparation prayer

Pray a preparatory prayer. This can be a spontaneous prayer or a read prayer like the one below:

> I am a creation of God
> I have a human face
> I laugh
> I weep
> I wait in hope
> I lift my eyes
> And stub my toe
> I love
> I struggle
> I fail
> I stand
> And always I will stand
> On trembling ground
> But God is God
> And Jesus is the Christ
> And the Spirit will lift up my feet
> God is at the centre
> God is at my endings
> Nothing lies beyond
> The love of God in Christ.[7]

Pray the psalm

- Turn in your Bible to the psalm you are going to pray.
- Focus on a specific aspect of personal distress.
- Pray slowly and aloud through a psalm of distress feeling free to repeat any part of the psalm if you want.[8]

Contemplate

- Sit quietly and reflect in silence.
- Notice whether your thoughts and feelings were drawn to any particular word or phrase in the psalm.

Meditate

- If there is a particular word or phrase that you find significant, as a result of your contemplation, spend some time repeating it slowly to see what it means for you.
- Notice how this affects your thoughts and feelings and become aware of any particular movements you notice in yourself as you do this.

Reflect

Record reflections in a personal journal responding to the following questions:

- What did the psalm enable me to express to myself and to God about my distress?
- What could I begin to assert about myself and about God amid my distress?
- In what way did praying the psalm help me to invest in my sense of well-being and in my relationship with God?
- How do I imagine my world differently?
- What was draining about the experience?
- What was life-giving about the experience?

After a few days you might want to use the following questions as a prompt to further reflection:

- Describe any movement in your thinking about self, God and others.
- Describe any movement in your feelings towards self, God and others.
- Describe any new sense of meaning in your experience of distress as you prayed the psalm.

Throughout this whole process it will be helpful for you to bear in mind the Matrix of Lament and its various features as a lens through which to view the psalms you are praying. It is not important to try to identify all the elements in each psalm but, rather, to remember the general direction of the flow from expressing, to asserting, to investing and, finally, imagining. You might also want to explore creative ways to ritualize your praying of these psalms. Here are a few suggestions to get you started:

- If you're a writer, try writing your own psalm of distress using the Matrix of Lament as a model.
- If you're musical, try composing a song.
- If you're an artist then try drawing, painting or sculpting your experience.
- If you're a dancer, try to choreograph some movements to express your distress.
- If you're an actor then create a script to act out your experience.

Conclusion

These are just a few suggestions to get you started, but feel as creative as you want to be and find ways to express yourself in prayer that align with your gifts and talents. Beyond this, you might want to consider praying some other psalms of distress. Now that you know what they look and feel like to pray, you will easily identify some others to try. It would also be valuable to intersperse praying these psalms with other types like psalms of praise and thanksgiving. That way you will be reflecting a more rounded practice of prayer that engages with the various parts of life experience.

My hope is that you will make the whole Psalter your prayer book, as it is for so many in the Judeo-Christian tradition. In doing this you will include the psalms of distress in your practice of prayer and, as you pray your sorrows in this way, you will begin to grapple with the question, 'Why, O Lord?' While the answer to this question may remain largely shrouded in the mysteries of life and faith, you will intentionally and creatively engage with your distress, embarking on a transformative journey through lament to praise.

Bibliography

Ackroyd, Peter R. *Doors of Perception: A Guide to Reading the Psalms* (London: SCM Press, 1978).

Allen, Ronald Barclay. *Praise: A Matter of Life and Breath* (Nashville: Thomas Nelson, 1980).

Alter, Robert. *The Art of Biblical Poetry* (New York: Basic Books, 1985).

Anderson, A.A. *Psalms Vols. 1 and 2*, New Century Bible Commentary (Grand Rapids, Michigan: Eerdmans, 1972).

Anderson, Bernhard W. *Out of the Depths: The Psalms Speak for Us Today* (Philadelphia: The Westminster Press, 1983).

Anderson, E. Byron. 'Liturgical Catechesis: Congregational Practice as Formation'. *Religious Education* 92 (1997): pp. 349–62.

Anderson, Herbert and Edward Foley. 'Experiences in Need of Ritual'. *Christian Century* 114, no. 31 (1997): pp. 1002–8.

———. *Mighty Stories, Dangerous Rituals* (San Francisco: Jossey-Bass, 1998).

———. 'Ritual and Narrative, Worship and Pastoral Care, and the Work of the Pastoral Supervision'. *Journal for Supervision and Training in Ministry* 19 (1999): pp. 13–24.

AP-Thomas, D.R. 'Some Notes on the Old Testament Attitude to Prayer'. *Scottish Journal of Theology* 9, no. 4 (1956): pp. 422–9.

Atkins, Peter. *Memory and Liturgy* (Aldershot: Ashgate, 2004).

Aune, Michael B. ' "But Only Say the Word": Another Look at Christian Worship as Therapeutic'. *Pastoral Psychology* 41, no. 3 (1993): pp. 137–44.

Austin, J.L. *How to Do Things with Words* (ed. J.O. Urmson and Marina Sbisà; Cambridge, Massachusetts: Harvard University Press, 2nd edn, 1975).

Baesler, E.J. *Theoretical Investigations and Empirical Confirmations of Communications and Prayer* (Lewiston, New York: Edwin Mellen Press, 2003).

Bakhtin, Mikhail. 'The Problem of Speech Genres'. Pages 121–32 in *The Discourse Reader* (ed. Adam Jaworski and Nikolas Coupland; London: Routledge, 1999).

―――. *Problems of Dostoevsky's Poetics* (trans. Caryl Emerson; ed. Wlad Godzich and Jochen Schulte-Sasse, 8 vols. Vol. 8, Theory and History of Literature; Minneapolis: University of Minnesota Press, 1984).

Bauman, Richard. *Verbal Art as Performance* (Rowley, Massachusetts: Newbury House, 1977).

Baumeister, Roy F. *Meanings of Life* (New York: Guilford Press, 1991).

Bell, Catherine. *Ritual Theory Ritual Practice* (Oxford: Oxford University Press, 1992).

Bellinger Jr, W.H. *Psalms: Reading and Studying the Book of Praises* (Peabody, Massachusetts: Hendrickson, 1990).

Billman, Kathleen D. and Daniel L. Migliore. *Rachel's Cry: Prayer of Lament and the Rebirth of Hope* (Cleveland, Ohio: United Church Press, 1999).

Bjorck, Jeffery P. 'Religiousness and Coping: Implications for Clinical Practice'. *Journal of Psychology and Christianity* 16, no. 1 (1997): pp. 62–7.

Blackwell, A.L. *The Sacred in Music* (Louisville: Westminster John Knox Press, 1999).

Blommaert, Jan. *Discourse* (Cambridge: Cambridge University Press, 2005).

Boivin, Michael J. 'The Hebraic Model of the Person: Toward a Unified Psychological Science among Christian Helping Professionals'. *Journal of Psychology and Theology* 19, no. 2 (1991): pp. 157–65.

Borditsky, Lera, Lauren A. Schmidt, and Webb Phillips. 'Sex, Syntax and Semantics'. Pages 61–80 in *Language in Mind* (ed. Dedre Gentner and Susan Goldin-Meadow; Cambridge, Massachusetts: Bradford, 2003).

Boulton, Matthew. 'Forsaking God: A Theological Argument for Christian Lamentation'. *Scottish Journal of Theology* 55, no. 1 (2002): pp. 58–78.

Briggs, Richard S. *Words in Action* (Edinburgh: T. & T. Clark, 2001).

Brock, Gary. 'Ritual and Vulnerability'. *Journal of Religion and Health* 29, no. 4 (1990): pp. 285–95.

Brooks, Claire Vonk. 'Psalm 51'. *Interpretation* 49, no. 1 (1995): pp. 62–6.

Brosschot, Jos F. and Julian F. Thayer. 'Worry, Perseverative Thinking and Health'. Pages 99–114 in *Emotional Health and Expression: Advances in Theory, Assessment and Clinical Applications* (ed. Ivan Nyklíček, Lydia Temoshok and Ad Vingerhoets; New York: Brunner-Routledge, 2004).

Brown, William P. *Seeing the Psalms: A Theology of Metaphor* (Louisville: Westminster John Knox Press, 2002).

Broyles, Craig C. *The Conflict of Faith and Experience in the Psalms: A Form-Critical and Theological Study* (Sheffield: JSOT Press, 1989).

Brueggemann, Walter. *Abiding Astonishment: Psalms, Modernity, and the Making of History* (Louisville, Kentucky: Westminster John Knox Press, 1991).

———. 'The Formfulness of Grief.' *Interpretation* 31, no. 3 (1977): pp. 263–75.

———. *Israel's Praise* (Philadephia: Fortress Press, 1988).

———. *The Message of the Psalms: A Theological Commentary* (Minneapolis: Augsburg Publishing House, 1984).

———. *The Psalms in the Life of Faith* (Minneapolis: Fortress Press, 1995).

———. 'Shape for Old Testament Theology, 1'. *Catholic Biblical Quarterly* 47, no. 1 (1985): pp. 28–46.

Buber, Martin. *Between Man and Man* (trans. Ronald Gregor Smith; New York: Macmillan, 1965).

———. *I and Thou* (trans. Ronald Gregor Smith; Edinburgh: T. & T. Clark, 1970).

Bucci, W. *Psychoanalysis and Cognitive Science: A Multiple Code Theory* (New York: Guilford Press, 1997).

Byrne, Patricia Huff. ' "Give Sorrow Words": Lament – Contemporary Need for Job's Old Time Religion'. *Journal of Pastoral Care and Counseling* 56, no. 3 (2002): pp. 255–64.

Calvin, John. *A Commentary on Psalms* Vol. 1 (trans. T.H.L. Parker; London: James Clark & Co., 1965).

Canda, Edward R. 'Therapeutic Transformation in Ritual, Therapy, and Human Development'. *Journal of Religion and Health* 27, no. 3 (1988): pp. 205–20.

Canfield, John V. *The Looking-Glass Self* (New York: Praeger, 1990).

Capps, Donald. 'Nervous Laughter: Lament, Death Anxiety, and Humour'. Pages 70–79 in *Lament: Reclaiming Practices in Pulpit, Pew, and Public Square* (ed. Sally A. Brown and Patrick D. Miller; Louisville: Westminster John Knox Press, 2005).

———. *Pastoral Care: A Thematic Approach* (Philadelphia: The Westminster Press, 1979).

———. *The Poet's Gift* (Louisville, Kentucky: John Knox Press, 1993).

———. 'The Psychology of Petitionary Prayer'. *Theology Today* 39, no. 2 (1982): pp. 130–41.

Carlsen, Mary Baird. *Meaning-Making* (New York: W.W. Norton, 1988).

Carney, Sheila. 'God Damn God: A Reflection on Expressing Anger in Prayer'. *Biblical Theology Bulletin* 13, no. 4 (1983): pp. 116–20.

Carol, L. Patrick and Katherine Dychman. *Inviting the Mystic, Supporting the Prophet: An Introduction to Spiritual Direction* (New York: Paulist Press, 1981).

Carroll, David W. *Psychology of Language* (Pacific Grove, California: Brooks/Cole Publishing Company, 1999).

Clinebell, Howard. *Basic Types of Pastoral Care and Counseling* (London: SCM Press, 1984).

———. *Counseling for Spiritually Empowered Wholeness* (New York: Haworth Press, 1995).

Cohen, Cynthia B., Sondra E. Wheeler, David A. Scott, Barbara Springer Edwards and Patricia Lusk. 'Prayer as Therapy'. *The Hastings Center Report* 30, no. 3 (2000): pp. 40–47.

Cohen, David J. 'A Prophet in Motion: The Counterpoint of Speaking, Acting and Reflecting'. Pages 15–35 in *On Eagles' Wings: An Exploration of Strength in the Midst of Weakness* (ed. Michael Parsons and David J. Cohen; Lutterworth Press, 2008).

———. 'Getting to the Heart of the Matter'. Pages 50–63 in *Text and Task: Scripture and Mission* (ed. Michael Parsons; Carlisle: Paternoster, 2005).

———. 'The Potential Function of the Lament Psalms and the Relevance of This to the Practice of Spiritual Direction with Both

Individuals and Communities of Faith'. Unpublished Masters dissertation. Murdoch University, 1999.

———. 'The Usage of the Psalms During the Post-Exilic Period up to 200 CE'. Unpublished Honours dissertation. Murdoch University, 1990.

Cooper-White, Pamela. 'The Ritual Reason Why: Explorations of the Unconscious through Enactment and Ritual in Pastoral Psychotherapy'. *Journal for Supervision and Training in Ministry* 19 (1999): pp. 68–75.

Craghan, John F. *Psalms for All Seasons* (Collegeville, Minnesota: Liturgical Press, 1993).

Craigie, P.C. *Psalms Vol. 1*, Word Biblical Commentary (Waco, Texas: Word Books, 1983).

Crites, Stephen. 'The Narrative Quality of Experience'. *Journal of the American Academy of Religion* 39, no. 3 (1971): pp. 291–311.

Crow, Loren D. 'The Rhetoric of Psalm 44'. *Zeitschrift für alttestamentliche Wissenschaft* 104, no. 3 (1992): pp. 394–401.

D'Aquili, Eugene G. 'The Myth-Ritual Complex: A Biogenetic Structural Analysis'. *Zygon* 18, no. 3 (1983): pp. 247–82.

Davis, Ellen F. 'Exploding the Limits'. *Journal for the Study of the Old Testament* 53 (1992): pp. 93–105.

Day, John. *Psalms* (Sheffield: Sheffield Academic Press, 1990).

Day, James M. 'Speaking of Belief: Language, Performance, and Narrative in the Psychology of Religion'. *International Journal for the Psychology of Religion* 3, no. 4 (1993): pp. 213–29.

Dombeck, Mary T. 'Learning through Symbol, Myth, Model and Ritual'. *Journal of Religion and Health* 28, no. 2 (1989): pp. 152–62.

Driver, Tom F. *Liberating Rites: Understanding the Transformative Power of Ritual* (Boulder, Colorado: Westview Press, 1998).

Duff, Nancy J. 'Recovering Lamentation as a Practice in the Church'. Pages 3–14 in *Lament: Reclaiming Practices in Pulpit, Pew, and Public Square* (ed. Sally A. Brown and Patrick D. Miller; Louisville: Westminster John Knox Press, 2005).

Duffy, Mervyn. *How Language, Ritual and Sacraments Work* (Rome: Gregorian University Press, 2005).

Eaton, John. *Psalms and the Way of the Kingdom: A Conference with Commentators* (Sheffield: Sheffield Academic Press, 1995).

Ellens, J. Howard. 'Communication Theory and Petitionary Prayer'. *Journal of Psychology and Theology* 15, no. 1 (1977): pp. 48–54.

Endres, John C. and Elizabeth Liebert. *A Retreat with the Psalms* (New York: Paulist Press, 2001).

Epperly, Bruce G. 'To Pray or Not to Pray: Reflections on the Intersection of Prayer and Medicine'. *Journal of Religion and Health* 34, no. 2 (1995): pp. 141–8.

Erickson, Richard C. 'Psychotherapy and the Locus of Control'. *Journal of Religion and Health* 22, no. 1 (1983): pp. 74–81.

Faber, Heije. 'The Meaning of Ritual in the Liturgy'. Pages 43–56 in *Current Studies on Rituals: Perspectives for the Psychology of Religion* (ed. Hans-Günter Heimbrock and H. Barbara Boudewijnse; Amsterdam: Rodopi, 1990).

Farmer, Kathleen A. 'Psalms'. Pages 137–44 in *The Women's Bible Commentary* (ed. Carol A. Newsom and Sharon H. Ringe; London: SPCK, 1992).

Fink, Peter E. 'Liturgical Prayer and Spiritual Growth'. *Worship* 55, no. 5 (1981): pp. 386–98.

Finney, John R. and H. Newton Malony Jr. 'Empirical Studies of Christian Prayer: A Review of Literature'. *Journal of Psychology and Theology* 13, no. 2 (1985): pp. 104–15.

Fløysvik, Ingvar. *When God Becomes My Enemy: The Theology of the Complaint Psalms* (Saint Louis: Concordia Academic Press, 1997).

Friedman, Maurice. *Religion and Psychology: A Dialogical Approach* (New York: Paragon House, 1992).

Fulghum, Robert. *From Beginning to End: The Rituals of Our Lives* (Sydney: Bantam Books, 1995).

Furnham, Adrian F. 'Locus of Control and Theological Beliefs'. *Journal of Psychology and Theology* 10, no. 2 (1982): pp. 130–36.

Galindo, Israel. 'Addressing the Needs of the Spirit'. *Journal of Pastoral Care* 51, no. 4 (1997): pp. 395–402.

Gass, Carlton S. 'Orthodox Christian Values Related to Psychotherapy and Mental Health'. *Journal of Psychology and Theology* 12, no. 3 (1984): pp. 230–37.

Gay, Volney P. 'Public Rituals Versus Private Treatment: Psychodynamics of Prayer'. *Journal of Religion and Health* 17, no. 4 (1978): pp. 244–60.

Georgakopoulou, Alexandra and Dionysis *Goutsos. Discourse Analysis* (Edinburgh: Edinburgh University Press, 1997).

Gerstenberger, Erhard S. *Psalms Part I*. Vol. 14, Forms of Old Testament Literature (Grand Rapids, Michigan: Eerdmans, 1988).

Goldingay, John. 'The Dynamic Cycle of Praise and Prayer in the Psalms'. *Journal for the Study of the Old Testament* 20 (1981): pp. 85–90.

Goldin-Meadow, Susan. 'Thought before Language: Do We Think Ergative?' Pages 493–522 in *Language in Mind* (ed. Dedre Genter and Susan Goldin-Meadow; Cambridge, Massachusetts: MIT Press, 2003).

Grainger, Robert. 'Forum: How Deep Is the Water?' *Worship* 76, no. 4 (2002): pp. 360–67.

Greenburg, Melanie A., Camille B. Wortman and Arthur A. Stone. 'Emotional Expression and Physical Health: Revising Traumatic Memories or Fostering Self-Regulation?' *Journal of Personality and Social Psychology* 71, no. 3 (1996): pp. 588–602.

Gunkel, Hermann. *The Psalms* (Philadelphia: Fortress Press, 1987).

Guthrie, Nancy. 'Can I Really Expect God to Protect Me? Divine Promises in the Midst of Suffering'. *Christianity Today* (October 2005), pp. 56–9.

Hall, Todd W. and Keith J. Edwards. 'The Spiritual Assessment Inventory: A Theistic Model and Measure for Assessing Spiritual Development'. *Journal for the Scientific Study of Religion* 41, no. 2 (2002): pp. 341–57.

Hall, Todd W. and Margaret Gorman. 'Relational Spirituality: Implications of the Convergence of Attachment Theory, Interpersonal Neurobiology, and Emotional Information Processing', *Newsletter of the Psychology of Religion* 28 (Spring 2003): pp. 1–12.

Hall, Todd W., Beth Fletcher Brokaw, Keith J. Edwards and Patricia L. Pike. 'An Empirical Exploration of Psychoanalysis and Religion: Spiritual Maturity and Object Relations Development'. *Journal for the Scientific Study of Religion* 37, no. 2 (1998): pp. 303–13.

Hayakawa, S.I. and Alan R. Hayakawa. *Language in Thought and Action* (San Diego: Harcourt Inc., 1990).

Heimbrock, Hans-Günter. 'Ritual and Transformation: A Psychoanalytic Perspective'. Pages 33–42 in *Current Studies on Rituals: Perspectives for the Psychology of Religion* (ed. Hans-Günter Heimbrock and H. Barbara Boudewijnse; Amsterdam: Rodopi, 1990).

Hill, P.C., K.I. Pargament, R.W. Hood Jr, M.E. McCullough, J.P. Swyers, D.B. Larson and B.J. Zinnbauer. 'Conceptualizing

Religion and Spirituality: Points of Commonality, Points of Departure'. *Journal for the Theory of Social Behaviour* 30 (2000): pp. 51–77.

Hine, Virginia H. 'Self-Generated Ritual: Trend or Fad?' *Worship* 55, no. 5 (1981): pp. 404–19.

Hogue, David A. 'Shelters and Pathways: Ritual and Pastoral Counseling'. *Journal for Supervision and Training in Ministry* 19 (1999): pp. 57–67.

Hogue, David A. and Pamela Cooper-White. 'Supervision of Ritual, Rituals of Supervision'. *Journal for Supervision and Training in Ministry* 19 (1999): pp. 9–12.

Holladay, William L. *The Psalms through Three Thousand Years* (Minneapolis: Fortress Press, 1993).

Holquist, Michael. *Dialogism: Bakhtin and His World* (New York: Routledge, 1990).

Howard Jr, J. Grant. 'Interpersonal Communication: Biblical Insights on the Problem and the Solution'. *Journal of Psychology and Theology* 3, no. 4 (1975): pp. 243–57.

Hughes, Graham. *Worship as Meaning: A Liturgical Theology for Late Modernity* (Cambridge: Cambridge University Press, 2003).

Hughes, Richard A. *Lament, Death, and Destiny.* Vol. 68, Studies in Biblical Literature (ed. Hemchand Gosai; New York: Lang, 2004).

Hustad, Donald P. 'The Psalms as Worship Expression: Personal and Congregational'. *Review and Expositor* 81 (1984): pp. 407–24.

Idelsohn, A.Z. *Jewish Music* (New York: Schoken, 1956).

Inch, Morris A. *The Psychology of the Psalms* (Waco, Texas: Word Books, 1970).

Iser, Wolfgang. *The Act of Reading: A Theory of Aesthetic Response* (London: Routledge & Kegan Paul, 1978).

Jackson, Laurence E. and Robert D. Coursey. 'The Relationship of God Control and Internal Locus of Control to Intrinsic Religious Motivation, Coping and Purpose in Life'. *Journal for the Scientific Study of Religion* 27, no. 3 (1988): pp. 399–410.

Jacobsen, Rolf. 'Burning Our Lamps with Borrowed Oil'. Pages 90–98 in *Psalms and Practice* (ed. Stephen B. Reid; Collegeville, Minnesota: Liturgical Press, 2001).

Jakobson, Roman. 'Linguistics and Poetics'. Pages 54–62 in *The Discourse Reader* (ed. Adam Couplan, and Nikolas Jaworski; London: Routledge, 1999).

James, Wendy. *The Ceremonial Animal: A New Portrait of Anthropology* (Oxford: Oxford University Press, 2003).

James, W. *The Varieties of Religious Experience* (New York: University Books, 1963).

Janssen, Jacques, Joep de Hart and Christine den Draak. 'Praying as an Individualized Ritual'. Pages 71–85 in *Current Studies on Rituals: Perspectives for the Psychology of Religion* (ed. Hans-Günter Heimbrock and H. Barbara Boudewijnse; Amsterdam: Rodopi, 1990).

Jennings, Theodore W. 'On Ritual Knowledge'. *Journal of Religion* 62, no. 2 (1982): pp. 111–27.

Jenson, Robert W. 'The Praying Animal'. *Zygon* 18, no. 3 (1983): pp. 311–25.

Johnson, Ben Campbell, and Andre Dreitcer. *Beyond the Ordinary: Spirituality for Church Leaders* (Grand Rapids, Michigan: Eerdmans, 2001).

Johnson, Elizabeth. *She Who Is: The Mystery of God in Feminist Theological Discourse* (New York: Crossroad, 1992).

Jones, Logan C. 'The Psalms of Lament and the Transformation of Sorrow'. *Journal of Pastoral Care and Counseling* 61, no. 1–2 (2007): pp. 47–58.

Jumonville, Robert Moore and Robert Woods. 'The Role-Taking Theory of Praying the Psalms: Using the Psalms as Model for Structuring the Life of Prayer'. *Journal of Biblical Studies* 3, no. 2 (2003): pp. 22–61.

Kelcourse, Felicity Brock. 'Prayer and the Soul: Dialogues that Heal'. *Journal of Religion and Health* 40, no. 1 (2001): pp. 231–42.

Kelley, Paige H. 'Prayers of Troubled Spirits'. *Review and Expositor* 81, no. 3 (1984): pp. 377–83.

Kidner, Derek. *Psalms 1–72*, Tyndale Old Testament Commentaries (Downers Grove, Illinois: InterVarsity Press, 1973).

———. *Psalms 73–150*, Tyndale Old Testament Commentaries (Downers Grove, Illinois: InterVarsity Press, 1975).

Klinghardt, Matthias. 'Prayer Formularies for Public Recitation: Their Use and Function in Ancient Religion'. *Numen* 46, no. 1 (1999): pp. 1–52.

Kraus, Hans-Joachim. *Psalms 1–59* (trans. Hilton C. Oswald; Minneapolis: Augsburg, 1988.

———. *Psalms 60-150* (trans. Hilton C. Oswald; Minneapolis: Augsburg, 1989).

————. *Theology of the Psalms* (Minneapolis: Augsburg Press, 1986).

Kselman, John S. 'A Note on Psalm 85:9–10'. *Catholic Biblical Quarterly* 46, no. 1 (1984): pp. 23–7.

Kubicki, Judith Marie. 'Using J.L. Austin's Performative Language Theory to Interpret Ritual Music Making'. *Worship* 73, no. 4 (1999): pp. 310–30.

Kugel, James. *The Idea of Biblical Poetry: Parallelism and Its History* (New Haven: Yale University Press, 1981).

Kundtz, David. *Stopping: How to Be Still When You Have to Keep Going* (Berkeley, California: Conari Press, 1998).

Ladd, Kevin L. and Bernard Spilka. 'Inward, Outward, Upward Prayer: Scale Reliability and Validation'. *Journal for the Scientific Study of Religion* 45, no. 2 (2006): pp. 233–51.

Ladrière, Jean. *Liturgical Experience of Faith* (ed. H. Schmidt and David N. Power; New York: Herder & Herder, 1973).

Lanigan, Richard L. *Speech Act Phenomenology* (The Hague, Netherlands: Martinus Nijhoff, 1977).

Le Roux, Jurie H. 'Augustine, Gadamer and the Psalms (Or: The Psalms as the Answer to the Questions)'. Pages 123–30 in *Psalms in Liturgy* (ed. Dirk J. Human and Cas J.A. Vos; London: T. & T. Clark International, 2004).

Leeming, David A. 'Myth and Therapy'. *Journal of Religion and Health* 40, no. 1 (2001): pp. 115–19.

Lefcourt, Herbert M. *Locus of Control: Current Trends in Theory and Research* (Hillside, New Jersey: Lawrence Erlbaum Associates, 1976).

Lefevere, Patricia. 'Poetry Opens a Window to Prayer, Healing'. *National Catholic Reporter* 38, no. 6 (2001): pp. 34–6.

Levine, Herbert J. *Sing Unto God a New Song: A Contemporary Reading of the Psalms* (Bloomington: Indiana University Press, 1995).

Lewis, C.S. *Reflections on the Psalms* (Glasgow: William Collins Sons & Co., 1978).

Lewis, Leslie C. 'Continuity and Meaning'. *Journal of Religion and Health* 37, no. 2 (1998): pp. 143–57.

Lowth, Robert. *De Sacra Poesie Hebraeorum Praelectiones Academicae Oxonii . . .* (1766).

Lusebrink, Vija Bergs. *Imagery and Visual Expression in Therapy* (ed. Carroll E. Izard and Jerome L. Singer; New York: Plenum Press, 1990).

Lustig, Andrew. 'Prescribing Prayer'. *Commonweal* (2004): pp. 32–3.

MacCormac, Earl R. *A Cognitive Theory of Metaphor* (London: Massachusetts Institute of Technology, 1985).

Madden, Kathryn Wood. 'From Speechlessness to Presence'. *Journal of Religion and Health* 40, no. 1 (2001): pp. 185–204.

Magaletta, Philip R. 'Prayer in Psychotherapy: A Model for Its Use, Ethical Considerations, and Guidelines for Practice'. *Journal of Psychology and Theology* 26, no. 4 (1998): pp. 322–30.

Martz, Louis L. *The Poetry of Meditation* (Yale: Yale University Press, 1962).

May, Gerald G. 'The Psychodynamics of Spirituality'. *Journal of Pastoral Care* 31, no. 2 (1977): pp. 84–90.

May, Rollo. *The Meaning of Anxiety* (New York: W.W. Norton, 1977).

Mays, James L. *The Lord Reigns: A Theological Handbook to the Psalms* (Louisville, Kentucky: Westminster John Knox Press, 1994).

Mazza, Nicholas. *Poetry Therapy: Interface of the Arts and Psychology* (ed. Charles R. Figley, Innovations in Psychology, Baton Rouge: CRC Press, 1999).

McCann, J. Clinton. *A Theological Introduction to the Book of Psalms – Psalms as Torah* (Nashville: Abingdon Press, 1993).

–––––. (ed.). The Shape and Shaping of the Psalter, *JSOT Dissertation Series* No. 159 (Sheffield: Sheffield Academic Press, 1993).

McCauley, R.N. and E.T. Lawson. *Bringing Ritual to Mind: Psychological Foundations of Cultural Forms* (Cambridge: Cambridge University Press, 2002).

McCullough, Michael E. 'Prayer and Health: Conceptual Issues, Research Review, and Research Agenda'. *Journal of Psychology and Theology* 23, no. 1 (1995): pp. 15–29.

McDargh, John. 'The Life of the Self in Christian Spirituality and Contemporary Psychoanalysis'. *Horizons* 11, no. 2 (1984): pp. 344–60.

Meisenhelder, Janice Bell and John P. Marcum. 'Responses of Clergy to 9/11: Posttraumatic Stress, Coping, and Religious Outcomes'. *Journal for the Scientific Study of Religion* 43, no. 4 (2004): pp. 547–54.

Merton, Thomas. *Contemplative Prayer* (London: Darton, Longman & Todd, 1981).

–––––. *The Signs of Jonas* (New York: Image Books, 1956).

Meserve, Harry C. 'The Human Side of Prayer'. *Journal of Religion and Health* 30, no. 4 (1991): pp. 271–6.

Metz, Johann Baptist. *A Passion for God: The Mystical-Political Dimension of Christianity* (trans. J. Matthew Ashley; New York: Paulist Press, 1990).

Miles, Jack. 'The Human Zoo: Adversaries and Alliances in the Psalms'. www.sbl-site.org/Newsletter/04_2003/Miles.html.

Miller Jr, Patrick D. *Interpreting the Psalms* (Philadelphia: Fortress Press, 1986).

———. 'Trouble and Woe'. *Interpretation* 37 (1983): pp. 32–45.

Miller, Patrick D. 'Heaven's Prisoners: The Lament and Christian Prayer'. Pages 15–26 in *Lament: Reclaiming Practices in Pulpit, Pew, and Public Square* (ed. Sally A. Brown and Patrick D. Miller; Louisville: Westminster John Knox Press, 2005).

———. 'The Psalms and Pastoral Care'. *Liturgy and Music*, no. 24 (1990): pp. 3.

———. *They Cried Unto the Lord: The Form and Theology of Biblical Prayer* (Minneapolis: Fortress, 1994).

Mitchell, Christina E. 'Internal Locus of Control for Expectation, Perception and Management of Answered Prayer'. *Journal of Psychology and Theology* 17, no. 1 (1989): pp. 21–6.

Mitchell, Leonel L. *The Meaning of Ritual* (Harrisburg, Pennsylvania: Morehouse, 1977).

Mitchell, Nathan D. 'The Amen Corner'. *Worship* 76, no. 1 (2002): pp. 67–77.

Moore, Gerald. 'Without Lament There Is No Life'. *Australian Journal of Liturgy* 10, no. 1 (2005): pp. 29–46.

Moore, R. Kelvin. *The Psalms of Lamentation and the Enigma of Suffering* (Lewiston, New York: Edwin Mellen Press, 1996).

Moore, Robert L. 'Contemporary Psychotherapy as Ritual Process: An Initial Reconnaissance'. *Zygon* 18, no. 3 (1983): pp. 283–94.

Morris, Pam, ed. *The Bakhtin Reader* (London: Edward Arnold, 1994).

Mowinckel, Sigmund. *The Old Testament as the Word of God* (trans. Reidar B. Bjornard; New York: Abingdon Press, 1959).

———. *The Psalms in Israel's Worship* (2 vols. Vol. 1; Oxford: Basil Blackwell, 1962).

Muck, Terry. 'Psalm, Bhajan and Kirtan'. Pages 7–27 in *Psalms and Practice* (ed. Stephen B. Reid; Collegeville, Minnesota: Liturgical Press, 2001).

Myers, Lyn B. and Nazanin Derakshan. 'The Repressive Coping Style and Avoidance of Negative Affect'. Pages 169–84 in *Emotional Expression and Health: Advances in Theory, Assessment and Clinical Applications* (ed. Ivan Nyklíček, Lydia Temoshok and Ad Vingerhoets; New York: Brunner-Routledge, 2004).

Nasuti, Harry P. 'The Sacramental Function of the Psalms in Contemporary Scholarship and Liturgical Practice'. Pages 78–89 in *Psalms and Practice* (ed. Stephen B. Reid; Collegeville, Minnesota: Liturgical Press, 2001).

Neufeld, Vernon H. *Reconceiving Texts as Speech Acts*, Biblical International Series (Leiden: E.J. Brill, 1994).

Neve, Lloyd. 'Realized Eschatology in Psalm 51'. *Expository Times* 80, no. 9 (1969): pp. 264–6.

Nunan, David. *Introducing Discourse Analysis* (ed. Ronald Carter and David Nunan; Penguin English Applied Linguistics. London: Penguin Books, 1993).

Ogelsby, William B. *Biblical Themes for Pastoral Care* (Nashville: Abingdon Press, 1980).

Ostriker, Alicia. 'Psalm and Anti-Psalm: A Personal Essay'. www.sbl-site.org/Newsletter/04_2003/Ostriker.html.

Paloma, Margaret M. 'The Effects of Prayer on Mental Well-Being'. *Second Opinion* (January 1993): pp. 37–51.

Paloma, Margaret M. and Brian F. Pendleton. 'The Effects of Prayer Experiences on Measures of General Well-Being'. *Journal of Psychology and Theology* 19, no. 1 (1991): pp. 71–83.

Pargament, K.I. *The Psychology of Religion and Coping: Theory and Practice* (New York: Guilford Press, 1997).

Parker, Paul P. 'Suffering, Prayer, and Miracles'. *Journal of Religion and Health* 36, no. 3 (1997): pp. 205–19.

Patrick, Carol L. and Katherine Dychman. *Inviting the Mystic, Supporting the Prophet: An Introduction to Spiritual Direction* (New York: Paulist Press, 1981).

Patterson, David. 'The Religious Aspect of Bakhtin's Aesthetics'. *Renascence* 46, no. 1 (1993): pp. 55–70.

Patton, John. 'Pastoral Ministry in a Fractured World'. *Journal of Pastoral Care* 42, no. 1 (1988): pp. 26–36.

Peterson, Eugene H. *Answering God* (San Francisco: Harper & Row, 1989).

Pleins, J. David. *The Psalms: Songs of Tragedy, Hope, and Justice* (Maryknoll, New York: Orbis Books, 1993).

Polanyi, Michael. *Knowledge and Being* (Chicago: University of Chicago Press, 1969).

———. *Personal Knowledge: Towards a Post-Critical Philosophy* (Chicago: University of Chicago Press, 1958).

Quesnell, Quentin. 'Interior Prayer and Ritual Drama'. *Dialogue and Alliance* 3, no. 4 (1989-90): pp. 64–70.

Quinn, Kenneth. *How Literature Works: The Nature of the Literary Experience* (Sydney: Australian Broadcasting Corporation, 1982).

Rappaport, Roy A. *Ritual and Religion in the Making of Humanity* (Cambridge: Cambridge University Press, 1999).

Reid, Stephen Breck. *Listening In: A Multicultural Reading of the Psalms* (Nashville: Abingdon, 1997).

———. 'Power and Practice: Performative Speech'. Pages 40–58 in *Psalms and Practice* (ed. Stephen B. Reid; Collegeville, Minnesota: Liturgical Press, 2001).

Renkema, Jan. *Discourse Studies* (Amsterim, The Netherlands: John Benjamins Publishing Company, 1993).

Renner, H.P.V. 'The Use of Ritual in Pastoral Care'. *Journal of Pastoral Care and Counseling* 23, no. 3 (1979): pp. 164–74.

Richards, Douglas G. 'The Phenomenology and Psychological Correlates of Verbal Prayer'. *Journal of Psychology and Theology* 19, no. 4 (1991): pp. 354–63.

Ricoeur, P. *Essays on Biblical Interpretation* (ed. Lewis S. Mudge; Philadelphia: Fortress Press, 1980).

———. *The Rule of Metaphor: Multidisciplinary Studies in the Creation of Meaning in Language* (London: Routledge & Kegan Paul, 1978).

Ritzema, Robert J. 'Attribution to Supernatural Causation: An Important Component of Religious Commitment?' *Journal of Psychology and Theology* 7, no. 4 (1979): pp. 286–93.

Robbins, Martha A. 'The Divine Dance: Partners in Remembering, Revisioning, and Reweaving'. *Journal of Pastoral Care* 51, no. 3 (1997): pp. 337–47.

Ross, James F. 'Job 33:14–30: The Phenomenology of Lament'. *Journal of Biblical Literature* 94, no. 1 (1975): pp. 38–46.

Roth, Andrew. ' "Men Wearing Masks": Issues of Description in the Analysis of Ritual'. *Social Theory* 13, no. 3 (1995): pp. 301–27.

Russell, D.S. 'Body Language in Worship and Prayer'. *Expository Times* 112, no. 4 (2001): pp. 123–5.

Sabourin, L. *Psalms* (New York: Alba, 1974).

Saliers, Don E. *Worship as Theology: Foretaste of Glory Divine* (Nashville: Abingdon, 1994).

Saur, Marilyn S. and William G. Saur. 'Transitional Phenomena as Evidenced in Prayer'. *Journal of Religion and Health* 32, no. 1 (1993): pp. 55–65.

Savran, George. 'How Can We Sing a Song of the Lord?' *Zeitschrift für die alttestmentilche Wissenschaft* 112, no. 1 (2000): pp. 43–58.

Scarry, Elaine. The Body in Pain (Oxford: Oxford University Press, 1985).

Schaller, Joseph J. 'Performance Language Theory: An Exercise in the Analysis of Ritual'. *Worship* 62 (1988): pp. 415–32.

Searle, John R. *Consciousness and Language* (Cambridge: Cambridge University Press, 2002).

———. *Speech Acts: An Essay in the Philosophy of Language* (Cambridge: Cambridge University Press, 1970).

Shannon, Martin. ' "A Certain Psychological Difficulty" or a Certain Spiritual Challenge: Use of the Integral Psalter in the Liturgy of Hours'. *Worship* 73, no. 4 (1999): pp. 290–309.

Sheppard, Gerald T. 'Theology in the Book of Psalms'. *Interpretation* 46 (1992): pp. 143–55.

Siegel, D.J. *How Relationships and the Brain Interact to Shape Who We Are* (New York: Guilford Press, 1999).

Simpson, John and Edmund Weiner, eds. *Oxford English Dictionary* (20 vols, London: Oxford University Press, 1989).

Smith, Barbara Herrnstein. *Poetic Closure* (Chicago: University of Chicago Press, 1968).

Smith, Jonathan Z. 'To Take Place'. Pages 26–50 in *Ritual and Religious Belief* (ed. Graham Harvey; London: Equinox, 2005).

Soskice, Janet Martin. *Metaphor and Religious Language* (Oxford: Clarendon Press, 1985).

Steere, Douglas V. 'Prayer in the Contemporary World' (Willington, Pennsylvania: Pendle Hill Publications, 1990).

Stoeber, Michael. 'Evelyn Underhill on Magic, Sacrament, and Spiritual Transformation'. *Worship* 77, no. 2 (2003): pp. 132–51.

Stucky-Abbott, Curtis. 'The Development of the Therapeutic Self within the Pastoral Person'. *Journal of Supervision and Training* 13 (1991): pp. 49–62.

Sutherland, Anne V. 'Worldframes and God-Talk in Trauma and Suffering'. *Journal of Pastoral Care* 49, no. 3 (1995): pp. 280–92.

Sweetman, Robert. 'Thomas of Cantimpré: Performative Reading and Pastoral Care'. Pages 133–67 in *Performance and Transformation* (ed. Mary Suydam and Joanne Ziegler; New York: St Martin's Press, 1999).

Swinton, John and Harriet Mowat. *Practical Theology and Qualitative Research* (London: SCM Press, 2006).

Tam, Ekman P.P. 'Faith Development Theory and Spiritual Direction'. *Pastoral Psychology* 44, no. 4 (1996): pp. 251–64.

Tanner, Beth LaNeel. 'How Long O Lord! Will Your People Suffer in Silence Forever?' Pages 143–52 in *Psalms and Practice* (ed. Stephen B. Reid; Collegeville, Minnesota: Liturgical Press, 2001).

Texter, Lynne A. and Janine M. Mariscotti. 'From Chaos to New Life: Ritual Enactment in the Passage from Illness to Health'. *Journal of Religion and Health* 33, no. 4 (1994): pp. 325–32.

Todorov, Tzvetan. *Mikhail Bakhtin: The Dialogical Principle* (trans. Wlad Godzich. Vol. 13, Theory and History of Literature. Manchester: Manchester University Press, 1984).

Tolson, Chester L. and Harold G. Koenig. *The Healing Power of Prayer* (Grand Rapids, Michigan: Baker Books, 2003).

Tostengard, Sheldon. 'Psalm 22'. *Interpretation* 46, no. 2 (1992): pp. 167–70.

Townsend, Loren L. 'Creative Theological Imagining: A Method for Pastoral Counselling'. *Journal of Pastoral Care* 50, no. 4 (1996): pp. 249–363.

Tracy, David. 'The Hidden God: The Divine Other of Liberation'. *Cross Currents* 46 (Spring 1996): pp. 5–16.

Trueman, Carl R. *The Wages of Spin: Critical Writings on Historic and Contemporary Evangelicalism* (Edinburgh: Christian Focus Publications, 2004).

Tull, Patricia K. 'Bakhtin's Confessional Self-Accounting and Psalms of Lament'. *Biblical Interpretation* 13, no. 1 (2005): pp. 41–55.

———. *Let Evil Speedily Hunt Down the Violent: Reflections on Troubling Psalms in Turbulent Times* (Louisville, Kentucky: Louisville Seminary, 2004).

Turner, Victor. *The Forest of Symbols: Aspects of Ndembu Ritual* (Ithaca: Cornell University Press, 1967).

Ulanov, Ann and Barry Ulanov. *Primary Speech: A Psychology of Prayer* (London: SCM Press, 1982).

Vall, Gregory. 'Psalm 22:17b: "The Old Guess."' *Journal of Biblical Literature* 116, no. 1 (1997): pp. 43–56.

VanKatwyk, Peter L. 'Healing through Differentiation: A Pastoral Care and Counseling Perspective'. *Journal of Pastoral Care* 51, no. 3 (1997): pp. 283–92.

Wallace, Howard Neil. *Words to God, Word from God* (Aldershot: Ashgate, 2005).

Watson, P.J., J. Trevor Milliron, Ronald J. Morris and Ralph W. Hood Jr. 'Locus of Control within a Religious Ideological Surround'. *Journal of Psychology and Christianity* 14, no. 3 (1995): pp. 239–49.

Weems, Ann. *Psalms of Lament* (Louisville, Kentucky: Westminster John Knox Press, 1995).

Weiser, Artur. *The Psalms* (London: SCM Press, 1962).

Wendland, Ernst R. *Analyzing the Psalms* (Dallas: Summer Institute of Linguistics, 1998).

West, William. *Spiritual Issues in Therapy: Relating Experience to Practice* (Basingstoke: Palgrave Macmillan, 2004).

Westermann, Claus. *Praise and Lament in the Psalms* (Edinburgh: T. & T. Clark, 1981).

———. *The Praise of God in the Psalms* (Richmond, Virginia: John Knox Press, 1965).

———. *The Psalms: Structure, Content and Message* (trans. Ralph D. Gehrke; Minneapolis: Augsburg, 1980).

———. 'The Role of the Lament in the Theology of the Old Testament'. *Interpretation* 28, no. 1 (1974): pp. 20–38.

Wheelock, Wade T. 'The Problem of Ritual Language: From Information to Situation'. *Journal of the American Academy of Religion* 50, no. 1 (1982): pp. 49–71.

Whitehead, James D. and Evelyn Eaton Whitehead. *Shadows of the Heart: A Spirituality of Negative Emotions* (New York: Crossroad, 1994).

Williamson, H.G.M. 'Reading the Lament Psalms Backwards'. Pages 3–15 in *A God So Near: Essays on Old Testament in Honor of Patrick D. Miller* (ed. B.A. Strawn and N.R. Bowen; Winona Lake, 2003).

Willimon, William H. *Worship as Pastoral Care* (Nashville: Abingdon, 1979).

Wolterstorff, Nicholas. *Divine Discourse: Philosophical Reflections on the Claim that God Speaks* (Cambridge: Cambridge University Press, 1995).

Woolery, Alison and Peter Salovey. 'Emotional Intelligence and Physical Health'. Pages 154–68 in *Emotional Expression and Health: Advances in Theory, Assessment and Clinical Applications* (ed. Ivan Nyklíček, Lydia Temoshok and Ad Vingerhoets; New York: Brunner-Routledge, 2004).

Wren, B. *Praying Twice: The Music and Words of Congregational Song* (Louisville: Westminster John Knox Press, 2000).

Endnotes

Preface

[1] Ann Weems, *Psalms of Lament* (Louisville, KY: Westminster John Knox Press, 1995), p. xvii.

1. The Journey Begins

[1] Thomas Merton, *The Signs of Jonas* (New York: Image Books, 1956), p. 248. Merton captures the concept well, stating, 'This is the secret of the Psalms. Our identity is hidden in them. In them we find ourselves, and God. In these fragments He has revealed not only Himself to us but ourselves in Him.'

[2] John Calvin, *A Commentary on the Psalms Vol. 1*, trans. T.H.L. Parker (London: James Clark & Co., 1965), p. 16.

[3] The phrase most commonly used in studies of the Psalter to describe the psalms' historical setting is the German, *Sitz im Leben*, literally meaning 'setting in life'. Notable scholars employing the phrase are Hans-Joachim Kraus, *Psalms 1–59* (trans. Hilton C. Oswald; Minneapolis: Augsburg, 1988) and *Psalms 60–150* (trans. Hilton C. Oswald; Minneapolis: Augsburg, 1989); and Artur Weiser, *The Psalms* (London: SCM Press, 1962).

[4] Cf. Walter Brueggemann, *The Message of the Psalms: A Theological Commentary* (Minneapolis: Augsburg, 1984); Erhard S. Gerstenberger, *Psalms Part I*, vol. 14, The Forms of Old Testament Literature (Grand Rapids, Michigan: Eerdmans, 1988); Hermann Gunkel, *The Psalms* (Philadelphia: Fortress Press, 1987).

[5] E.g. Kathleen D. Billman and Daniel L. Migliore, *Rachel's Cry: Prayer of Lament and the Rebirth of Hope* (Cleveland, Ohio: United Church Press, 1999).

6   David J. Cohen, 'Usage of the Psalms During the Post-Exilic Period up to 200 CE' (Murdoch University, 1990). This study explored the issue from an historical perspective.

7   It could be argued that both the Baptist and Churches of Christ traditions, with which I have experience, have historically made some use of lectionary readings, including readings from the Psalter. How- ever, a systematic and intentional employment of the Psalter gener- ally, and psalms of distress specifically, as a part of personal devotion or corporate worship has clearly diminished from the latter part of the twentieth century.

2. Signpost 1 – What is Lament?

1   Hermann Gunkel, *The Psalms* (Philadelphia: Fortress Press, 1987). He was the first of many to coin this term to describe one of the *Gattungen* (genres) that he identified within the Psalter.

2   Although the focus here is on individual laments, and the benefit they can have for individuals, the conclusions reached are, most likely, equally applicable to groups using these psalms for prayer.

3   Claus Westermann, *Praise and Lament in the Psalms* (Edinburgh: T. & T. Clark, 1981), p. 266.

4   Walter Brueggemann, *The Psalms in the Life of Faith* (Minneapolis: Fortress Press, 1995), p. 33.

5   Westermann, *Praise and Lament*, p. 267.

6   Of interest here is the decreasing number of lament psalms and the increasing number of praise psalms present as one moves towards the end of the Psalter.

7   Erhard S. Gerstenberger, *Psalms Part I*, vol. 14, The Forms of Old Testament Literature (Grand Rapids, Michigan: Eerdmans, 1988), p. 14.

8   H.P.V. Renner, 'The Use of Ritual in Pastoral Care', *JPCC* 23, no. 3 (1979): pp. 164–74.

9   Craig C. Broyles, *The Conflict of Faith and Experience in the Psalms: A Form-Critical and Theological Study* (Sheffield: JSOT Press, 1989), p. 13.

10 Brueggemann, *The Psalms*, p. 8. See this reference for a detailed description of how Brueggemann applies Ricouer's thinking to the characterization of various types of psalms (P. Ricoeur, *The Rule of Metaphor, Multidisciplinary Studies in the Creation of Meaning in Language* (London: Routledge & Kegan Paul, 1978).

11 These examples have been selected from among many similar expressions found in most lament psalms.

12 By the term 'intrapsychic', I mean the movement within oneself between thinking, feeling and sensing our experiences of living.

13 This kind of expression could be viewed as a dialogue but is probably more accurately identified as dialectic. Dialectic seems the more appropriate term here because the dialogue is often argumentative or polemical in style.

14 Of course, processes of lament without the use of these psalms are entirely possible.

15 Claus Westermann, 'The Role of the Lament in the Theology of the Old Testament,' *Interpretation* 28, no. 1 (1974): p. 27.

3. Signpost 2 – Lament and Ritual

1 Hermann Gunkel, *The Psalms* (Philadelphia: Fortress Press, 1987); Sigmund Mowinckel, *The Psalms in Israel's Worship* (2 vols; Oxford: Basil Blackwell, 1962), p. 1; Artur Weiser, *The Psalms* (London: SCM Press, 1962); Hans-Joachim Kraus, *Theology of the Psalms* (Minneapolis: Augsburg, 1986); et al. It should also be noted that this approach was, in no sense, limited to examining just psalms of distress. Rather, the scope included the whole Psalter.

2 The significance of the presence of titles in some psalms of distress is beyond our exploration here. However, despite doubt concerning their authenticity and accuracy of attributions in the psalms' original form they do, at the very least, suggest a real-life origin for the experiences recorded in the text.

3 David J. Cohen, 'Usage of the Psalms During the Post-Exilic Period up to 200 CE' (Murdoch University, 1990). The psalms' importance as a basis for individual and communal expression to God is also reinforced by the later identification of the Psalter as the hymnbook of the Second Temple.

4 Of course this kind of grappling activity is not limited to lament psalms found in the Psalter. Lament is freely expressed on a number of occasions by the prophet Jeremiah in chapters 11 – 20 (David J. Cohen, 'A Prophet in Motion: The Counterpoint of Speaking, Acting and Reflecting', in *On Eagles' Wings:An Exploration of Strength in the Midst of Weakness* [ed. Michael Parsons; Lutterworth Press, 2008], pp.

15–35). The main characters in Ecclesiastes, Job and Jonah also express lament in various ways but, in contrast to these examples, the individual psalms of distress in the Psalter are not connected directly to historical events or persons; notwithstanding the titles which were added at a later date.

5 While the focus here is the individual's response to ritual it could also suggest a dynamic present for worshipping communities as well.

6 An example today might be the act of baptism, which is a significant and intentional ritual and which has a meaning that can be clearly explained. On the other hand, we can sometimes observe the person who sits in the same seat in the congregation every week but could not necessarily give any meaningful reason for this action.

7 Tom F. Driver, *Liberating Rites: Understanding the Transformative Power of Ritual* (Boulder, Colorado: Westview Press, 1998), p. xi. Of course many others have made attempts at defining ritual. Among them are Herbert Anderson and Edward Foley, *Mighty Stories, Dangerous Rituals* (San Francisco: Jossey-Bass, 1998); Edward R. Canda, 'Therapeutic Transformation in Ritual, Therapy, and Human Development', *JReligHealth* 27, no. 3 (1988); Roy A. Rappaport, *Ritual and Religion in the Making of Humanity* (Cambridge: CUP, 1999); Victor Turner, *The Forest of Symbols: Aspects of Ndembu Ritual* (Ithaca: Cornell University Press, 1967). I have chosen Driver's definition of ritual function as it provides a comprehensive coverage of the issues related to the efficacy of psalms of distress.

8 Driver, *Liberating Rites*, p. 6.

9 Driver, *Liberating Rites*, p. 16. It is interesting that while emphasizing the repetitive nature of ritual Driver also allows for the incorporation of improvisation within the form. Thereby, ritual can accommodate the need for the familiar and the new; fixed, prescribed activity, with the innate human desire to be creative. According to Driver this should not be ignored but, rather, nurtured.

10 Theodore W. Jennings, 'On Ritual Knowledge', *JR* 62, no. 2 (1982): p. 115.

11 Jennings, 'On Ritual Knowledge', p. 117. Jennings' conclusion reinforces the perspectives of Driver and Turner in particular.

12 Rappaport, *Ritual and Religion*, p. 72.

13 Rappaport, *Ritual and Religion*, p. 143.

14 Of course the expression of words alone can also constitute a ritual act.

[15] Turner, *Forest of Symbols*, p. 19.

[16] Driver, *Liberating Rites*, p. 19.

[17] Driver, *Liberating Rites*, p. 22. As an example of this transcendence, Driver uses a personal example of him washing his hands before a meal, saying that he learnt and practised the ritual of this long before he had cognitively apprehended its significance yet he did it because it is 'the way it is done'.

[18] Jonathan Z. Smith, 'To Take Place', in *Ritual and Religious Belief* (ed. Graham Harvey; London: Equinox, 2005), p. 33.

[19] Herbert J. Levine, *Sing Unto God a New Song: A Contemporary Reading of the Psalms* (Bloomington, IN: Indiana University Press, 1995), p. 24.

[20] Anderson and Foley, *Mighty Stories*, p. xii.

[21] Anderson and Foley, *Mighty Stories*, pp. xi–xii.

[22] Anderson and Foley, *Mighty Stories*, p. xi.

[23] Anderson and Foley, *Mighty Stories*, p. 14.

[24] The interesting exception here is Ps. 88, which could be characterized as being exclusively parabolic in nature.

[25] Anderson and Foley, *Mighty Stories*, p. 3.

[26] Anderson and Foley, *Mighty Stories*, p. 5.

[27] Leonel L. Mitchell, *The Meaning of Ritual* (Harrisburg, PA: Morehouse, 1977), p. 28.

[28] Anderson and Foley, *Mighty Stories*, p. 20.

[29] Jennings, 'On Ritual Knowledge', p. 112.

[30] Stephen Crites, 'The Narrative Quality of Experience', *JAAR* 39, no. 3 (1971): p. 291. In doing this Crites wants to inextricably link life experience and story to each other. Therefore the articulation of this narrative becomes possible because the experience is a story.

[31] Canda, 'Therapeutic Transformation', p. 206.

[32] Driver, *Liberating Rites*, p. 28.

[33] Driver, *Liberating Rites*, p. 28; and also Virginia H. Hine, 'Self-Generated Ritual: Trend or Fad?', *Worship* 55, no. 5 (1981): p. 412. She argues that, 'the greater the psychic change required, the greater the investment in ritual must be'.

[34] Driver, *Liberating Rites*, p. 113.

[35] Driver, *Liberating Rites*, p. 5.

[36] Driver, *Liberating Rites*, p. 117.

[37] Lynne A. Texter and Janine M. Mariscotti, 'From Chaos to New Life: Ritual Enactment in the Passage from Illness to Health,' *JReligHealth* 33, no. 4 (1994): p. 326.

38 E.g. Ps. 10:1, 'Why, O L ORD, do you stand far off? Why do you hide yourself in times of trouble?' Ps. 13:1–2, 'How long, O L ORD? Will you forget me forever? How long will you hide your face from me? How long must I bear pain in my soul, and have sorrow in my heart all day long? How long shall my enemy be exalted over me?' Ps. 22:1, 'My God, my God, why have you forsaken me? Why are you so far from helping me, from the words of my groaning?' Et al.

39 Quentin Quesnell, 'Interior Prayer and Ritual Drama', *Dialogue and Alliance* 3, no. 4 (1989–90): p. 70.

40 Robert Sweetman, 'Thomas of Cantimpré: Performative Reading and Pastoral Care', in *Performance and Transformation* (ed. Mary Suydam and Joanne Ziegler; New York: St Martin's Press, 1999), p. 134.

41 Turner, *Forest of Symbols*, p. 19.

42 Anderson and Foley, *Mighty Stories*, p. 37.

43 Robert W. Jenson, 'The Praying Animal', *Zygon* 18, no. 3 (1983): pp. 314–16.

44 Gary Brock, 'Ritual and Vulnerability', *JReligHealth* 29, no. 4 (1990): p. 291.

4. Signpost 3 – The Language of Lament

1 Jan Renkema, *Discourse Studies* (Amsterdam, The Netherlands: John Benjamins, 1993), p. 2. It is interesting to note Jan Blommaert's (*Discourse*, Cambridge: CUP, 2005, p. 14) observation that, 'We can, and must, start from the observation that language matters to people, that people make investments in language, and that this is a crucial part of what they believe language does for them and what they do with language'.

2 Of course in individual psalms of distress all the characters are anonymous, including the person in distress, but are nonetheless portrayed as characters.

3 The climax could be articulated in a variety of ways including the plea or a cry of imprecation against the enemies.

4 More will be said about the nature and function of poetic language later.

5 E.g. while Ps. 22 is one of the most dramatic examples of this type of movement, others also reflect a similar movement.

6 E.g. Ps. 22:4–5 (NIV), 'In you our ancestors put their trust; they trusted and you delivered them. To you they cried out and were saved; in

you they trusted and were not put to shame.' Ps. 44 also provides an example of an extended appeal to history as the basis of lament. Though this is generally categorized as a communal psalm of distress its content clearly emphasizes an historical focus on the action of God as a starting point for expressing distress. The individual psalms of distress tend not to describe history in such detail, as found in Ps. 44, but still focus on the idea that, because God has saved in the past (e.g. as in Ps. 44), it is worthwhile calling on God in the present.

7 Claus Westermann, *Praise and Lament in the Psalms* (Edinburgh: T. & T. Clark, 1981), pp. 193–4. The term 'dialectic', as opposed to 'dialogue', is helpful in this context as it highlights the tension between the voices which are active within the lament.

8 Martin Buber, *Between Man and Man* (trans. Ronald Gregor Smith; New York: Macmillan, 1965). In discussing this concept Buber refers to the definition of dialectic provided by Feuerbach as far back as 1843 who said, 'True dialectic is not a monologue of the solitary thinker within himself (*sic*), it is a dialogue between *I* and *Thou*'.

9 In this sense desolation and consolation can be viewed as two sides of the one coin.

10 For example, in Ps. 10:4 the distressed person quotes the enemy who says, 'There is no God', and in v. 6 'We shall not be moved'. In Ps. 22:14–17 the distressed person says, 'I am poured out like water, and all my bones are out of joint; my heart is like wax; it is melted within my breast; my mouth is dried up like a potsherd, and my tongue sticks to my jaws; you lay me in the dust of death. For dogs are all around me; a company of evildoers encircles me. My hands and feet have shrivelled; I can count all my bones. They stare and gloat over me.'

11 P. Ricoeur, *The Rule of Metaphor: Multidisciplinary Studies in the Creation of Meaning in Language* (London: Routledge & Kegan Paul, 1978). Note my usage of this concept in a different sense from Brueggemann (Walter Brueggemann, *The Psalms in the Life of Faith* [Minneapolis: Fortress Press,1995], p. 8). He uses Ricoeur's terms as descriptive categories for discrete psalms.

12 William P. Brown, *Seeing the Psalms: A Theology of Metaphor* (Louisville, KY: Westminster John Knox Press, 2002), p. 2.

13 P. Ricoeur, *Essays on Biblical Interpretation* (ed. Lewis S. Mudge; Philadelphia: Fortress Press, 1980), p. 90.

14 Ricoeur, *Essays*, p. 80.

15 Robert Alter, *The Art of Biblical Poetry* (New York: Basic Books, 1985), p. 112.

16 James Kugel, *The Idea of Biblical Poetry: Parallelism and Its History* (New Haven: Yale University Press, 1981), pp. 69–70. While his comments describe poetry in the Hebrew Bible generally, they obviously include the material of Psalter as significant examples of this.

17 Much debt is owed to Robert Lowth for his seminal work on Hebrew poetry: *De Sacra Poesie Hebraeorum Praelectiones Academicae*, published in 1766. Lowth coined the term 'parallelism' as a way of describing the two-line couplets prominent in Hebrew poetry where the second line in some way reflects the content of the first.

18 Erhard S. Gerstenberger, *Psalms Part I*, vol. 14, The Forms of Old Testament Literature (Grand Rapids, Michigan: Eerdmans, 1988), p. 14. He suggests the presence of a five-syllable stress feature which he identifies as a 'dirge rhythm' in the psalms of distress.

19 The assumption here is usage of the psalms in a regular ritual manner.

20 Brown, *Seeing the Psalms*, p. 7. It should be noted that Brown does not limit the function of any psalms to didactic function. However, what he helpfully highlights is the potential effect this kind of discourse might have on those who engage with it.

21 Brown, *Seeing the Psalms*, p. 7.

22 Brown, *Seeing the Psalms*, p. 5.

23 Earl R. MacCormac, *A Cognitive Theory of Metaphor* (London: Massachusetts Institute of Technology, 1985), pp. 192–3.

24 Janet Martin Soskice, *Metaphor and Religious Language* (Oxford: Clarendon Press, 1985), pp. 38–9. She argues, on the basis of work by cognitive literary theorists, that metaphors act as 'cognitive meditation', suggesting that poetic metaphor engages both affective and cognitive responses.

25 Jurie H. Le Roux, 'Augustine, Gadamer and the Psalms (Or: The Psalms as the Answer to the Questions)', in *Psalms in Liturgy* (ed. Dirk J. Human and Cas J.A. Vos; London: T. & T. Clark International, 2004), p. 124.

26 Le Roux, 'Augustine', p. 127. In doing this, Le Roux acknowledges the formative work by Gadamer in this regard. In saying this Le Roux is not suggesting that the text is therefore a closed-ended discourse such as a catechetical question-and-answer process. He elucidates this by arguing that, 'The dialogue does not comprise of propositions but of questions and answers, which *always give rise to new questions and different answers*' (italics mine).

27 Wade T. Wheelock, 'The Problem of Ritual Language: From Information to Situation', *JAAR* 50, no. 1 (1982): p. 49.

28 Kenneth Quinn, *How Literature Works: The Nature of the Literary Experience* (Sydney: Australian Broadcasting Corporation, 1982), p. 93.

29 Tom F. Driver, *Liberating Rites: Understanding the Transformative Power of Ritual* (Boulder, CO: Westview Press, 1998), p. 31.

30 Herbert J. Levine, *Sing Unto God a New Song: A Contemporary Reading of the Psalms* (Bloomington, IN: Indiana University Press, 1995), p. 81.

31 Mikhail Bakhtin (*Problems of Dostoevsky's Poetics*, trans. Caryl Emerson, ed. Wlad Godzich and Jochen Schulte-Sasse; 8 vols; Minneapolis: University of Minnesota Press, 1984, p. 8) uses the term 'dialogical' rather than 'dialectical'. Despite the use of different words the functions of dialogue that Bakhtin and others have identified apply equally well to the dialectic in psalms of distress.

32 Although it must be acknowledged that Bakhtin developed these ideas primarily from analyzing fictional novels, namely those written by Dostoyevsky, a number have seen the relevance to the psalms (cf. Patricia K. Tull, 'Bakhtin's Confessional Self-Accounting and Psalms of Lament', *Biblical Interpretation* 13, no. 1 [2005]: pp. 41–55).

33 Levine, *Sing Unto God*, p. 82.

34 In some ways this reflects what could be characterized as the difference between a biographical view of self which views others, and relationships with those others, in a different way from an autobiographical view of self and relationships with others.

35 Bakhtin, *Problems*, 8:183.

36 Levine, *Sing Unto God*, p. 82.

37 Bakhtin, *Problems of Dostoevsky's Poetics*, pp. 72, 73, 185–6. For example, God is quoted in Ps. 35:3b saying, 'I am your salvation', while the enemy is quoted Ps. 10:11 saying, 'God has forgotten, he has hidden his face, he will never see it'. There are many other examples of these kinds of quotes throughout individual psalms of distress.

38 Levine, *Sing Unto God*, p. 115.

39 This deepening of self-understanding seems to derive in part from individuals being able to articulate both their own words about themselves and the words of God and others about them.

40 David Patterson, 'The Religious Aspect of Bakhtin's Aesthetics', *Renascence* 46, no. 1 (1993): p. 63. In this article Patterson is specifically dealing with the relevance of Bakhtin's theories to religious understanding.

41 Levine, *Sing Unto God*, p. 105.

42 E.g. Ps. 12:5, ' "Because the poor are despoiled, because the needy groan, I will now rise up", says the Lord; "I will place them in the safety for which they long." '

43 E.g. Ps. 22:8, 'Commit your cause to the Lord; let him deliver – let him rescue the one in whom he delights!'

44 James L. Mays, *The Lord Reigns: A Theological Handbook to the Psalms* (Louisville, KY: Westminster John Knox Press, 1994), p. 30. He discusses this description at length. See for example Ps. 34:6, 'This poor soul cried, and was heard by the Lord, and was saved from every trouble'; Ps. 40:17, 'As for me, I am poor and needy, but the Lord takes thought for me. You are my help and my deliverer; do not delay, O my God'; and Ps. 69:29, 'But I am lowly and in pain; let your salvation, O God, protect me.'

45 E.g. Ps. 4:3, 'But know that the Lord has set apart the faithful for himself; the Lord hears when I call to him'; Ps. 7:10, 'God is my shield, who saves the upright in heart'; and Ps. 10:8, 'They sit in ambush in the villages; in hiding-places they murder the innocent. Their eyes stealthily watch for the helpless.'

46 Cf. Ps. 38:12–14, 'Those who seek my life lay their snares; those who seek to hurt me speak of ruin, and meditate treachery all day long. But I am like the deaf, I do not hear; like the mute, who cannot speak. Truly, I am like one who does not hear, and in whose mouth is no retort'; and Ps. 130:3, 'If you, O Lord, should mark iniquities, Lord, who could stand?' et al.

47 Ps. 22:1 (NET).

48 E.g. Ps. 4:8, 'I will both lie down and sleep in peace; for you alone, O Lord, make me lie down in safety.'

49 Craig C. Broyles, *The Conflict of Faith and Experience in the Psalms: A Form-Critical and Theological Study* (Sheffield: JSOT Press, 1989), pp. 62–3.

50 Ps. 17:1–5, 'Hear a just cause, O Lord; attend to my cry; give ear to my prayer from lips free of deceit. From you let my vindication come; let your eyes see the right. If you try my heart, if you visit me by night, if you test me, you will find no wickedness in me; my mouth does not transgress. As for what others do, by the word of your lips I have avoided the ways of the violent. My steps have held fast to your paths; my feet have not slipped.'

51 Kathleen A. Farmer, 'Psalms', in *The Women's Bible Commentary* (ed. Carol A. Newsom and Sharon H. Ringe; London: SPCK, 1992), p. 140.

52 Gerstenberger, *Psalms*, p. 14.

53 In Ps. 3:2–3, for example, this dialectic can be clearly observed: 'many are saying to me, "There is no help for you in God." *Selah* But you, O LORD, are a shield around me, my glory, and the one who lifts up my head.' It is not in the form of a direct conversation between the two parties but, rather, the enemy's jibes are quoted and then followed by the distressed person's contrary viewpoint on the situation.

54 Cf. Ps. 3:1–2, 'O LORD, how many are my foes! Many are rising against me; many are saying to me, "There is no help for you in God"; and Ps. 10:2–11, 'In arrogance the wicked persecute the poor – let them be caught in the schemes they have devised. For the wicked boast of the desires of their heart, those greedy for gain curse and renounce the LORD. In the pride of their countenance the wicked say, "God will not seek it out"; all their thoughts are, "There is no God." Their ways prosper at all times; your judgements are on high, out of their sight; as for their foes, they scoff at them. They think in their heart, "We shall not be moved; throughout all generations we shall not meet adversity." Their mouths are filled with cursing and deceit and oppression; under their tongues are mischief and iniquity. They sit in ambush in the villages; in hiding-places they murder the innocent. Their eyes stealthily watch for the helpless; they lurk in secret like a lion in its covert; they lurk that they may seize the poor; they seize the poor and drag them off in their net. They stoop, they crouch, and the helpless fall by their might. They think in their heart, "God has forgotten, he has hidden his face, he will never see it"' et al.

55 Patrick D. Miller Jr, *Interpreting the Psalms* (Philadelphia: Fortress Press, 1986), p. 50.

56 An interesting example of this is found in Ps. 130:3 (NIV), where the individual, by implication, is an enemy to oneself due in this case to one's 'sins'.

5. Signpost 4 – Shape and Function

1 In the form-critical approach, psalms of distress are referred to as psalms of lament (both communal and individual) and the form itself is often identified with the German word, *Gattungen*.

2 Erhard S. Gerstenberger, *Psalms Part I*, vol. 14, The Forms of Old Testament Literature (Grand Rapids, Michigan: Eerdmans, 1988), p.

12. It should be noted that these ten elements are present in communal laments as well. However, not all of the ten elements identified by Gerstenberger appear in every psalm of distress. Claus Westermann (*Praise and Lament in the Psalms*; Edinburgh: T. & T. Clark, 1981, p. 52), suggests five elements as constituents of individual psalms of distress, identifying the presence of address, lament, confession of trust, petition, and vow of praise. While this is also a helpful way of viewing the form of lament, Gerstenberger's approach is more all-encompassing.

³ The only notable exception to this is Ps. 88.

⁴ Walter Brueggemann, 'Shape for Old Testament Theology, 1,' *CBQ* 47, no. 1 (1985): p. 31. Admittedly here he is addressing the theology expressed in psalms rather than directly describing the emotional experience of distress from phenomenological distress.

⁵ Brueggemann, 'Shape', p. 31.

⁶ It is interesting to note Nathan D. Mitchell's ('The Amen Corner', *Worship* 76, no. 1, 2002, p. 67) observation at this point that 'our participation expresses both our worship of God and solidarity with one another'. Notwithstanding the fact that here, we are focusing on individuals, as they engage with personal distress through individual psalms of lament, the aspect of communal resonance, in whatever form that takes, cannot be ignored.

⁷ Leslie C. Lewis, 'Continuity and Meaning', *JReligHealth* 37, no. 2(1998): p. 143.

⁸ Martha A. Robbins, 'The Divine Dance: Partners in Remembering, Revisioning, and Reweaving', *Journal of Pastoral Care* 51, no. 3 (1997): pp. 344–6.

⁹ John Swinton and Harriet Mowat, *Practical Theology and Qualitative Research* (London: SCM Press, 2006), p. 107.

¹⁰ Swinton and Mowat, *Practical Theology*, p. 106. In presenting this idea, Swinton and Mowat consider that, 'Phenomenology is a philosophy of experience that attempts to understand the way in which meaning is constructed through human experience'.

¹¹ Graham Hughes, *Worship as Meaning: A Liturgical Theology for Late Modernity* (Cambridge: CUP, 2003), p. 79. As part of his discussion Hughes relates the ideas of understanding and comprehension to the work of Mink on the function of narrative in the meaning-making process.

¹² In this regard Hughes (*Worship as Meaning*, p. 90) refers to Derrida's comments on dialogue: 'I must first hear myself. In soliloquy as in

dialogue, to speak is to hear oneself. As soon as I am heard, as soon as I hear myself, the I who hears *itself*, who hears me, becomes the I who speaks and takes speech from the I who thinks that he speaks and is heard in his own name.'

13   Anne V. Sutherland, 'Worldframes and God-Talk in Trauma and Suffering', *Journal of Pastoral Care* 49, no. 3 (1995): pp. 285–6.

14   Patricia Huff Byrne, ' "Give Sorrow Words": Lament – Contemporary Need for Job's Old Time Religion', *JPCC* 56, no. 3 (2002): p. 262.

15   J.L. Austin, *How to Do Things with Words* (ed. J.O. Urmson and Marina Sbisà; Cambridge, MA: HUP, 2nd edn, 1975).

16   Wade T. Wheelock, 'The Problem of Ritual Language: From Information to Situation', *JAAR* 50, no. 1 (1982): p. 49.

17   Judith Marie Kubicki, 'Using J.L. Austin's Performative Language Theory to Interpret Ritual Music Making', *Worship* 73, no. 4 (1999): p. 312. She sees that spoken language is not only just language of assertion but also language of action. This reinforces both the idea of speech acts *doing something* and *indicating* the existence of a relationship between speaker and hearer.

18   In fact on the issue of speech and relationship, James M. Day ('Speaking of Belief: Language, Performance, and Narrative in the Psychology of Religion', *IJPR* 3, no. 4 (1993): p. 215) states categorically that, 'language arises and is meaningful in and because of relationship, and there is no place outside the social realm where it could function'.

19   Richard S. Briggs, *Words in Action* (Edinburgh: T. & T. Clark, 2001), p. 51.

20   The idea of a 'permissive' could be included in this category as well, indicating a nuanced concept of expression where the person's speech act is present by virtue of a form (i.e. in this case lament form) which gives permission for such an utterance to be made.

21   Terms such as 'locutionary', 'illocutionary' and 'perlocutionary' as developed and used by Austin (*How to Do Things*) and John R. Searle (*Speech Acts: An Essay in the Philosophy of Language*, Cambridge: CUP, 1970) et al., need to be carefully defined even though there is still some disagreement as to definitions presented by the various theorists.

22   The implication here is that the request itself brings about the action on another's (in this case God's) part. It is notable that while the first four categories of speech are almost innumerable within the psalms of distress, declaratives are not so prevalent. Rather than declare change

through one's own words, the change is expressed as a direct request (plea) or a wish for something the individual desires God to do. In biblical Hebrew this is most often expressed by using the jussive form of the verb in either the singular or plural which specifically identifies the idea as a wish or desire. It is a nuanced, softer form of the imperative.

23 Searle, *Speech Acts*.
24 Wheelock, 'The Problem of Ritual Language', p. 59.
25 Day, 'Speaking of Belief', p. 217.
26 Kubicki, 'Using J.L. Austin's Performative Language Theory', p. 320.
27 Kubicki, 'Using J.L. Austin's Performative Language Theory', p. 320.
28 Day, 'Speaking of Belief', p. 215. He suggests that, 'Without a voice, there is no reality, let alone the prospect of representing or making it meaningful.'
29 Briggs, *Words in Action*, p. 7. Briggs, as a caution, rightly argues for a distinction in levels of self-involvement in speech acts while recognizing that participation in any speech act suggests at least a superficial level. Later (p. 148) he argues that, 'The basic point about self-involvement is that the speaking subject invests him or herself in a state of affairs by adopting a stance towards the state of affairs. Where self-involvement is most interesting and significant is in cases where the stance is logically entailed by the utterance itself. This is most obvious in cases where the language is present-tense first person language.'
30 Wheelock, 'The Problem of Ritual Language', p. 60.
31 Jurie H. Le Roux, 'Augustine, Gadamer and the Psalms (Or: The Psalms as the Answer to the Questions)', in *Psalms in Liturgy* (ed. Dirk J. Human and Cas J.A. Vos; London: T. & T. Clark International, 2004), p. 124.
32 Le Roux, 'Augustine', p. 127.
33 Wheelock, 'The Problem of Ritual Language', p. 66. Day ('Speaking of Belief', p. 214) expands on this idea stating that, 'we are created by the words as well as being creators of them'.
34 John R. Finney and H. Newton Malony Jr, 'Empirical Studies of Christian Prayer: A Review of Literature', *JPsychTheol* 13, no. 2 (1985): pp. 104–15.
35 Finney and Malony Jr, 'Empirical Studies', p. 104. This definition is taken from W. James, *The Varieties of Religious Experience* (New York: University Books, 1963), p. 464.
36 Finney and Malony Jr, 'Empirical Studies', p. 104.
37 Finney and Malony Jr, 'Empirical Studies', p. 107.

38 Cynthia B. Cohen et al., 'Prayer as Therapy', *Hastings Center Report* 30, no. 3 (2000): p. 3.

39 Kevin L. Ladd and Bernard Spilka, 'Inward, Outward, Upward Prayer: Scale Reliability and Validation', *JSSR* 45, no. 2 (2006): p. 234.

40 Ladd and Spilka, 'Inward, Outward', pp. 234, 237.

41 Ladd and Spilka, 'Inward, Outward', p. 234.

42 Bruce G. Epperly, 'To Pray or Not to Pray: Reflections on the Intersection of Prayer and Medicine', *JReligHealth* 34, no. 2 (1995): p. 147.

43 Marilyn S. Saur and William G. Saur, 'Transitional Phenomena as Evidenced in Prayer'. *JReligHealth* 32, no. 1 (1993): p. 63. They also concluded that, for some, body posture was also a significant mode of expressing relational connection in prayer.

44 Volney P. Gay, 'Public Rituals Versus Private Treatment: Psychodynamics of Prayer', *JReligHealth* 17, no. 4 (1978): p. 250.

45 Margaret M. Paloma, 'The Effects of Prayer on Mental Well-Being', *Second Opinion* (January 1993): p. 41.

46 Paloma, 'The Effects of Prayer', p. 41.

47 Margaret M. Paloma and Brian F. Pendleton, 'The Effects of Prayer Experiences on Measures of General Well-Being', *JPsychTheol* 19, no. 1 (1991): pp. 80–1.

48 I would not choose to use Paloma and Pendleton's description of affect as 'negative'. In my view, such a term can suggest a pejorative value judgement being placed on a quality which is a normal part of human experience.

49 Patrick D. Miller, *They Cried Unto the Lord: The Form and Theology of Biblical Prayer* (Minneapolis: Fortress, 1994), p. 134.

50 Ladd and Spilka, 'Inward, Outward', p. 234.

51 Felicity Brock Kelcourse, 'Prayer and the Soul: Dialogues that Heal', *JReligHealth* 40, no. 1 (2001): p. 240.

52 Hans-Joachim Kraus, *Psalms 1–59* (trans. Hilton C. Oswald; Minneapolis: Augsburg, 1988), p. 301.

6. The Matrix of Lament: A Model

1 These images and ideas are taken from definitions of the terms as found in the *Oxford English Dictionary* (ed. John Simpson and Edmund Weiner, *Oxford English Dictionary*, 20 vols; London: OUP, 1989).

2 I.e. Expressing – 'I *to* self' / 'I *to* Thou', Asserting – 'I *about* self' / 'I *about* Thou', Investing – 'I *in* self' / 'I *in* Thou' and Imagining – 'I *with* self' / 'I *with* Thou'. The significance of these will be explained in the discussion to follow.

3 In fact, the jarring shifts in expression found in this psalm have not passed unnoticed by scholars. As a result some have proposed that the psalm was originally two separate psalms which have been fused together (cf. P.C. Craigie, *Psalms Vol. 1*, WBC; Waco, Texas: Word Books, 1983, p. 197). While it may well be the case that this psalm was originally two separate psalms, the fact remains that it is present in the biblical text as one complete unit. Clearly, this is how it was recorded and probably used liturgically. Therefore, the discussion of the psalms' earlier form must, in my view, always be subordinated to its present form in the Psalter.

4 Ellen F. Davis, 'Exploding the Limits', *JSOT* 53 (1992): p. 93.

5 E.g. Pss. 10:1; 22:1 (Why . . .?) and 13:1 (How long . . .?) are typical interrogative forms used in lament.

6 E.g. Ps. 41:3, 'The Lord sustains them on their sickbed; in their illness you heal all their infirmities' (vindication); Ps. 51:1, 'Have mercy on me, O God, according to your steadfast love; according to your abundant mercy blot out my transgressions' (have mercy); Ps. 88:1–2, 'O Lord, God of my salvation, when, at night, I cry out in your presence, let my prayer come before you; incline your ear to my cry' (listening); Ps. 140:1, 'Deliver me, O Lord, from evildoers; protect me from those who are violent' (deliverance).

7 Claus Westermann, *Praise and Lament in the Psalms* (Edinburgh: T. & T. Clark, 1981), pp. 35–6. He cites Ps. 86 as an example of the writer using the Hebrew form *'attâ*.

8 E.g. Ps. 102:1, 'Hear my prayer, O Lord; let my cry come to you' (positive); Ps. 10:1, 'Why, O Lord, do you stand far off? Why do you hide yourself in times of trouble?' (negative).

9 E.g. Ps. 17:1, 'Hear a just cause, O Lord; attend to my cry; give ear to my prayer from lips free of deceit'; Ps. 55:1, 'Give ear to my prayer, O God; do not hide yourself from my supplication' (positive action); Ps. 38:1, 'O Lord, do not rebuke me in your anger, or discipline me in your wrath' and Ps. 83:1; 'O God, do not keep silence; do not hold your peace or be still, O God!' (negative action) et al. It should be noted that this positive or negative is not exclusively found in the invocation of psalms of distress.

10 The desired response is formulated later in more detail with a plea.

11 Craig C. Broyles, *The Conflict of Faith and Experience in the Psalms: A Form-Critical and Theological Study* (Sheffield: JSOT Press, 1989), p. 80. He explores the 'Why?' question of lament as an expression of an absence of the Hebrew concept of *shalom*.

12 Martin Buber, *I and Thou* (Edinburgh: T. & T. Clark, 1970).

13 Note that in psalms of distress one of these is often present but not both.

14 The plea can also be called a petition.

15 E.g. Ps. 51:3–4, 'For I know my transgressions, and my sin is ever before me. Against you, you alone, have I sinned, and done what is evil in your sight, so that you are justified in your sentence and blameless when you pass judgement.'

16 E.g. Ps. 59:3–4, 'Even now they lie in wait for my life; the mighty stir up strife against me. For no transgression or sin of mine, O LORD, for no fault of mine, they run and make ready. Rouse yourself, come to my help and see!'

17 E.g. Ps. 6:5, 'For in death there is no remembrance of you; in Sheol who can give you praise?'

18 Due to the historical details surrounding most psalms of distress being sketchy at best, it is impossible to conclude whether or not God in fact acted in accordance with the psalmist's petition/plea. However, based on the historical accounts found elsewhere in the Hebrew Bible is seems logical to conclude that God would have responded in line with God's compassion, justice and mercy.

19 When these kinds of psalms were prayed in a communal setting it is also significant that these assertions about self and God were made to the community of faith.

20 Note here the use of *Yahweh*, the *name* of the Israelite God, as opposed to the more generic *Elohim*.

21 E.g. Ps. 69:22–8, 'Let their table be a trap for them, a snare for their allies. Let their eyes be darkened so that they cannot see, and make their loins tremble continually. Pour out your indignation upon them, and let your burning anger overtake them. May their camp be a desolation; let no one live in their tents. For they persecute those whom you have struck down, and those whom you have wounded, they attack still more. Add guilt to their guilt; may they have no acquittal from you. Let them be blotted out of the book of the living; let them not be enrolled among the righteous.' See also Pss. 137:7–9; 139:19–22, et al.

22 Westermann, *Praise and Lament*, p. 265.

23 Paige H. Kelley, 'Prayers of Troubled Spirits', *RevExp* 81, no. 3 (1984): p. 377. E.g. Pss. 13:5; 22:3; 31:14.

24 E.g. Ps. 58:10–11, 'The upright will rejoice when they see vengeance done; they will bathe their feet in the blood of the wicked. People will say, "Surely there is a reward for the righteous; surely there is a God who judges on earth."' 'See also Pss. 61:5; 130:7–8.

25 E.g. Ps. 40:1–3, 'I waited patiently for the LORD; he inclined to me and heard my cry. He drew me up from the desolate pit, out of the miry bog, and set my feet upon a rock, making my steps secure. He put a new song in my mouth, a song of praise to our God. Many will see and fear, and put their trust in the LORD.'

26 Westermann, *Praise and Lament*, pp. 58–9. He points out that the confession of trust at times *leads to* a point where the individual can actually praise God (e.g. Ps. 74:12, 'Yet God my King is from of old, working salvation in the earth' leading to verses 13–17, 'You divided the sea by your might; you broke the heads of the dragons in the waters. You crushed the heads of Leviathan; you gave him as food for the creatures of the wilderness. You cut openings for springs and torrents; you dried up ever-flowing streams. Yours is the day, yours also the night; you established the luminaries and the sun. You have fixed all the bounds of the earth; you made summer and winter').

27 Westermann, *Praise and Lament*, p. 27.

28 E.g. Pss. 6, 27, 28, 35.

29 Although the term 'intrapsychic' is perhaps more appropriate here, 'psychological' is Westermann's preferred way of describing this notion.

30 Westermann, *Praise and Lament*, p. 27.

31 Heb. *'ānî*.

32 James L. Mays, *The Lord Reigns: A Theological Introduction to the Book of Psalms – Psalms as Torah* (Louisville, KY: Westminster John Knox Press, 1994), p. 30.

33 E.g. Ps. 4:3, 'But know that the LORD has set apart the faithful for himself; the LORD hears when I call to him.'

34 Of course psalms of distress do not record a verbal response from God, yet there is an implicit understanding that God has spoken and continues to speak in the situation.

35 Even in Ps. 22:1 where a feeling of abandonment is expressed it is still, incongruently, expressed to God.

36 E.g. Ps. 88:7, 'Your wrath lies heavy upon me, and you overwhelm me with all your waves'; Ps. 13:1, 'How long, O LORD? Will you forget me for ever? How long will you hide your face from me?'

37 Kathleen A. Farmer, 'Psalms', in *The Women's Bible Commentary* (ed. Carol A. Newsom and Sharon Ringe; London: SPCK, 1992), p. 140.

38 Mays, *The Lord Reigns*, pp. 27–30. As a reinforcing image to the idea of divine sufficiency, Mays argues that the idea of God's kingship is a given for the psalmist facing distress and, therefore, acknowledgement of God's ability to change the situation is significant.

39 This may be indicative of a typical oscillation between faith and doubt in response to distress. For example, Ps. 17:1–5, 'Hear a just cause, O LORD; attend to my cry; give ear to my prayer from lips free of deceit. From you let my vindication come; let your eyes see the right. If you try my heart, if you visit me by night, if you test me, you will find no wickedness in me; my mouth does not transgress. As for what others do, by the word of your lips I have avoided the ways of the violent. My steps have held fast to your paths; my feet have not slipped.'

40 Erhard S. Gerstenberger, *Psalms Part 1*, vol. 14, The Forms of Old Testament Literature (Grand Rapids, Michigan: Eerdmans, 1988), p. 14.

41 An example of other people as the enemy can be seen in Ps. 35:11–12: 'Malicious witnesses rise up; they ask me about things I do not know. They repay me evil for good; my soul is forlorn', et al. An example of God as the enemy can be seen in Ps. 60:1–3, 'O God, you have rejected us, broken our defences; you have been angry; now restore us! You have caused the land to quake; you have torn it open; repair the cracks in it, for it is tottering. You have made your people suffer hard things; you have given us wine to drink that made us reel.'

42 John Day, *Psalms* (Sheffield: Sheffield Academic Press, 1990), p. 29.

43 For Christians, the expression of violence through imprecation can be viewed as contrary to Jesus' teaching and other parts of the New Testament. However, in my view, imprecation is an expression of emotions and thoughts which can be, although unpalatable, a natural response towards those who violently oppose us. Expression of these emotions and thoughts in prayer is a more desirable outcome than physical violence of some kind enacted against one's enemies.

44 Walter Brueggemann, *The Psalms in the Life of Faith* (Minneapolis: Fortress Press, 1995), p. 69.

7. The Practice of Lament

[1] This is notwithstanding the fact that some settings in the Christian tradition have discontinued their usage in more recent times.

[2] Kathleen D. Billman and Daniel L. Migliore, *Rachel's Cry: Prayer of Lament and the Rebirth of Hope* (Cleveland, OH: United Church Press, 1999), p. 111.

[3] Billman and Migliore, *Rachel's Cry*, p. 82. Billman and Migliore see here that lamenting can be understood in terms of grief and mourning.

[4] As an example of this, one could consider how the widespread usage of Ps. 23, though not a lament, has brought comfort to many people regardless of their articulated sense of faith.

[5] John F. Craghan, *Psalms for All Seasons* (Collegeville, MN: Liturgical Press, 1993), p. 100.

[6] Herbert J. Levine, *Sing Unto God a New Song: A Contemporary Reading of the Psalms* (Bloomington, IN: Indiana University Press, 1995), p. 81.

[7] In doing this Levine takes the 'in between' ideas of Buber from being a dynamic of the text to being a function of a process of lament.

[8] Levine, *Sing Unto God*, pp. 81–2.

[9] Levine, *Sing Unto God*, p. 82.

[10] Claus Westermann, *Praise and Lament in the Psalms* (Edinburgh: T. & T. clark, 1981), p. 27.

[11] Patrick D. Miller, 'Heaven's Prisoners: The Lament and Christian Prayer', in *Lament: Reclaiming Practices in Pulpit, Pew, and Public Square* (ed. Sally A. Brown and Patrick D. Miller; Louisville, KY: Westminster John Knox Press, 2005), p. 18.

[12] Rolf Jacobsen, 'Burning Our Lamps with Borrowed Oil', in *Psalms and Practice* (ed. Stephen B. Reid; (Collegeville, MN: Liturgical Press, 2001), p. 93.

[13] Beth LaNeel Tanner, 'How Long O Lord! Will Your People Suffer in Silence Forever?', in *Psalms and Practice* (ed. Stephen B. Reid; Collegeville, MN: Liturgical Press, 2001), p. 150.

[14] Billman and Migliore, *Rachel's Cry*, p. 67.

[15] Billman and Migliore, *Rachel's Cry*, p. 67.

[16] Billman and Migliore, *Rachel's Cry*, p. 91.

[17] Walter Brueggemann, 'The Formfulness of Grief', *Interpretation* 31, no. 3 (1977): p. 265. Notwithstanding this idea of lament form limiting the experience as suggested by Brueggemann, Ellen F. Davis ('Exploding the Limits', *JSOT* 53, 1992: p. 93) in contrast describes psalms of

distress as 'exploding the limits'. Her concept is focused on the idea that these psalms go beyond what some might see as a reasonable limit in expressing personal experience to God in prayer. So there is a tension here in lament form between limitation and freedom.

[18] Donald Capps, 'Nervous Laughter: Lament, Death Anxiety, and Humour', in *Lament: Reclaiming Practices in Pulpit, Pew, and Public Square* (ed. Sally A. Brown and Patrick D. Miller; Louisville, KY: Westminster John Knox Press, 2005), p. 71. It should be noted of course that, though a comparison is helpful, Kübler-Ross' work was particularly in bereavement and loss whereas Brueggemann is addressing the more generalized experience of distress.

[19] It is interesting to note the use of the term 'structures' by Brueggemann in discussing Kübler-Ross and psalms of distress which could give this impression.

[20] Richard A Hughes, *Lament, Death, and Destiny* (ed. Hemchand Gosai, vol. 68, SBL, New York: Lang, 2004), p. 7.

[21] Hughes, *Lament*, p. 155.

[22] Elaine Scarry, *The Body in Pain* (Oxford: OUP, 1985), p. 4.

[23] Billman and Migliore, *Rachel's Cry*, p. 105.

[24] Hughes, *Lament*, p. 155.

[25] Tanner, 'How Long O Lord!', p. 150.

[26] While the focus here is to examine the psychodynamic effect on individuals utilizing the psalms of distress as found in the biblical text, Hoffman makes an important observation saying that one 'may begin with the text but must eventually go beyond it – to people, to their meanings, to their assumed constructs, and to their ritualized patterns that make their words uniquely their own' (quoted in Don E. Saliers, *Worship as Theology: Foretaste of Glory Divine*, Nashville: Abingdon, 1994), p. 141). The comment highlights the nature and function of individual psalms of distress as a beginning point but not necessarily an end in themselves.

[27] Billman and Migliore, *Rachel's Cry*, p. 80.

[28] Billman and Migliore, *Rachel's Cry*, p. 83.

[29] Billman and Migliore, *Rachel's Cry*, p. 86.

[30] Stephen Breck Reid, 'Power and Practice: Performative Speech', in *Psalms and Practice* (ed. Stephen B. Reid; Collegeville, MN: Liturgical Press, 2001), p. 53.

[31] Martha A. Robbins, 'The Divine Dance: Partners in Remembering, Revisioning, and Reweaving', *Journal of Pastoral Care* 51, no. 3 (1997), p. 339. It is interesting to note that Robbins calls this Divine dance the

Divine dance emphasizing the significance of its ubiquitous place in human experience.

32   Cf. note 129.

33   Jacobsen, 'Burning Our Lamps', p. 95.

34   Hughes, *Lament*, p. 165. Admittedly Hughes is referring specifically here to a response to violence in lament and the distress caused by it. However, the term is useful in describing the restorative nature of revisiting the distress whatever it might have been.

35   E.g. Ps. 22:22, 'I will tell of your name to my brothers and sisters; in the midst of the congregation I will praise you.'

36   Robert Moore Jumonville and Robert Woods, 'The Role-Taking Theory of Praying the Psalms: Using the Psalms as Model for Structuring the Life of Prayer', *JBS* 3, no. 2 (2003): p. 43.

37   Robert Fulghum, *From Beginning to End: The Rituals of Our Lives* (Sydney: Bantam Books, 1995), p. 21.

38   Peter L. VanKatwyk, 'Healing through Differentiation: A Pastoral Care and Counseling Perspective', *Journal of Pastoral Care* 51, no. 3 (1997): p. 286. He goes even further than this suggesting that, 'This baseline in the wounded person is represented by a line of interaction between suffering and knowing the wound. Knowing is found in the ongoing process of naming, interpreting, and representing the wound through such narrative and symbolic expressions as story, lamentation, prayer and symptom. The knowing and suffering interaction keeps the wound, though dated in precipitating events in the past, hurting in the present and projected through anticipation into the future.'

39   Hughes, *Lament*, p. 166. It should also be noted that, words as ritual are a useful tool for reflection and meaning-making. However, it is also important to consider the combining of words with ritual symbols. This then adds a 'multivocality' as identified by Turner, *The Forest of Symbols*, 1–47 and indicates that there is the possibility of multiple levels of reflection. Therefore, meaning-making for different individuals from the same ritual process is possible.

40   Saliers, *Worship as Theology*, p. 145.

41   E.g. in Ps. 10:17 the psalmist clearly states an expectation of a result saying, 'O LORD, you will hear the desire of the meek; you will strengthen their heart, you will incline your ear.' In Ps. 42:9, indignation is clearly evident through usage of the interrogative as the psalmist struggles with distress: 'I say to God, my rock, "Why have

you forgotten me? Why must I walk about mournfully because the enemy oppresses me?"'

42 While other literature may also be pertinent and helpful to the process of lament, it would not be considered Scripture.

43 Billman and Migliore, *Rachel's Cry*, p. 83.

44 Cf. Howard Neil Wallace, *Words to God, Word from God* (Aldershot: Ashgate, 2005), p. 79. He says of Ps. 13, 'In this prayer there is the assumption that God is powerful enough to effect some change in the psalmist's plight. It is the way of God to effect transformation in life.'

45 Billman and Migliore, *Rachel's Cry*, p. 114.

46 Billman and Migliore, *Rachel's Cry*, p. 114.

47 Saliers, *Worship as Theology*, p. 69.

48 Hughes, *Lament*, p. xvi.

49 Saliers, *Worship as Theology*, p. 119.

50 See Terry Muck, 'Psalm, *Bhajan* and *Kirtan*', in *Psalms and Practice* (ed. Stephen B. Reid; Collegeville, MN: Liturgical Press, 2001), p. 7. He says that 'from the history of religions point of view, psalm, *bhajan*, and *kirtan* are religious devotional songs used in liturgical and individual's worship by adherents of Christianity, Hindu, and Sikh, respectively, as aides to think, feel and act in ways appropriate to their traditions' understanding of transcendent reality.'

51 Reid, 'Power and Practice', p. 54.

52 It is interesting to note that this concept is possibly embedded in the name Israel itself. One of its possible translations is 'one who struggles with God'.

53 Reid, 'Power and Practice', p. 53.

54 Billman and Migliore, *Rachel's Cry*, p. 112. They are referring here in part to the observations of David Tracy, 'The Hidden God: The Divine Other of Liberation', *Cross Currents* 46 (Spring 1996): pp. 5–16.

55 In this sense the psalms of distress approach the age-old dilemma of theodicy. It is beyond our scope here to explore this in depth. However, Richard Hughes presents some helpful historical perspectives on this issue together with the emergence of a doctrine of providence evident in the Christian Scriptures and developing significantly in the writings of biblical scholars and theologians ever since (Hughes, *Lament*).

56 Jumonville and Woods, 'Role-Taking Theory', p. 36.

57 Jumonville and Woods, 'Role-Taking Theory', p. 36.

8. The Psychodynamics of Lament

1. I have purposely chosen the term 'psychodynamic' rather than 'intrapsychic' as the former term incorporates more comprehensively the significance of individuals in relationship with others, as reflected in psalms of distress.

2. Michael J. Boivin, 'The Hebraic Model of the Person: Toward a Unified Psychological Science among Christian Helping Professionals', *JPsychTheol* 19, no. 2 (1991): p. 161.

3. Rollo May, *The Meaning of Anxiety* (New York: W.W. Norton, 1977), p. 390. It is also interesting in the light of this study to note that May's comments are made in relation to people who are experiencing some kind of anxiety.

4. John McDargh, 'The Life of the Self in Christian Spirituality and Contemporary Psychoanalysis', *Horizons* 11, no. 2 (Fall 1984): pp. 355–6.

5. Thomas Merton, *Contemplative Prayer* (London: Dartman, Longman & Todd, 1981), p. 82.

6. Gerald G. May, 'The Psychodynamics of Spirituality', *Journal of Pastoral Care* 31, no. 2 (1977): p. 85.

7. Eugene G. D'Aquili, 'The Myth-Ritual Complex: A Biogenetic Structural Analysis', *Zygon* 18, no. 3 (1983): p. 256.

8. D'Aquili, 'Myth-Ritual Complex', p. 259.

9. Robert J. Ritzema, 'Attribution to Supernatural Causation: An Important Component of Religious Commitment?', *JPsychTheol* 7, no. 4 (1979): p. 288.

10. D'Aquili, 'Myth-Ritual Complex', p. 260.

11. This openness and honesty is perhaps even more graphically illustrated in the Jeremianic laments found in Jer. 11 – 20 and in the book of Lamentations.

12. Todd W. Hall and Margaret Gorman, 'Relational Spirituality: Implications of the Convergence of Attachment Theory, Interpersonal Neurobiology, and Emotional Information Processing', *Newsletter of the Psychology of Religion* 28 (Spring 2003): pp. 1–12.

13. James D. Whitehead and Evelyn Eaton Whitehead, *Shadows of the Heart: A Spirituality of Negative Emotions* (New York: Crossroad, 1994), p. 139. They use the specific emotion of anger as an example here, concluding that the articulation of this particular emotion 'separates a person from the protective cocoon of depression' and, instead, presents a different pathway with hope for the future.

14 Hall and Gorman, 'Relational Spirituality', p. 10. Another perspective on this is provided by Michael Polanyi, *Personal Knowledge: Towards a Post-Critical Philosophy* (Chicago: UCP, 1958), p. 303. Here he describes this as the 'coherence of commitment' which comes about through a process of intentional reflection.

15 Hall and Gorman, 'Relational Spirituality', p. 7. It should be noted here that while agreeing with the sentiment expressed at this point the usage of the term 'negative' is not altogether helpful. Use of this term can suggest a pejorative standpoint whereas I see distress, for example, as a given, not needing a value judgement to be added. It should also be noted that Hall and Gorman's usage of the terms 'symbolic' and 'subsymbolic' appear to be based on Fowler and Newell's earlier work in distinguishing between thoughts that simply exist in the mind (non-symbolic or subsymbolic) and thoughts that are then expressed through speech or act (symbolic).

16 D'Aquili, 'Myth-Ritual Complex', p. 261.

17 Hall and Gorman, 'Relational Spirituality', p. 9. See also Michael Polanyi, *Knowledge and Being* (Chicago: UCP, 1969), p. 132.

18 Hall and Gorman, 'Relational Spirituality', p. 8.

19 See my comments on Westermann in Chapter 2.

20 Janice Bell Meisenhelder and John P. Marcum, 'Responses of Clergy to 9/11: Posttraumatic Stress, Coping, and Religious Outcomes', *JSSR* 43, no. 4 (2004): p. 548. This is based on studies by Koenig, McCullough and Larson in 2001.

21 Meisenhelder and Marcum, 'Responses', p. 553.

22 Meisenhelder and Marcum, 'Responses', p. 553.

23 Laurence E. Jackson and Robert D. Coursey, 'The Relationship of God Control and Internal Locus of Control to Intrinsic Religious Motivation, Coping and Purpose in Life', *JSSR* 27, no. 3 (1988): p. 399.

24 Jackson and Coursey, 'Relationship', p. 407. These conclusions are also supported by Adrian F. Furnham ('Locus of Control and Theological Beliefs', *JPsychTheol*, 10, no. 2, 1982, pp. 130–6) in his literature review of research on this issue concluding that numerous studies demonstrate the same result.

25 Douglas G. Richards, 'The Phenomenology and Psychological Correlates of Verbal Prayer', *JPsychTheol* 19, no. 4 (1991): p. 361.

26 Jackson and Coursey, 'Relationship', p. 399.

27 Christina E. Mitchell, 'Internal Locus of Control for Expectation, Perception and Management of Answered Prayer', *JPsychTheol* 17, no. 1 (1989): p. 21.

[28] Todd W. Hall et al., 'An Empirical Exploration of Psychoanalysis and Religion: Spiritual Maturity and Object Relations Development', *JSSR* 37, no. 2 (1998): p. 304.

[29] Hall et al., 'Empirical Exploration', p. 310.

[30] On the other hand Hall et al. also suggest that individuals with 'disturbed relationships with other people' are more likely to display a more 'pathological relationship with God' ('Empirical Exploration', p. 311).

[31] May, 'Psychodynamics', p. 84.

[32] May, 'Psychodynamics', p. 85.

9. The Journey of a Few

[1] In this chapter and the next the names have been changed to protect each person's identity but the gender has been retained.

[2] The ritual is described in more detail in Chapter 11.

[3] The three evaluation instruments were the *Depression, Anxiety and Stress Scale (DASS), Locus of Control* (LOC), and the *Spiritual Assessment Inventory* (SAI).

[4] The verbatim words and phrases from the group members are italicized for ease of identification in this chapter.

[5] John noted on numerous occasions, both in his journal and during our discussions, that the preparatory prayer at the start of each ritual was particularly helpful as reaffirming the safety and security of relationship with God in all experiences of life.

[6] It should be noted that in the context of her journaling the concept of relinquishment did not indicate an abrogation of personal responsibility but, rather, recognition that some things cannot be altered by human response.

[7] Sandra also noted that knowing the author and the receivers would help to contextualize the psalms for herself a little better.

10. The Final Destination

[1] Note that all vignettes can be identified by the usage of italics. In this chapter, along with the six group members' stories we heard in the previous chapter, observations of others in the group have also been included.

2   The words of this prayer are included for your use in the next chapter.
3   Again these will be described in the next chapter for your use.
4   Or, in two cases, in the place of the enemy.
5   The idea of blaming became more problematic for one person in Ps. 88 with the idea that God was to blame. One person chose only to blame 'Satan' and one person chose only to blame 'self'.
6   This could be observed in the comparison of the psychometric evaluations before and after the six weeks of prayer.
7   Anne also noted at this point that the hand movement associated together with the investing constellation was particularly strong in reinforcing the shift in affect that she had experienced.
8   In fact two group members indicated that the whole of v. 14 was significant in providing a new perspective. In full it states, 'But you do see! Indeed you note trouble and grief, that you may take it into your hands; the helpless commit themselves to you; you have been the helper of the orphan.'
9   It is important to stress that the movements indicated here describe the *general trend* of the whole group and do not reflect specific individuals whose experience was different.
10 Indicated by a general trend towards a stronger internal locus of control for most people.

11. Now It's Your Turn

1   This is where the psalmist requests that God act violently towards the enemy.
2   Ps. 10:12.
3   Ps. 55: 6b–8.
4   Ps. 102:3–11.
5   Ps. 102:13–14.
6   Ps. 102:15–23.
7   This is an anonymous prayer.
8   You can include different physical movements for each constellation as long as it is not distracting you from the prayer and your reflections.

ND - #0092 - 090625 - C0 - 216/138/12 - PB - 9781842277546 - Gloss Lamination